PELICAN BOOKS

ORNITHOLOGY:
AN INTRODUCTION

Austin L. Rand was born in Nova Scotia, Canada,
and was educated at Acadia University and
Cornell University, from which he received his
Ph.D. degree. His publications include *Handbook
of New Guinea Birds* and *Birds from Nepal*. Dr
Rand is at present Chief Curator of Zoology at the
Field Museum of Natural History, Chicago.

AUSTIN L. RAND

Ornithology:
An Introduction

PENGUIN BOOKS

Penguin Books Ltd, Harmondsworth, Middlesex, England
Penguin Books Australia Ltd, Ringwood, Victoria, Australia

—

First published in the U.S.A. by W. W. Norton & Co. 1967
Published with revisions in Great Britain by Penguin Books Ltd 1974

—

Copyright © W. W. Norton & Co. Inc., 1967

—

Made and printed in Great Britain
by Richard Clay (The Chaucer Press) Ltd
Bungay, Suffolk
Set in Linotype Plantin

FOR RHEUA

CONTENTS

Contents

LIST OF ILLUSTRATIONS

PREFACE

ONCE while I was planning exhibits for museum halls, a transparent dog was put on temporary display. It was carved from clear plastic and made larger than life, with the vital organs so portrayed that they were illuminated one by one. A tape recording gave a synchronized talk. The visitor response was not quite what we had expected. I remember especially one small boy whose mother dragged him away from a stuffed buffalo, saying, 'Come, Freddie, see the transparent dog and its insides.' Freddie watched, wide-eyed, as lungs, stomach, liver, kidneys, and gonads lighted up in succession and the loudspeaker blared out an explanation. Freddie turned and asked, peevishly, 'Mamma, where is the dog?'

And so in this book I have tried to present the subject of birds so that no one will ask, 'Where is the bird?' The diversity of the forms and the functions of birds of the world is presented for the general reader, and the patterns that emerge are viewed against the background of the birds' environment and their evolutionary history. Technical language is avoided as much as possible, and the treatment is as comprehensive as space permits. The limitations of space have necessitated careful selection of material and examples from all that are available. For those who would go more deeply into different aspects of the subject, references to more specialized works are provided.

Some of my own observations made in the field on living birds or in museums on specimens appear in the following pages. But by far the greater part of the information and ideas used here comes from the writings of other students of birds, past and present. Their contributions have been recorded in scientific journals, in memoirs of learned societies, and in books.

These have given me material to think about, and have shaped my thinking. Here is my story of birds, which have evolved to assume a conspicuous place in animate nature. The basic problems of birds – to reproduce themselves and to occupy as much as possible of the globe – are the basic problems of all animals. But the way in which birds have met many of the difficulties confronting them is unique. Yet within this framework is a wealth of diversity of detail. Both the uniqueness and the diversity provide the fascination of bird study.

Though I can acknowledge only *en bloc* the help other ornithologists have given me, some indication of the extent of this is provided by the references listed for the various chapters. On a more immediate, personal level I want to thank the Field Museum of Natural History for supporting my work with its world-wide collections of birds and its library to match. To the staff of the Division of Birds there, Curator Emmet R. Blake and Associate Curator Melvin A. Traylor, I have often gone for information, advice, and criticism. For assistance in preparing this manuscript I have to thank Mrs Wanda O. Harrison of the Department of Zoology of the Field Museum of Natural History. For the illustrations I am indebted to Mr E. John Pfiffner, Chicago artist.

Finally, it is an especial pleasure to acknowledge the help of my wife, Rheua Medden Rand, throughout the whole enterprise.

A. L. RAND

Chicago, Illinois
June 1964

CHAPTER 1

Introducing
Birds

EVERYONE knows at least one bird, whether it is a canary singing in a cage, a rooster crowing on a farm, a pigeon pattering on a city street, a robin feeding on a lawn, a gull riding the up-draught of air behind a steamer, or even a penguin moping in a zoo or an ostrich pacing behind the fence of its enclosure. 'How does one know they are birds?' is a question easily answered. These and all other birds have one infallibly identifying character shared with no other animal. They are unique in having feathers.

Feathers may seem superficial structures to be emphasized in this way as the key distinguishing mark of birds, whose many salient characters are given in Figure 1. But birds' feathers, which evolved from reptiles' scales, played a major role when evolution produced flying birds from running reptiles. The role of feathers is much greater than the simple one of protecting the bird against the elements or of providing colour for use in social communication and in protection.

The coat of feathers is intimately associated with flight, for it smooths the angular contours of the bird's body and gives it the streamlined shape so important in flying. A row of long feathers on the back edge of the forelimb provides the greater part of the wing area by which a bird flies. Another row of long feathers, attached to the fleshy stub of a tail, provides the greater part of the length of the tail. This is important at least to some species

107°F Bird
98.4°F Man

in steering the bird's flight. Also important is the role of the feather coat in providing insulation. This prevents the loss of heat and is essential for the effectiveness of the warm-blooded condition. It is this warm-blooded condition, which is sustained by the feathers, that makes possible the high and continuous rate of activity and the alertness of birds. Other similar multiple uses of a single set of characters are seen commonly in other aspects of birds' lives. For instance, feet are used in walking and in grasping prey; wings are used for flight and in fighting; and the respiratory structures serve in breathing and as a cooling system.

Birds look very different from the snakes, turtles, lizards, and crocodiles that are their nearest relatives. But the arrangement of bone and tissue in the bird's body is the basic vertebrate one inherited from its lizard-like reptile ancestors.[1] The chief structural changes have been adaptations associated with the power of flight. The forelimbs have been modified into wings; the body has been shortened; the extremities lightened; and the centre of gravity lowered for stability. Lightness has been provided by slender, often hollow bones. Strength and rigidity have been provided by the fusion of parts of the skeleton, especially in the outer ends of the wings and legs and in the hip region, and by bony braces, especially in the shoulder region. The great mass of the breast muscles that power the wings has necessitated the enlargement of the breast bone, or sternum, into a large plate with a projecting blade or keel for muscle attachment. These are some of the bodily changes that are discussed in more detail in Chapter 3.

However, it is not mainly in major changes in bone and muscle that birds are more advanced organisms than reptiles. Rather it is in the less tangible but very real factors of awareness – a new readiness to respond, a speeding-up of bodily processes, and a quickening behaviour. The factors associated

Figure 1. *What is a bird? An animal* (a) *that has a skeleton* (b); *has a high body temperature* (c); *is covered with feathers* (d); *flies with its forelimbs, i.e., wings* (e); *runs or hops with its hind limbs* (f); *has jaws elongated into a toothless beak* (g); *has large eyes and eye sockets* (h); *lays eggs in a nest* (i); *incubates eggs* (j); *and cares for young* (k).

with these include a relatively larger brain and an improvement of sight, hearing, and voice. These are accompanied by a continuous high temperature (warm-bloodedness) associated with a four-chambered heart, high metabolism, and the insulating covering of feathers, mentioned above, which retains bodily heat.

Birds still lay eggs, like reptiles, but the small number of their young and the elaborate care given the eggs and later the young, and the considerably more elaborate social behaviour of adults, are all great advances from their reptile ancestors.

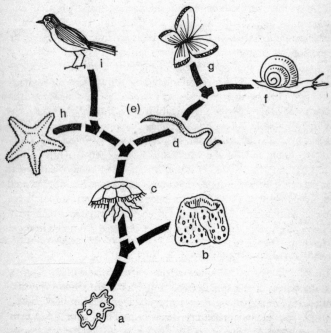

Figure 2. *Diagrammatic relationship of the main phyla, or groups, in animal kingdom:* (a) *Protozoa (amoebae, etc.);* (b) *Porifera (sponges);* (c) *Coelenterata (jellyfishes, etc.);* (d) *Annelida (segmented worms);* (e) *several phyla, represented by such organisms as roundworms, flatworms, lamp shells, etc.;* (f) *Mollusca (snails, etc.);* (g) *Arthropoda (insects, etc.);* (h) *Echinodermata (starfishes, etc.);* (i) *Chordata (birds, etc.).*

Birds and mammals are shown at the top of the evolutionary tree (Figures 2 and 3) to indicate their advanced status. Groups of reptiles, now extinct, gave rise to each. The advances embodied in mammals parallel those of birds in some ways; mammals too are characterized by warm blood, high metabolism, an insulating coat, good hearing and sight (usually), much care

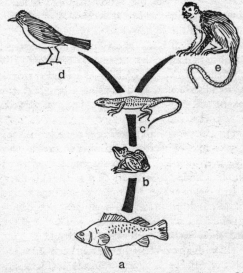

Figure 3. *Family tree of vertebrates:* (a) *fishes,* (b) *amphibians,* (c) *reptiles,* (d) *birds,* (e) *mammals.*

of the young, and a large brain. However, there are notable differences. Among the most obvious are the characteristic mammalian coat of hair instead of feathers; and the teeth which arm the mammalian jaw, teeth that show an advance over reptile teeth in being more complex in structure, i.e., the milk teeth appear first and are subsequently shed and replaced by permanent teeth. No modern bird has teeth. In addition to fine sight and hearing, many mammals have an effective sense of smell, a sense almost lacking in birds. The mammalian brain is large,

but differs from that of birds in the great development of the
centres for coordinating all impressions, activities, learning, and
memory. By contrast, in birds' brains the most highly developed
centres are those governing stereotyped instinctive behaviour.

In mammalian reproduction an external egg like that of birds
has generally been abandoned, and the young, nourished within the mother's body by her bloodstream, are born alive. Much
parental care is given, but the young mammal is fed on milk
secreted by the parent instead of receiving at once the food
which will be eaten throughout life, as birds do.

The student of fossil birds who would trace the step-by-step
ancestry of birds is plagued by the scarcity of early fossils.[2] Most
of our knowledge of the rise of birds is deduced from a small
amount of fossil evidence. Bird bones are generally small and
easily broken, and few of them have been preserved in the
record in the rocks.

Accordingly, it seems little short of a miracle that amazingly
complete specimens of a crow-sized bird called *Archaeopteryx*
should have been found. These fossils come from the Jurassic
lithographic limestone of Germany (Table I). This fine-grained
stone was laid down 192 to 136 million years ago in a shallow,
quiet coral sea, and has preserved even such fine details as the
imprints of the feathers of *Archaeopteryx*. The fossil specimens
of this bird show it had reptile-like teeth and a long, bony,
lizard-like tail with a row of feathers down each side. The wings
– of which both bones and prints of the feathers have been
preserved – and breast bone indicate that this ancient bird had
small breast muscles and a weak flight. There were three fingers,
each equipped with a claw. Probably *Archaeopteryx* used its
claws in climbing among the branches of trees, and its wings in
gliding from tree to tree, flapping them but little. Palaeontolo-
gists, who study fossils, have pointed out that except for its
feathers there was little to separate it from some reptiles of the
period. But since *Archaeopteryx* did have feathers, ornithologists are justified in claiming it as an early bird. Two well-
preserved specimens, another partial one, and a single isolated
feather print, four specimens in all, of *Archaeopteryx* are all we
know of birds from the Jurassic.

TABLE I
Geological Time Scale

Eras	Periods	Epochs	Years ago (in millions of years)
Cainozoic	Recent		·02
	Quaternary	Pleistocene	1·5
	Tertiary	Pliocene	7
		Miocene	26
		Oligocene	37
		Eocene	54
		Palaeocene	65
Mesozoic	Cretaceous		136
	Jurassic		192
	Triassic		225
Palaeozoic	Permian		280
	Carboniferous		345
	Devonian		395
	Silurian		435
	Ordovician		500
	Cambrian		570

Pre-Cambrian

The next period, the Cretaceous, which extended from 136 to 65 million years ago, is somewhat richer in birds. Two ancient types have been found as fossils in the rocks of Kansas: one, *Hesperornis*, the 'western bird', was a diver-like, flightless swimming bird with small wings and with jaws armed with teeth like those of *Archaeopteryx*. The other, *Ichthyornis*, the 'fish bird', had long, strong wings and evidently flew over the water snatching fish from the surface in a manner still used by terns today. Whether or not the fish bird had teeth is an open question. No one has found the fossil jaw bones.

These three – lizard-tail, western, and fish – are the only types of ancient bird we know. One was a climbing and gliding bird, one a flightless, swimming bird, and one a strong-winged bird. The character of their bodily structure unquestionably supports the idea of the evolution of birds from reptiles, but these birds provide little direct information about the evolution of flight. Judging by the great differences between the three types, we assume that a considerable diversity existed among ancient birds, and we can hope that some day more fossil birds will be found so that we can actually trace the way flight developed. Until then we are left with two theories, each equally plausible.

One is that birds' ancestors were tree-climbing lizards which used their developing feathers and wings in gliding and parachuting to extend their jumps and to break the force of their landings. Gradually wings and flight developed.

The other theory is that birds' ancestors were running lizards and the developing feathers and wings served as planes adding to the speed of running and finally allowing them to glide and, at last, to fly.

However bird flight originated, it was very successful, especially when it was combined with an efficient bipedal means of progress – walking, hopping, or swimming. Early in the mainstream of the evolution of birds a balance was struck between aerial and terrestrial locomotion, that is, between the use of wings and the use of legs.

Not all birds maintained this balance and some went up evolutionary blind alleys. Birds such as *Hesperornis*, ostriches, and penguins lost their powers of flight. Others, such as frigate birds and swifts and perhaps *Ichthyornis*, almost lost the powers of bipedal locomotion and their feet became useful only for perching. However, most birds have retained effective use of both their wings and their feet. This gives them a wonderful advantage, for they can share in two worlds. Like the reptiles they can hop about or run on the ground, and climb about in the shrubbery and the trees, or swim in the ocean. Also, without losing this ability, they have achieved the freedom of the air, and distance means little to them.

Perhaps no one can appreciate what this freedom means better than a naturalist who is trying to study the life in a tropical forest. Here the habitats are most complex and life is the richest in the world. However, much of what is going on is happening in the treetops a hundred feet or more overhead, where the birds hop from twig to twig and fly from branch to branch while man is earthbound and frustrated below.

The need to escape competition and population pressure from the reptiles that were dominant in the Jurassic period may well have been a factor that caused the birds of that time to specialize as light, active, flying animals of the trees. The vegetation of the period was dominated by cycads, ferns, and conifers; insects flourished and there were fish in the seas. These provided food for birds.

But great and far-reaching changes came in the next period, the Cretaceous. With its close, the age of reptiles ended and extinction came to all but the few types – lizards, snakes, turtles, and crocodiles – that we know today. Most important to birds, there no longer were flying reptiles to compete with them in the air.

At the same time there was also a great change in the vegetation. The angiosperms, or flowering plants, became dominant. These included types resembling the familiar plants of today: broadleaf trees very much like maples and beeches, shrubs like roses and blackberries, and herbs like columbines, sunflowers, and grasses. Their leaves, flowers, fruits, and seeds, as well as their attendant insects, provided a lavish array of food. To use these, both birds and mammals evolved into many different types.

Already in the Cretaceous the first modern bird types had appeared, as we know from the fragmentary fossil bones of flamingos, pelicans, cranes, and ducks. By the early part of the Cainozoic era, in the Palaeocene and the Eocene, many of our present-day bird families had become established. Mammals had evolved along with birds, and were their main competitors.

The most familiar mammals are terrestrial quadrupeds – mice, cows, and elephants; climbing cats, squirrels, and monkeys; and burrowing moles. But there are also the fish-like whales and the flying bats. The birds easily met the problems of competing with most of these by their greater alertness and their use of the power of flight. They rested and nested in places difficult of access on foot. Birds came to occupy all the habitats used by mammals except the soil, which moles burrow into, but which birds, such as the domestic hen and the woodcock, only scratch or probe.

In only one habitat, the air, were birds in serious competition with a mammal – the bat. Here the competition recalls that between the early flying reptiles, pterosaurs, and the primitive birds. Both the pterosaur and the bat had wings of skin supported by elongated fingers: the pterosaur's wing by a single long finger, the bat's, by several. The wing so constructed is more liable to serious injury by accident than is a bird's wing, in which a broken feather can be replaced by moult. This skin-covered wing is also less flexible than that of a bird, and in addition both flying reptiles and bats sacrificed the effectiveness of their hind limbs as organs of locomotion. The flying reptiles could use their hind limbs, judging by their structure, for little but hanging up at rest. Bats, we know, can shuffle about on feet and wrists, but only to a limited extent.

How different a bird is, with its alternative effective modes of locomotion. Agile in the air, it can alight, fold its wings within the shelter of its fluffed-out feathers, and be a nimble biped.

It may have been the competition with diurnal birds that forced bats to be creatures of the night. Even in the tropics, where bats are most numerous and diversified, both the mouse-sized insect-eating bats and the squirrel-sized fruit-eating bats avoid direct competition with birds. They do this by obtaining their food – insects on the wing or fruit gathered from the trees – in the darkness, thus avoiding birds which feed on the same food in the same area.

While mammals have been dominant in the Cainozoic, the 'Age of Mammals', birds have been runners-up, and in many parts of the world they are the most conspicuous animals.

CHAPTER 2

Size and Shape of Birds

FACTS about extremes in size – or in speed, fighting ability, or age – have a fascination in themselves. They are concrete bits of information that outline definitely certain aspects of our world (Figure 4).

The smallest bird is the bee humming-bird of Cuba, *Mellisuga helenae*. It is a red, green, and blue mite only two and a half inches long including its long bill. Its weight appears not to have been recorded, but compared with the known weight of larger humming-birds it must be about one gramme (there are just over twenty-eight grammes in one ounce). Naturalists who have watched this bird in Cuban gardens say that it is much more likely to be mistaken for a bee than recognized as a bird. Not only is this the smallest bird, but it is probably also the smallest warm-blooded vertebrate. The only mammal approaching its tiny size is the diminutive shrew which weighs about two grammes.[1]

The largest flying birds, to judge by their wing-spreads, are the great wandering and royal albatrosses of the southern oceans, whose wing-spreads reach eleven and a half feet. Not far behind are the white pelicans and the trumpeter swans, with wing-spreads reaching nearly ten feet, and the condors, reaching nine and a half feet. Their weights range from twenty to forty pounds.

The real giants of the bird world today are the flightless birds.

Figure 4. *Range in bird sizes:* (a) *ostrich,* (b) *pelican,* (c) *rooster,* (d) *robin,* (e) *humming-bird.*

Because their wings are rudimentary, a wing-spread measurement is meaningless for comparison, but their weights can be compared. The largest flightless water bird is the emperor penguin. It weighs up to ninety-four pounds and stands about three and a half feet high. Among the flightless land birds the ostrich is the largest. It weighs up to three hundred pounds and stands as much as eight feet high. When the ostrich feeds along with the herds of zebras, wildebeests, and antelope on the plains of Africa, its head is high above them. This gives it an advantage in watching for enemies and it often serves as a sentinel, its alarmed movements alerting the other animals.

That larger species than those living today existed in the past we know from the fossil record. Estimates of the wing-spreads and weights of these species are based on a comparison of fossil bones with the corresponding bones of living species. However, the larger fossil flying birds were only slightly larger than our present-day ones. There was a flying sea bird of the Miocene, *Osteodontornis,* that must have had a wing-spread of fifteen feet, and a vulture, *Teratornis,* of the North American Pleistocene that had nearly as great a wing-spread and a weight of fifty pounds.

Among the extinct flightless birds, a moa of New Zealand and the *Aepyornis*, or 'elephant bird', of Madagascar reached the greatest size, much greater than that of the ostrich. It is from the bones of these that Dr Dean Amadon of the American Museum of Natural History in New York has calculated that a large moa may have weighed five hundred pounds, and *Aepyornis* twice that, or half a ton.[2] While we group these two giants with the fossil birds, they missed by very little being part of our present-day fauna. The first men to colonize New Zealand from other South Pacific islands must have found some moas still living, and it is possible that when the first native peoples reached Madagascar, living *Aepyornis* were still there.

Comparing the sizes of other vertebrates with those of birds, we find that the smallest species of fish, amphibians, reptiles, and mammals are all in the same range, about one to three grammes. Presumably the organization of a vertebrate is not functionally efficient below this size.

At the upper range of size, however, the largest birds are much smaller than the largest mammals – the hundred-ton aquatic whale and the six-ton terrestrial elephant. The largest birds are also much smaller than the largest reptiles, such as the fifty-ton extinct dinosaur, *Brontosaurus*.

It may be that flying birds, which must alternately support their weight by a single pair of wings in flight and by their two legs on the land, have reached the upper limit of weight possible for them. This limit is a result of structural requirements in terms of ratios of weight and strength and diameter of bone, a simple matter of physics.

In the course of their evolution, birds developed their present type of structural organization as early as the Cretaceous, and this fitted them extremely well for their way of life. But in this specialization for a life involving both walking and flying, they became incapable of further radical change and as a result they represent an evolutionary conservatism, unlikely to produce any further basic differences.

Compared to the diversity in shape that is found among

mammals and even among reptiles, the basic shape of birds is remarkably uniform. Mammals, typically quadrupeds, have also
evolved as winged bats and fish-like whales. Even the living
reptiles include legless snakes, four-legged slender lizards, and
turtles with bulky box-like bodies borne on four legs. But birds
are all bipeds with wings, even those which have lost the power
of flight.

In discussing the shape of birds it is advisable to take up the
different elements separately: first, the body, which varies little;
second, the organs of locomotion, the wings and legs, whose
great adaptations are intimately correlated with the birds' preferred habitat and general way of life; and third, the necks and
bills, which are adapted to a particular type of food. Figure 5
shows some of the different combinations of bills, necks, and
legs which have arisen.

The meagre range in body shape is well illustrated by a
comparison of three kinds of birds – the turkey, which tapers
backward in a more or less triangular shape from its broad
'shoulders' and its enormous breast muscles to the 'parson's
nose', the stubby, fleshy remnant of the tail; the duck, which is
more elongate, like a broad-beamed boat, as befits a bird that
swims; and the herons and rails of the marshes, whose some-

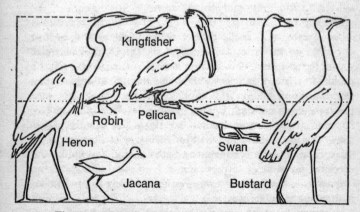

Figure 5. *Different combinations of bills, necks, and legs.*

what laterally compressed bodies aid them in slipping between the reeds. Our common garden birds, swallow, robin, sparrow, and the like, have bodies much like the turkey's. As special cases there are the flightless birds, with little or no breast muscle. But all are basically similar in body shape. Whatever pronounced diversity in shape exists is to be found in the extremities of birds – in their wings, legs, and feet, and in their necks and bills.

A skilled ornithologist or a talented observer can examine an unfamiliar bird and deduce its way of life. Adaptations to a particular habitat modify each bird in certain ways, and specialization for a certain type of food causes corresponding evolutionary changes. For example, an eagle will soar on its broad wings, a duck swim with its webbed feet, and a tiny humming-bird probe deep into a flower with its long, slender bill.[3]

The many and various types of birds are treated at some length in Appendix I, which includes a classification of birds into twenty-seven main groups, or orders, with illustrations of each order. These groups are formed of closely related species presenting a natural, or phylogenetic, classification.

But a broader, ecological classification of birds, by the major habitats to which they have become adapted, gives a better understanding of the diversity of their wings and feet. There are four major habitats: the trees and other vegetation, the ground, the water, and the air.

In attempting to choose four types of birds, each typical of one of these four habitats, one is faced with an embarrassment of riches, for so many different birds live in each habitat. Also, the problem of living in a certain habitat may be solved in more than one way. For instance, gulls fly over the ocean and pick their food from the surface, while auks and divers swim and dive for theirs. Again, where one habitat changes to another, where water changes to land through mud flats, sand beaches, grassy marshes, or tree-filled swamps, we find special conditions and special types of birds.

Even so, a few types of bird from each habitat can be chosen to illustrate the main extremes of adaptation. Tree birds are well represented by the passerine, or perching birds, such as our familiar song-thrush and robin. With well-developed grasping or perching feet and well-developed wings, these birds hop and flit and fly, using their wings and legs alternately in moving about to feed. A few birds that ordinarily perch in trees do not feed there but watch for food on the ground or in the water and dart down for it, as does the kingfisher.

Ground birds, such as the gallinaceous birds, which include the pheasant and the domestic fowl, have stout legs and toes suitable for scratching as well as for walking, their usual method of getting about when they feed. Their short, rounded wings are used chiefly for flying short distances to escape their enemies.

Running birds of the plains are typified by the bustards, with the elongated legs and short toes which befit birds that run over a hard surface. Their large, broad wings are used to travel long distances. In the ostrich-like birds, the running type of leg and foot is the sole means of locomotion and the wings have degenerated and are no longer useful for flight.

Along the ocean beaches are found the waders, such as the sandpipers and plovers, with slender legs and short toes. These birds feed as they trot over the ground, and their long, pointed wings carry them from one feeding place to another as well as on spectacular long migrations.

On shores where the water is shallow and the bottom is soft and muddy, herons with long legs and long toes are at home, watching, or stalking along, or flying from place to place with measured strokes of their long, broad wings. Cranes, storks, and ibis are superficially similar to the herons.

Where rich herbaceous vegetation grows at the edge of the water, the rails, with rather short legs but long toes, walk over the floating vegetation. When alarmed, they run into the shelter of the reeds or grass, seldom using their short, rounded wings. Jacanas somewhat resemble rails in habits but have longer toes and usually fly rather than hide when disturbed.

Swimming birds, such as divers and ducks and swans, have waterproof plumage, short legs, and webbed feet. Their rather small, pointed wings beat rapidly as they carry their owners in direct flights to distant places. Auks use their wings for swimming under water, and the somewhat similar penguins have adapted their wings to stubby paddles which are no longer useful for flight. In contrast, pelicans also swim and eat fish but have long, broad wings, and some species fly slowly over the water seeking their prey.

Aerial birds spend much of their time on the wing when looking for food. Their wings are large, their feet small. Swallows and swifts catch their food, insects in flight, over the land; frigate birds, albatrosses, and often gulls and terns hunt over the sea, taking food from the surface.

While the length of the neck and the size and shape of the bill are important in determining the shape of the bird, they may or may not correlate with the size and shape of the wings and the legs (Figure 5). The diversity of size, shape, and structure of the bill does correlate with the type of food preferred by the bird. Each habitat provides many kinds of food, and to use these and avoid competition, different bills have arisen.

The bill is basically comparable to the grasping end of a pair of tweezers, the upper mandible more or less a fixed part of the skull, the lower mandible hinged to the bottom of the skull and operated by the jaw muscles. Despite many details of variation in size and shape, there seem to be just three main types of bill: plain tweezers, used for seizing and probing; tweezers with a hook at the end for the additional use of snatching and tearing; and tweezers broadened and lengthened, with a fringe around the edge so that with the aid of the tongue they can be used as a sieve to collect small food items from mud or water.

The plain-tweezers type of bill may be short or long, slender or stout, blunt or sharp-pointed, straight or curved. The cutting edge of the upper mandible may be smooth or may have tiny serrations or a single notch near the tip. Some extreme forms of this bill with special uses may be mentioned: the long, slender bills of the humming-bird, creeper, and snipe, used respectively for probing into flowers, into crevices in bark, or into the earth; the long, stout bills of herons and storks, for catching fish and other live prey; the short, stout bills of finches, for cracking seeds; the fine, pointed bills of warblers for picking insects off leaves; and the very short bills, reduced to little more than rims around the mouths of swallows and swifts, which catch insects on the wing in their widely opened mouths. Most birds' bills are somewhere in between and are adapted for use in a wide variety of ways rather than for one special purpose.

The tweezers type of bill with a single hook at the tip may be short, as in hawks and owls, whose bills are all hook and are used primarily for tearing flesh from a mammal or bird caught in the bird's feet; or the hook may be at the end of a long, rather slender bill, as in cormorants and frigate birds, where it is used for snatching fish, or at the end of a stout bill such as the shrike's, where it aids in holding large insects.

The sieve-like, or filtering, type of bill is not common among birds and is restricted to those whose habitat is the water and the mud. It is well illustrated by the bills of ducks. The bills of flamingos and a group of small petrels called prions are similar.

The diversity of fine structural detail of the bill, some of which can be correlated with feeding habits, is great. But the diversity in the use of bills of the same general structure is much greater. The interesting thing is not that bills are so varied in detail, but that bills of the same general type can be used for so many purposes. The wonder of adaptation lies not only in the evolution of structure, but in the wonder of the adaptive behaviour.

CHAPTER 3

The Bird Body

JUST as it is possible to drive a motor car without knowing much about an internal-combustion engine, gears, and electric wiring, so it is possible to watch birds and even study their behaviour with little knowledge of their anatomy. But a survey of the structural organization of a bird's body will help in understanding what has taken place in the course of bird evolution as well as how birds live and behave today.

In this chapter, after a brief look at the outside of a bird, the organ systems are discussed in the following order: the skeleton, the muscles, the alimentary canal, the excretory system, and the reproductive, circulatory, respiratory, nervous, and endocrine systems.

These are the same organs and systems that one finds in other vertebrate animals. They have been inherited from the reptile and modified to meet the bird's needs. Much of the bird's internal economy is parallel to that of the human body, but the basic vertebrate plan is beautifully adapted inside and out for the bird's own way of life. In this chapter space permits examination of only a sampling of the more notable adaptations.

In looking at the living bird, one is seldom aware of its skin because of the feathers. The skin itself is tender, and protection for the body is provided by the coat of overlapping feathers. This is so dense and full that the shape of the body and limbs is concealed. How different a plucked bird in a market looks! The body is short and thick, the neck long and thin, topped by a large head. Without their quills the wings and legs are slender and the tail is a fleshy stub.

The only skin gland of birds is the uropygial gland, present in most birds, which is found on the lower back just above the tail. The gland secretes an oily substance through nipple-like structures. Traditionally this substance has been regarded as useful in dressing the plumage, but this idea has been questioned and the view put forward that the secretion may be a source of vitamin D. Though birds certainly seem to use it in preening, they could ingest some at the same time, and the gland may serve a dual purpose.

The skeleton, which is the supporting framework of the bird and provides the levers on which the muscles work, has evolved striking adaptations for both flight and bipedal locomotion. The general adaptations have already been mentioned: the lightness and rigidity, achieved by slender hollow bones and by fusion of different bones and reduction of the number of parts. However, each section of the skeleton has its particular specialization.[1]

The most distinctive aspect of the skull is the beak, or bill. This is formed by the elongation of the bony jaws, which are covered with horny sheaths and are quite without teeth in modern birds. Though a few birds, such as hawks, grasp food in their feet, most birds use the bill in grasping and manipulating food and nest material, and in preening. If the bill is considered functionally as equivalent to the pair of forceps used for picking up things, the neck must be considered as the arm that moves the forceps about. To serve effectively in this way, the neck is very flexible, and in some birds it is very long. The flexibility is achieved in two ways. First, the cervical, or neck, vertebrae that make up this part of the backbone are more numerous than in mammals – all of which have seven vertebrae in the neck, the whale and man as well as the long-necked giraffe. Some birds have as few as eight vertebrae; fourteen is a common number; and some long-necked birds have as many as twenty-five. In the second place, flexibility of the neck is increased by the peculiar saddle shape of the articulating surfaces of the vertebrae, which allows maximum bending forwards and backwards as well as sideways.

This ease of movement of the neck is seen to advantage in

a swan, which reaches out with its long neck for food, or folds it back in graceful curves when it is at rest, and in the owl, which can rotate its head through nearly a whole circle. This ability is the basis of the old tale that by walking completely around an owl that is watching, one can make it wring its own neck.

The forepart, or thoracic region, of the skeleton of the bird's trunk, like that of a man, has a backbone, ribs, and a breast-bone, or sternum. But in birds these have been modified along with the forelimbs, which have become wings.

The great breast muscles that power the wings have dictated an increase in size of the sternum and it has become a flat plate with a projecting keel for muscle attachment. Rigidity is given the ribs by a strap-shaped projection on each rib that overlaps the one behind and so forms a brace, and by the immovability of the vertebrae, which have become a nearly solid column, very different from the flexible neck vertebrae. Since the breast muscles and the wings support the whole weight of the bird in flight, extra bracing in addition to that of the ribs is neces-sary. This is provided by the two collar bones, or clavicles, which fuse just in front of the breast bone to form the 'wish-bone', and by another pair of bones, the coracoids, especially well developed in birds. These are stout braces that run up-wards from the front of the sternum and converge on each side with the clavicle and the slender shoulder blade to form the socket in which the basal bone of the wing, the humerus, fits and articulates.

The humerus, which is comparable to man's upper-arm bone, and the radius and the ulna, comparable to the two bones of man's forearm, support the basal and central parts of the wing, the ulna bearing the long flight feathers called secondaries.

The bony elements of the bird's 'wrist' and 'hand' are much reduced in number and fused together. The 'fingers' are re-duced to remnants of three, only one of which is important. None of these ordinarily has claws. These greatly modified 'hand' bones support the long flight quills called primaries.

The bones of the forelimbs have developed as a supporting framework for the wing surface, and the thoracic region of the skeleton has become a rigid frame for supporting the wings themselves, somewhat similar to the corresponding section of an aeroplane. But in addition this frame has a quality possessed by no aeroplane frame: it is flexible enough so that the wings can also be moved to supply the power for flying.

In contrast with the adaptations for flying in the forepart of the skeleton of the trunk, the adaptations of the hind part are for supporting the bird's weight on a single pair of legs, for achieving rigidity without weight. The most obvious change that has taken place is the fusion into a single unit of the lower-back vertebrae and the hip bones which correspond to those forming the pelvis in man. This unit, called the synsacrum, forms a roof over the viscera in the abdomen and is open below; it can also be likened to an inverted, keel-less sternum or an inverted basin. This synsacrum, joining the immovable thoracic vertebrae, gives a remarkable absence of flexibility to the whole shortened trunk of the bird. This rigidity has eliminated the need for elaborate body muscles such as those that brace the more flexible back of a mammal and hold up the forepart of its body. There is no 'tenderloin' on a bird.

There is also an adaptive feature of this open, inverted-basin shape of the synsacrum which has nothing to do with locomotion, but is concerned rather with the laying of a large egg. The hip bones of mammals unite below to form a pelvic ring through which the young are born, an arrangement which would be impractical for birds, for their relatively large, hard-shelled eggs cannot safely be subjected to pressure.

It has been said that the knee of a bird, unlike that of a man, bends backwards. This indicates a lack of understanding of the structure of both human and bird legs. Superficially, the bird's leg is more like the hind leg of the horse than the leg of a man, though the same bones are involved in all three. The human leg is the most generalized, the bird's is the most modified. The bird's thigh – with its thigh bone, or femur, which articulates with a socket in the synsacrum – is completely concealed in the coat of feathers, as is the real knee joint of the bird. The shin bone, or tibia – with its associated bone, the fibula, which is reduced to a mere splint – is the 'drumstick' of the roast turkey. This is the first visible section of the bird's leg. Then comes the slender shank, or tarsus, usually covered with horny scales and bearing the toes, usually four in number. This tarsus has no counterpart as a single bone in man, but is formed by the fusion and elongation of certain ankle bones. The one visible joint of the leg is thus comparable to the ankle joint in man.

A fusion of bones and a reduction of the number of parts also appears in the tail of modern birds. The ancestral long tail as seen in *Archaeopteryx* has been reduced to a few free vertebrae; the remaining vertebrae have been fused into a short plate-like bone, the pygostyle, to which the long tail quills are attached. Again we see repeated the reduction of weight in the extremities.

Some of the modifications of muscles have been mentioned in connection with the bones they move.[2] The stiffness of the skeleton of the trunk, eliminating movement within it, has reduced the need for muscles there, and in the slender extremities the muscles have changed to less bulky tendons. The need for powering the wings and legs for locomotion has resulted in the enlargement of the muscle masses of the breast and the upper leg. This concentration of muscles is evident to anyone who carves a fowl. There is the white meat of the breast and the dark meat of the legs in a domestic fowl or a turkey. In the goose and the duck the meat is all dark. The colour of the meat is due to the number of red blood cells in it and correlates with the use the muscles get. White meat tends to occur where the muscles are used only for short, sudden bursts of movement, while dark-red meat indicates muscles used for long-continued efforts.

Food enters the digestive system through the gape, or maw, passes down the gullet to the stomach, and moves on through the small intestine, where the nutrients are absorbed.[3] The waste material is emptied into the large intestine, passes into the cloaca, and is expelled through the vent, or anus. A pair of slender caeca may or may not be present at the hind end of the small intestine, but their function is obscure.

Since the bird has no teeth, food must be swallowed whole

or in roughly broken or torn pieces. To facilitate swallowing large pieces, the bones of the lower jaw are flexible, bending outwards and increasing the size of the gape when required. It is surprising what large fruit some pigeons can eat at a gulp, and what large fish certain ducks can swallow. When a food item sticks in the gape, the tongue, with barbs on its base, can help to pull it through. This raw food may be stored in the thin-walled, extensible gullet when the stomach is full. In some species, such as gallinaceous birds, doves, and sparrows, there is a special enlargement of part of the gullet into a thin-walled crop to increase this storage capacity.

Birds that feed on hard food have compensated for the lack of grinding teeth by evolving a gizzard. The gizzard is a modified ventriculus, the rear, non-glandular part of the stomach. The walls of the opposite sides become enormously thickened and muscular, and the lining becomes tough and horny. To this equipment the bird adds grinding stones by swallowing grit or gravel. Muscular action of the gizzard wall is very effective in grinding up the hardest foods. Certain diving ducks swallow molluscs whole and the gizzard grinds them up, shells and all. Other species can grind up hard nuts.

Adaptation may not always lead to complexity or advances; it sometimes results in degeneration. This is exemplified by the stomachs of certain birds whose food needs no preparation at all. There is a South American passerine bird, a euphonia tanager, in which the soft, sweet fruit eaten passes directly from the glandular forepart of the stomach (the proventriculus) into the intestine. The ventriculus has nearly atrophied in the course of evolution into a small, useless projection on the wall of the digestive tube. Some of the flower-peckers (*Dicaeum*) of the East Indies that eat sweet berries and spiders show an intermediate condition. The ventriculus has become a small sac on the wall of the digestive system. When the flower-pecker eats spiders they are routed to the ventriculus, where presumably they receive some mechanical treatment before they are passed on to the intestines for digestion. However, when the bird eats berries, which consist of sweet pulp needing no treatment, they pass directly from proventriculus to intestines. These seem to be examples of the progressive loss of an organ as its use decreases.

Birds have two methods of excreting liquid wastes.[4] They have no urinary bladder, but the wastes from the kidneys are emptied as semi-solids into the cloaca, where they are mixed with the faeces and expelled with them. More unusual is the excretion of excessive salts in the system through a pair of nasal glands, one located above each eye. These glands, which are well developed only in birds living close to the sea, take salt from the system and discharge it in a highly concentrated solution through the nostrils. It is the action of these glands that allows birds to drink salt water, as discussed in Chapter 7.

The sex organs become enlarged and active for only part of each year.[5] Then they dominate the activities of the bird for weeks and months, from courtship through nesting to fledging the young. These conspicuous and complicated behaviour patterns have supplied a great deal of natural-history data for the student of living birds, and the changes in the reproductive system within the bird and the related physiological changes have been a fruitful source of experimentation for the biologists. The reproductive systems of both birds and mammals evolved from that of reptiles, but the two have followed diverging paths. The difference is well illustrated by the product as it is brought into the world: the bird's 'young' at birth is a hard-shelled, food-filled egg with only a tiny speck of living protoplasm in it; the mammal's young at birth is a living, breathing small mammal, even if it is blind, naked, and nearly helpless in many cases.

The gonads, or sex glands, lie in the body cavity on the forward edge of the kidneys – a pair of oval testes in the male and a single ovary on the left side in the female. The sperm of the male pass from the testes to the cloaca by way of the paired deferent ducts and are transferred from the male to the female at mating by contact of the cloacae. Sometimes an organ of intromission, a penis, is present in the male. In the female the egg is fertilized by one of the mobile sperm, which swims to the upper part of the single oviduct. After this, the germ cell with its yolk passes down the oviduct and receives its outer layers as it descends. It then passes to the cloaca and is expelled through the vent.

The fertilized egg is a reproductive cell containing a minute blastoderm that develops into an embryo.[6] The blastoderm is located on the side of the yolk, which contains the mass of the food for the embryo. This is enclosed in the albumen, or white of the egg, which is an elastic, shock-absorbing, insulating semi-solid with a high water content. It is the chief source of water for the embryo. A two-ply parchment-like membrane lies between the egg contents and the eggshell. Between these two layers, usually at the larger end of the egg, an air cell develops when the egg cools after laying. This air cell increases in size with the age of the egg because of water loss during incubation. It supplies air to the embryo when breathing starts. The shell is a hard, brittle calcareous (limy) layer which protects the contents and through the pores permits gaseous exchange, of both water vapour and air, between the egg and surrounding air.

Of major importance in maintaining the bird's warm-blooded condition is the four-chambered heart.[7] This is the pump, really two pumps in one, whose muscular contractions send the blood in a series of spurts out through the arteries and back through the veins of the closed circulatory system. To tissues throughout the body the blood carries food from the intestines and oxygen from the lungs, to be used in metabolism. It also carries waste products of metabolism to the kidneys and, as carbon dioxide, to the lungs for expulsion, and, as we shall see, it carries hormones as well.

Reptiles and other lower vertebrates have at most a three-chambered, or an imperfectly four-chambered, heart. This is an inefficient pumping system, allowing the dark-red, oxygen-poor venous blood carrying carbon dioxide to mix in the heart with the bright-red, oxygen-rich arterial blood. The four-chambered heart that birds share with mammals (there are minor differences in detail) prevents the mixing of in-coming and out-going blood and consequently is much more efficient.

The general circulatory system of all vertebrates is similar and the differences outlined above for birds and mammals are obviously adaptive. They correlate with the speeding-up of the life processes – the heightened metabolism that makes possible the continually active, agile life of the birds. However, there is one respect in which the bird's blood resembles that of all lower vertebrate animals and differs from that of mammals. The bird's red corpuscles are oval and have a nucleus, while in mammals they are round (except for camels) and lack a nucleus. The adaptive significance is obscure. However, it is one of those curious facts of nature which have been picked up and used in general literature. In this case it is a stock-in-trade item of the 'scientific' detective of fiction who focuses his microscope on the reddened handkerchief to find out whether the stain is really human blood or is a clue faked with chicken blood.

The main function of the lungs is to provide the blood with oxygen and to remove carbon dioxide from it.[8] The bird's warm-blooded condition demands a high rate of gaseous exchange for metabolism, much greater than the sluggish reptiles require and comparable to that found among mammals. But the bird's lungs, compared to those of mammals, are relatively small and capable of little expansion. Air enters the respiratory system through the external nostrils, passes down a tube-like trachea, or windpipe, and through its two branches, or bronchia, to the lungs. These fit against the backbone and adjacent parts of the ribs, much as in mammals.

To compensate for the smallness and rigidity of the lungs, birds have elaborated a new way of increasing their efficiency. This is by means of air sacs. These are thin-walled projections of the respiratory system. Some were present in a primitive form in the reptiles from which birds arose, emphasizing the close bird–reptile relationship, but they are absent in mammals. The number and arrangement of the air sacs varies with the species of bird; in the well-studied pigeon there are nine. The most important for breathing is the abdominal pair, which occupies the space round the viscera. The others are in the regions of the chest and the neck.

When a mammal breathes, air is drawn into the lungs and then forced back out by action of a muscular diaphragm across the body cavity. In birds the air passes through the lungs twice.

It is drawn through the lungs into the air sacs and then out through the lungs again. The air sacs act as a bellows, operated by the movement of the muscles of the body wall. The muscles raise and lower the rear end of the sternum and increase and decrease the size of the abdominal cavity and with it the size of the air sacs. Whether gaseous exchange is most effective in the lungs during inflow or outflow has been much discussed by scholars, who still disagree. As the arrangement is a very effective one, judging by results, it probably takes place both times.

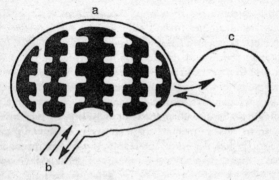

Figure 6. *Diagram of the cross-section of a lung and one of the abdominal air sacs, to show how air passes through the lungs twice: (a) lungs, with major passageways through lung tissue; (b) bronchia, leading to trachea (windpipe); (c) an abdominal air sac, which when expanded causes an inflow of air, and when reduced in size by pressure of the body wall causes an outflow of air.*

The breathing rate of birds, like the rate of heartbeat, varies with the size of the bird, as one might expect. Both processes are concerned with supplying oxygen to the system. The rates are faster in small birds, slower in large ones. Also, as in man, the rates increase with stepped-up activity, which requires the burning of more fuel.

An increase in the breathing rate in the individual bird is also caused by rises in temperature. A pigeon at rest may have a rate of thirty respirations a minute, while a pigeon panting from the heat may have a rate ten times that. Heat does not cause a corresponding rate increase in man, whose sweat glands wet his skin so that evaporative cooling goes on over his whole body surface. Such body-surface cooling is impossible in birds, for they have no sweat glands and their coat of feathers prevents loss of heat from the skin. However, the inner surfaces of the air sacs are moist and provide areas for internal evaporative cooling. It is probable that the air sacs in the forepart of the bird serve mainly as cooling organs, while the abdominal air sacs, so essential to the effective functioning of the lungs, may at the same time help in cooling the body.

Two functions of the respiratory system have been outlined – gaseous exchange and cooling. There is yet a third. The respiratory system is modified in birds, as it is in mammals, to produce the voice. But there is a difference in the location of the voice-producing apparatus in the two groups. In mammals the 'voice box' is the larynx, found in the upper part of the windpipe and associated with the 'Adam's apple' in the neck. In birds the 'voice box' is the syrinx, located at the lower end of the windpipe, at the point where it branches to send tubes to the lungs. Thus it is within the chest. At this fork there is a membrane, and the air stream vibrates it to produce the sound, a sound controlled by a variable number of muscles of the syrinx.[9]

The greatest evolutionary change in the bird's nervous system as compared with that of the reptile has been in the brain, which has become relatively larger.[10] It is short and broad, with large, smooth cerebral hemispheres in the front and a large cerebellum just behind them. The olfactory lobes are small and the optic lobes large, as one would expect in animals with little sense of smell and with great reliance on vision. Birds' brains are remarkably uniform throughout the group, while those of mammals vary enormously from group to group.

The nervous system shares with the endocrine system the function of coordination, which enables the whole animal to act as a unit.[11] These two systems are intimately related in the cooperative enterprise of sending messages throughout the body, but they work in quite different ways. The messages sent as electrochemical impulses along the neurons – the nerve cells and their nerve fibres – have been likened to telephone messages; they produce immediate action. The messages sent by the endocrine system are carried by hormones travelling in the blood and have been likened to messages sent by letter. They are usually concerned with gradual changes in the body – growth, metabolism, sexual and seasonal changes – and resultant behaviour, such as breeding and migration.

The increase in our knowledge of the endocrine system is one of the great advances in biology of the twentieth century. Much of our knowledge comes from experimental work which is still continuing. We now know that the effects of these glands are out of all proportion to their small size. Minute quantities of hormones, secreted directly into the blood, act far from their place of origin, and the glands may even influence each other. One gland may have multiple effects. Some are stimulating and some are inhibiting. The great amount of recent work that has been done on the endocrines of birds has helped bird watchers to understand many of the changes in behaviour and appearance which they have observed.

The endocrine glands in birds are the pituitary, or hypophysis, the thyroid, the parathyroid, the pancreatic islets, the adrenals, and, in part, the gonads.

The pituitary is situated below the brain in the floor of the skull. It is the master gland, affecting general metabolism, and influences other glands, including the thyroid and the gonads. It can be influenced by light and may be an important element in the timing system that controls cyclic activities such as migration and breeding. The thyroid is in the mid-line low in the neck, and can be influenced by diet. Its hormones govern metabolism and affect feather growth and pigmentation. Thyroid deficiency may cause goitre in chickens just as it does in man. The parathyroids, just behind the thyroid, have functions that include governing the calcium level in the blood and the excretion of phosphorus by the kidneys.

The adrenals are a pair of glands on the underside of the kidneys, near the forward edge. One of the functions of the adrenals is to prepare the body to withstand stress by causing additional blood to be sent from the viscera to the brain and muscles so that the bird is ready either to fight or to flee. These glands are unique in being under nervous control. The gonads, on the undersurface of the kidneys near the adrenals, have the primary function of producing sex cells; their endocrine functions include the release of hormones that affect secondary sexual characters and breeding behaviour.

The pancreas is a gland of external secretion and produces digestive juices. In this gland are the pancreatic islets, whose hormones include insulin, which controls the sugar content in the blood. The thymus and the pineal are often discussed with the endocrine glands, but no endocrine function has yet been shown for them. There seem to be hormones secreted by certain parts of the intestines, and hormones appear early in the egg yolk.

This brief survey has not touched on the organs of sight and hearing, which will be discussed in the next chapter.

CHAPTER 4

The Senses
of Birds

MOST birds are animals of the light. They flit from twig to twig; they plunge from the air to seize fish in the water or mice on the ground, or dart in among the branches to snatch insects from the leaves. After moving at high speed, a bird suddenly stops and perches on the top of a high tree. Small wonder that vision predominates in the bird world. But many birds also live among vegetation, in the shade of the leafy treetops, in the shrubbery, or among the grass stems. To keep in touch with each other and to be aware of enemies, birds need keen hearing, too. These are the aspects of the bird's life that have dictated specialization, first in vision and secondarily in hearing. Only occasionally do we see night-birds that reverse this order of importance and sometimes hunt by ear rather than by eye. There are a few birds as well, such as kiwis, that use a sense of smell, and a few, such as snipes, that use a tactile sense in obtaining their food from the earth.

The main everyday function of the eye is to act as an organ of vision, that is, to see. The eye of the bird, like that of other vertebrates, is of the camera type.[1] A lens focuses the image on the retina, which lines the back of the eyeball; there two different types of cells, called rods and cones, act as receptors and transmit the information to the central nervous system.

A structure characteristic of birds but not of mammals is the pecten. This is a folded, richly vascular membrane projecting from the back of the eyeball near the optic nerve into the humour (liquid) which fills the eyeball. Its edge is often comb-like in outline, whence its name. Its functions are still not clear. A physiological one has been suggested. The bird's retina has little of the vascularity (blood supply) so evident in the mammalian eye, and the pecten, with its rich supply of blood, may have taken over the job of providing nutrients to the eye. These foodstuffs are diffused through the humour to the cells of the retina. This may well have been the original function of the pecten, and may continue to be an important one. But a further optical use in vision has been suggested. The diverse shapes of the pecten in various types of birds correlate with differences in the birds' habits. It may aid in detecting movements of prey and enemies and perhaps in the little-understood use of the stars in celestial navigation. This seems to be a field in which experimental work is particularly difficult, and the arguments are abstruse.

The avian eye has one or more foveae, which are depressions on the retina, but they do not seem to be directly comparable to those in man. They have been said to be the areas of clearest vision; as the visual image must change as it crosses these, because of the slope of the walls of the pits and the change in distance from the lens, the foveae may aid in detecting the motion of distant objects against a featureless background like the sky. If so, they could share this function with the pecten.

The faculty of vision in the bird is comparable to that of man, but there are two striking differences. First, because of the flattened rather than globular shape of the eyeball, the bird's whole visual field is in focus at one time, while in man only the small area about the optical axis is in sharp focus. A bird sees everything in its whole field of vision sharply and in detail; a man must build up a similar detailed picture by focusing on various parts of the visual field. Second, the bird's eyes are usually placed on the sides of the head, so that the visual field is very wide, in some birds including practically the entire horizon. This vision, however, tends to be monocular. With a few exceptions such as owls, birds have only a restricted overlap in the vision of the two eyes. As a result there is no perspective, no idea of depth or of distance. The picture a bird gets is two-dimensional; that received by man, three-dimensional. As the foremost student of the senses of birds, Dr R. J. Pumphrey, of the University of Liverpool, has said, if a man had a bird's eyes he would be incapable of threading a needle; if a bird had a man's eyes he would be at the mercy of any cat that had the sense not to make a frontal attack.

One result of the lack of depth of vision is seen in the way a robin or a heron may cock its head to look at an object from two different angles before pecking at it. It is using parallax to estimate distance, to build up a three-dimensional picture.

While monocular vision is the basic type in birds, there is some modification towards binocular vision. The bird's eyeball, being relatively large, has little mobility, but it does have some in most birds, and some binocular vision seems not only possible but necessary for those – like certain swifts, swallows, and hawks – which pursue moving prey on the wing.

Before going on with more general aspects of the bird's vision, it is necessary to take up some details of light perception in the eye. As has been mentioned, the light-receptor cells in the retina that pass on the picture to the brain are of two kinds: cones for day vision and rods for night vision. But there are other differences between them besides the very great differences in sensitivity to the amount of light. Cones, effective in good light, give acuity, resolution of detail, and colour vision – that is, a clear, sharp picture in colour. Rods, effective when the light is so dim that the cones are quite blind, are poor in resolution power and in registering colour. The picture the rods give is a soft one, the images with indefinite edges and of various shades of grey.

In the human eye, there is a compromise, with some rod cells and some cone cells present, giving both day and night vision. In birds there is an adaptive difference in the relative number of rods and cones from species to species. In some diurnal birds the retina has many cones, though they are variable in distribution, and few or no rods. This gives poor night vision. In some nocturnal birds, such as owls, the rods predominate and the cones are few, giving good night vision.

Figure 7. *Birds' eyes: (a) external ear and nostril in relation to eye as seen in the bare head of a guinea fowl; (b) owl, with large, forward-looking eyes – much binocular vision; (c) diver with relatively small eyes on the sides of the head – vision largely monocular; (d) eye with nictitating membrane, a translucent, white 'third eyelid' that can be drawn across from inner corner; (e) eye partly closed, showing how lower lid is more movable than upper one.*

In resolution, the ability to see detail, the birds with the sharpest eyes are said to have vision with two or three times the acuity of man's day vision, though there are complications in comparing such abilities because of the differences in the field of vision and the grouping of the cone cells.

In night vision it has been estimated that an owl can see a hundred times better than a human can. This means that an owl can see by starlight about as well as a man does by bright moonlight. But the owl has sacrificed acuity and colour vision for its night vision. This sort of vision enables an owl to fly about and find perches, but it is hardly enough to enable it to find its prey, and for this hearing has taken over in part. As a protection against the brightness of a sunny day, the owl, like the cat, can cut down on the amount of light that enters the eye by expanding the iris, but the pupil stays round in the owl and does not become slit-like, as in the cat.

Accommodation is the ability to focus at different distances by means of muscles acting on the lens of the eye. For close vision it has been estimated that the ability of many birds is twice that of a twenty-year-old man, while in a cormorant, which dives and catches fish under water, accommodation is said to be five times as great.

Current research suggests that birds are capable of celestial navigation, of finding their way on long migrations and in their long-distance homing flights by utilizing visual clues in the sky – the sun by day and perhaps some star patterns by night. If this is true (and it may well be) birds have a visual ability and a power to coordinate such visual data which man has been able to equal only with the use of instruments.

The wide range of bird coloration and its use in species recognition, courtship, and display had prepared us for the psychologists' conclusion, based on careful experiments, that birds see colour much as we do. Indeed, it has been suggested that certain oil droplets coloured red, orange, and yellow which occur in the cones of the bird's eye may enable the bird to distinguish mixed or pigmentary colours to an extent possible to man only with the aid of filters.

It may be that the cryptic coloration of many birds has been developed entirely as a camouflage against other birds' keen colour vision, and this need for protection from sharp-eyed birds may also have been a major factor in the development of the many striking cases of insect mimicry and camouflage.

The suggestion that owls use infra-red light for hunting in darkness seems completely without foundation. For them to do so is theoretically impossible, and the owls' ability to hunt in complete darkness has been demonstrated to depend on hearing rather than on sight. Some insects, like bees, are able to see polarized light and act according to its pattern. The successful use of polaroid spectacles by fishermen for seeing fish in the water has raised the possibility that fishing birds, such as king-fishers and herons, which stab into the water for their prey, may use polarized light. Theoretically this seems quite possible and useful, but we have no evidence whatever that it occurs.

The ears of a bird are on the sides of its head, more or less where a man's are in relation to his eyes.[2] But where most mammals have external ears, especially developed in such animals as rabbits and donkeys, birds lack these 'ear trumpet' aids. The 'ears', or 'horns', of owls have no relation to hearing; they are simply ornamental tufts of feathers. The ear opening is normally covered with a special set of feathers, the auriculars, or ear coverts, except in bald species such as vultures and ostriches. These feathers normally lack barbules and therefore permit the more ready passage of sounds.

The bird's ear, like that of man, is divisible into an outer, a middle, and an inner ear. The outer ear is a tube through which sound waves enter to act on the ear-drum, or tympanic membrane, that closes the inner end. The sound is transferred across the air-filled middle-ear cavity by a single slender bone, the columella, which transfers the vibrations to the liquid, the endolymph, filling the coiled tube of the inner ear, or cochlea. There hair cells, receptors of various frequencies, pick them up and send them on to the central nervous system. The single biggest difference between the bird's and the man's ear seems to be in the middle ear, where the columella of the bird replaces the three bones – malleus, incus, and stapes – of man.

The performance of the bird's ear is inferred from bird behaviour. Presumably birds hear their own voices, which often are somewhat higher than ours, so it has been concluded that their hearing range is somewhat higher than ours. But experimental work (with only a limited number of species, it is true) indicates an outside range of from 40 to 28,000 cycles per second, with the greatest sensitivity in the middle ranges, from about 1,000 to 3,000 cycles per second. This is not very different from the hearing range in man. There is no evidence that birds utter ultra-high-frequency sounds comparable to those of bats.

Nevertheless, birds that nest in the complete darkness of the far interior of caves, like the oil-birds (*Steatornis*) of South

America and probably the swiftlets (*Collocalia*) of the Orient, have an echo-location method of finding their way in the dark. This system was first discovered in the bat, which uses ultrasonic (to human ears) cries. The oil-bird, however, uses audible calls as it flies, and these, echoing back from the rocky walls to the bird's ears, give it an awareness of the details of the interior of the cave and enable it to find its nest ledge.

Another equally amazing refinement has been demonstrated in the barn owl's hearing. For some time it has been known that this bird can catch mice in complete darkness. This led to the idea that the owl could see by infra-red light. But further experiments showed that the owl listened to the scampering of the mouse, and when the sounds ceased, flew on silent wings and with widespread claws to strike at the correct spot and grab the mouse. Hearing has replaced vision for this special type of hunting.

The study of the anatomy of the nasal passages of birds reveals no reason why many birds could not have a useful sense of smell, even if the olfactory lobes of the brain are small.[3] But the experimental evidence has been either negative or unconvincing, and field observation lends little support to the idea of a generally useful sense of smell in birds.

However, it has been well established that the kiwi does have a sense of smell that helps it in hunting for the worms it eats, and thus is an exception to the general rule. Moreover, for over a hundred years, since the time of Audubon, there has been a controversy over whether or not American vultures find the carrion on which they feed by using scent as a clue. Certainly here, if anywhere, it would be useful for the birds to be able to smell. Only in 1962 did Dr K. E. Stager, of the Los Angeles County Museum, demonstrate by an experiment that the controversy was probably the result of not separating the two American species, the turkey vulture and the black vulture.[4] The turkey vulture (or turkey buzzard) proves to have an effective sense of smell and uses it; the American black vulture and also several tested Old World vultures do not.

Then Dr Stager made another and rather amusing discovery. The gas maintenance men in southern California are well aware of the olfactory ability of the turkey buzzard, and use it in their work. An extremely smelly substance is added to the gas so that leakage from a household appliance can be detected at once. This odour is also detected by turkey buzzards, and is attractive to them. When a break in a gas pipe is reported, the men drive along the pipe until they see a congregation of buzzards over the line. The chances are that there they find the leak.

As one would expect, taste plays only a small part in a heron's catching and swallowing minnows, or in a pigeon's swallowing dry, hard seeds, but parrots biting off pieces of fruit and starlings eating cherries apparently do enjoy the taste. The theory that noxious flavours of insects developed as a protection against predation by birds leans heavily on the assumption that birds generally have a sense of taste. Research in this field is limited, but does indicate that some birds distinguish flavours. Experiments on colour discrimination too sometimes use ill-tasting substances to see how quickly birds learn to reject certain colours when they are accompanied by bitter tastes.

The taste buds are located in the fleshy part of the tongue and in the palate. As one would expect, the number is variable – from twenty-seven in some pigeons to three hundred or four hundred in some parrots, while none at all have been found in the domestic fowl.

The hard, horny bills of many birds provide little opportunity for exercise of a tactile sense in feeding. The tongue too is often horny at the tip. But some birds have a bill covered with soft skin and have a fleshy tongue provided with tactile organs, and they use these in finding food entirely by touch. Notable are the ducks, which sieve edible items from the mud by random dabbling, and the snipes, which probe into the mud for worms which they pull out and swallow.

Of course, much of the sensory equipment of all vertebrate animals is similar. They all feel heat, cold, and pressure, and respond to taste and gravity, but it is in sight and hearing that the greatest advances have been evolved in the higher vertebrates. Other senses have been postulated – a sense of direction, an ability to detect the earth's magnetic field, and the Coriolis force – but there seems no proven basis of fact for any of these. These are discussed in relation to direction finding in a later chapter (p. 148).

Birds, depending primarily on sight and secondarily on hearing, have proved to be remarkably like man and his anthropoid cousins in their perceptions of the world about them. The world of smell, which is so meaningful to many mammals, is practically closed to birds, as it is to the anthropoids. It is this similarity of the perceptual worlds of man and birds that has enabled man to appreciate the activities of birds and has contributed so much to our realization and appreciation of their complex ways of life.

CHAPTER 5

Patterns of
Diversity

THE wealth of differences separating species from species involves variations in details of plumage and behaviour more often than in structure. Exploring these details is at once the delight and despair of the student of birds. There is such an array of diversity that remembering all the particulars is impossible, and patterns must be sought as an aid to memory if for no other reason. To add meaning, these patterns must also codify principles underlying the biology of birds.

The patterns taken up in this chapter are those of adaptations to environment correlated with patterns of blood relationships among birds. But one must not ask too much of patterns. Perhaps we do not see clearly enough, but there always seem to be some details that do not fit into any pattern. As we learn more and more, we may be able to emend the patterns or formulate new, more satisfactory ones.

Each species of bird differs more from some of its relatives than from others. These degrees of difference indicate degrees of relationship. As an example, the mallard duck is more like a wood duck than it is like a swan or goose, but ducks, swans, and geese are more alike and more closely related to each other than they are to hawks, eagles, falcons, buzzards, and vultures, which form another group. Patterns of relationship can be worked out along these lines. All birds belong in one class, Aves (birds).[1] Within this class a number of *orders* are recognized, of which some of the most familiar are ducks and their relatives; Galliformes, or gallinaceous birds (domestic fowl, pheasants, quail, and the like); hawks and their near relatives; wader, gull, and auk assemblage; petrel and albatross assemblage; pelicans and their near relatives; woodpeckers and their relatives; and Passeriformes, or passerine birds (including the familiar perching birds and song-birds). The order of passerine birds in its turn includes a number of *families*, such as larks, swallows, sparrows, shrikes, wrens, warblers, and thrushes.

The thrush family has various *genera*, including the chats, (*Saxicola*), the wheatears (*Oenanthe*), the nightingales (*Luscinia*), the American blue-birds (*Sialia*), and the 'typical' thrushes (*Turdus*). The genus *Turdus* includes among other *species* the American robin (*Turdus migratorius*), the European blackbird (*Turdus merula*), and the song-thrush (*Turdus philomelos*).

This pattern, or system of classification, is based on similarities and differences and indicates actual blood relationships. All birds are descended from one group of ancient birds, which in its turn was descended from one pre-bird group of reptiles. That is, birds are monophyletic. In the course of the 200 million years of their evolution, they developed different types, from which different sub-types evolved, and this process has continued until we have some ten thousand or so species of birds today.

The guiding principle that has determined the course of this evolution is adaptation both of structure and of way of life to as many habitats and habitat niches as possible, in order to use to the full the available food. This adaptation was accomplished in ways that reduced competition. The functioning of this principle is deduced from fossil evidence viewed in the light of what we can see today in bird lives and interrelationships.

The evolution of adaptation will be discussed with respect to the following topics: adaptive radiation, specialization, convergence, ecological counterparts, ecological competition, correlation of structure and habits, pre-adaptation, and generalized feeding.[2]

In the early days of bird evolution, when the species were still few in number, many habitat niches probably were empty or at least much less crowded than they are today. Conditions were favourable for a single type of bird to spread out into several new habitat niches, and in adapting to them, the bird might evolve into a number of new divergent types. That is, adaptive radiation took place, and at that time was probably more common on a large scale than it is today. One of our oldest orders, that of the crane-like birds, shows that this has happened. Fossils of this order are known from the Cretaceous, a period from which very few fossil birds are known. The living crane-like birds include among others the families of cranes, rails, fin-feet, and bustard quail.

The cranes, adapted to walking and wading in open grass plains, and marshes, are long-legged, long-toed, long-necked birds that superficially resemble the herons and storks of another order. Rails are adapted to living among the vegetation of marshes, to running over floating vegetation and mud. They are much smaller, more compact birds than cranes, with shorter legs but with long toes. They find an unrelated parallel in the lily-trotters (*Jacana*) of another order. The fin-feet (*Podica*), adapted to a swimming life, have become somewhat duck-like, but with lobed instead of webbed toes. The bustard quail (*Turnix*) are adapted to walking on dry ground amid dense grass. They are small, compact birds with short toes, and recall small, true quail of the order of gallinaceous birds.

Another ancient order, the one which includes the diverse assemblage of waders, auks, and gulls, is an equally striking example of adaptive radiation. It now includes a family of long-winged flying birds (gulls and terns), a family of short-winged, web-footed swimming and diving water birds (auks), several families of running birds whose habitat is the water's edge (sandpipers and the like), a family of quail-like birds (seed snipe), and a family of marsh birds superficially recalling rails (jacanas or lily-trotters).

These two orders, the crane-like birds and the wader, gull, and auk assemblage, have successfully occupied water, land, and air habitats through adaptive radiation. The only major habitat they have not mastered is that of trees.

Trees and shrubbery provided the major habitat for the order of passerine birds. These seem to have radiated relatively late in geological time, in the Miocene or the Pliocene. This order alone now contains about half of the living species of birds, most of them in a sub-group called song-birds, which includes many of the familiar garden birds. Besides the warblers and tits, which have well-developed wings and grasping feet and flit and hop about, the order also includes the long-winged swallows, which feed on the wing in the air, and the larks, which with little structural modification have adopted a terrestrial life in the open plains.

But the most intriguing song-bird is the dipper (*Cinclus*). It looks like a short-tailed thrush or a large wren. Without any adaptation in structure, without the webbed or lobed toes that characterize ducks, divers, grebes, gulls, and most other water birds, the dipper has become entirely aquatic in its feeding habits. It is a song-bird that swims, dives, and walks on the bottom of swift mountain streams, seeking insect larvae, crustaceans, and small fish. There are water birds in plenty in other orders, but they all live in larger bodies of water. The dipper is a specialist among the song-birds that has moved into a vacant habitat niche. This bird seems to be one of nature's recent experiments. As yet the five species live only in the Americas, in Europe, and in Central Asia. Many of the world's small streams still lack a thrush-sized swimming and diving bird. Perhaps the dipper will develop into a new structural type of song-bird with webbed feet or lobed toes. If so, and this should make it more successful than it is now, it might spread to other areas as well.

The term adaptive radiation refers to a condition in which a single group of birds has evolved a number of quite different specialists, as discussed above. But a relatively uniform group may evolve a single specialized member, or sub-group. A few examples of such specialization can be briefly described. The members of the sparrow family are notable for their thick bill, adapted to cracking seeds. But in one genus (the crossbills) the tips of the mandibles are crossed, and thereby adapted for prying open the scales of pine and spruce cones and securing the seeds. Among the waders, most sandpipers and their near relatives have a rather slender bill that acts as a pair of tweezers or a probe, but one related genus, the oyster-catcher (*Haematopus*), has a bill which is laterally compressed and blunt at the tip. This makes a useful organ for prying limpets off rocks and for opening oysters and mussels, prey safe from most other waders.

In the petrels the bill is typically rather slender, has a hook at the tip, and is used in seizing food. However, the whale-birds, or prions, in this same order, have a broadened and fringed bill and use it to sieve small crustaceans from the sea. Hawks generally have short legs, but one species, the secretary bird (*Sagittarius*), has long, slender legs and, instead of flying to seize its prey, hunts by walking about in the open plains of Africa.

Food or habitat specialists such as these are commonplace. It seems as if evolution takes the form of continual experimentation, a search for new ways to make sure that all habitats and all foods are being used. But, in comparing the adaptive radiation of one group with that of another, one soon realizes that the same sort of adaptation has been evolved independently time after time. That is, the divergence within particular groups may result in convergence between them. In the discussion of the adaptive radiation of the crane-like birds and of the wader, auk, and gull assemblage, a number of such cases of convergence were mentioned: cranes and storks, rails and jacanas (Figure 8), bustard quail and true quail, and seed snipe and true quail.

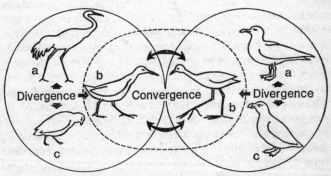

Figure 8. *Divergence in the order Gruiformes (left): (a) crane, (b) rail, and (c) bustard quail; and in the order Charadriiformes (right): (a) gull, (b) jacana, and (c) auk. Convergence between the two groups is evident in the similarity of the rail and the jacana.*

When they have evolved in different areas, birds like these – alike in appearance, but unrelated – are called ecological counterparts.[3] The resemblance between them may be amazingly detailed. The meadowlark of America and the longclaw of Africa are a classic example. Both are song-birds, but the meadowlark (*Sturnella*) is a member of the American family of icterid blackbirds, while the longclaw (*Macronyx*) is a member of the pipit family, of world-wide distribution. Both are thrush-sized birds of the grassland with upper parts streaked with black, brown, and tan; white outer tail feathers; and under parts yellow with a broad, black crescent on the breast. Both feed on the ground, make domed nests of dead grass on the ground, and utter plaintive whistled calls. The similarity is such that one who knows the meadowlark and sees the longclaw for the first time finds it difficult to believe they are not related. But a comparison of bill, feet, and wing details quickly establishes their true relationships.

Ecological counterparts may involve only two genera, like the longclaws and the meadowlarks, or they may involve whole families, with many species in each. The specialized flower-feeders are striking examples of this.

The development of flowering plants provided birds with a whole new niche in which to forage and find a new food – nectar. The humming-birds in the Americas, the sun-birds in Africa, and the honey eaters in Australia evolved to occupy this new niche. Though the humming-birds are related to the swifts, and the sun-birds and honey eaters belong to different families of song-birds with separate origins, all three evolved the same type of bill and tongue for feeding on nectar (Figure 9). The bill is long and slender and can probe the depths of the blossoms. The tongue, as long as the bill, has edges which curl inwards to provide a tube through which nectar can be sucked. This is the fundamental adaptation in all three families, and it has been so successful that the humming-birds have evolved over 300 species, the sun-birds over 100 species, and the honey eaters over 150. Besides drinking the nectar, the flower-feeders also eat small insects attracted to the blossoms, and they may assist in the pollination of the plants, thus forming another strand in the interrelationships that form the web of life.

Figure 9. *Ecological counterparts in flower feeding:* (a) *sun-bird, of Africa;* (b) *honey eater, of Australia;* (c) *humming-bird, of America.*

These three flower-feeding ecological counterparts consume the same sort of food in the same sort of place but in different parts of the world, so there is no ecological competition between them. But in the Australian area where the honey eaters live there has developed another group of flower-feeders, certain parrots, called the brush-tongued lories. Both may feed in the same flowering tree, but each has specialized for flower feeding in quite a different way. While the honey eaters suck up the nectar with a long, tubular tongue in a long, slender bill, the brush-tongued lories, with typically short, hooked parrot bill, have evolved their flower-feeding adaptation in the tongue only. When this is retracted into the mouth, it looks not unlike the rather fleshy tongue of other parrots, but when it is stretched out, the tip unfolds into a brush, somewhat as the fingers of an unclenched fist extended. This is used to collect nectar and flower parts from the blooms; then the tongue is retracted and the brush tip folded up, and the food is squeezed into the mouth. So deeply is the habit fixed in these birds that when captive lories are fed fleshy fruit, they scoop up the juice and soft pulp with the brush-tipped tongue instead of biting pieces from the fruit as other parrots would.

The honey eaters and the lories provide a picture of convergence between two distantly related groups, each specialized in a different way for flower feeding. The forests in which the birds live have a great many species of flowering trees. While both honey eaters and lories may be adaptable enough to feed at times in the same profusely flowering tree, each is presumably adapted especially for feeding on the flowers of different kinds of trees which they prefer. This is advantageous in reducing competition for food between the two groups.

Differences in feeding methods, correlated with structure and time of feeding, also reduce competition between two closely related groups: the skimmer (*Rynchops*) and the tern. Both feed on small fish from the surface of the water where certain kinds of fish are more common by day, others by night. A tern locates a fish by sight and seizes it with its sharp, pointed bill or plunges head first into the water after it. The skimmer, however, has a bill that is unlike any other in the bird world. It is compressed vertically to blade-like thinness, and the lower mandible is much longer than the upper. It is a very unlikely bill for picking up food, and the skimmer feeds in an unlikely way. It flies with half of the lower, bladelike mandible of its wide-open bill in the water. 'Ploughing the seas' is one of the ways this manoeuvre has been described. When the bird's mandible makes contact with a fish, the head snaps down and back as the bill closes. Presumably the skimmer may never see the fish before it is caught.

The skimmer feeds over coastal waters, large rivers, and lakes in the warmer parts of the world. Competition with the tern is reduced by the skimmer's habit of feeding during the twilight hours and after dark, which is made possible by the peculiarly adapted bill.

The reduction of competition by feeding at different times of day is perhaps best exemplified in the division of the twenty-four hours between the hawks and the owls. Both have hooked, grasping claws and hooked beaks for feeding on prey such as mice, birds, and reptiles. Both groups are of world-wide distribution. The hawks are diurnal, feeding in the daylight hours, while the owls take over the night shift, most of them hunting only while the hawks are asleep.

Structure and habits sometimes develop together, sometimes do not. In one bird group changes may have taken place in physical equipment to match alterations in the way of life. This is illustrated by the crossbill's method of feeding on the seeds of pine and spruce cones, the hawk's way of capturing mice, and the oyster-catcher's means of obtaining oysters.

In other groups of birds a new type of behaviour may develop with little corresponding change in the structure of the bird. There are cases where the bird may be handicapped in some degree. The clearest example is the cormorant. This is a swimming and diving bird, a relative of the pelican, and one would expect waterproof plumage to be indispensable. But the cormorant's plumage is not waterproof. Periodically it must leave the water and fly to a perch to dry its feathers. Obviously it cannot sleep on the water, for its plumage would become waterlogged and it would perish.

There are other cases of specialized behaviour that has developed with little corresponding change in the structures of the bird. For example, the dipper, mentioned earlier, is an unmodified song-bird although it has become aquatic in its habits. This type of change is exemplified also by a vulture and a duck, which alight in palm trees to eat the fruit. The palm vulture (*Gypohierax*) of Africa, with bill and feet much like those of other vultures, depends largely on the kernel of the oil palm for food. In the West Indies there is a tree duck (*Dendrocygna*) which also perches in the tops of palm trees and eats the fruit there. To look at these two birds, one with its bill shaped for seizing and tearing meat and the other with its bill shaped for sieving small items from mud and water, one would never expect them to alight in palm trees and eat fruit there.

On the other hand, widely different structures may be used for taking the same kind of food. This is especially well shown

by the many different ways birds use in catching fish. The
fishing methods of the tern and the skimmer have already been
mentioned. The diver, with its webbed feet and dagger-like bill,
pursues the fish under the water by swimming after it. The
long-legged heron wades in shallow water and spears the fish
it sees. The kingfisher, with its short legs, perches on a limb
over the water and dives headlong for its prey, while the osprey,
or fish hawk, seizes fish in its taloned feet (Figure 10).

Pre-adaptation is a further ecological concept. The idea is
that a species may develop a structure before there is a specialized use for it. Then, when the opportunity arises, the bird
changes its habits in accordance with the new conditions, for
which it is already adapted. In effect, pre-adaptation simply
means that the structure of a species allows it to change its
habits. While the usefulness of the concept may seem limited,
there are a few cases where it may apply. The kea parrot
(*Nestor*) of New Zealand is a case in point. It has a hooked bill,

Figure 10. *Fish eaters of different types:* (a) *kingfisher*, (b) *osprey*, (c)
tern, (d) *pelican*, (e) *diver*, (f) *heron*.

used by most parrots for eating fruits and seeds. But the kea is as omnivorous as a crow. When sheep were introduced into New Zealand, the bird, by trial-and-error type of learning, found out how to kill sheep and eat their flesh and fat. For this the hooked bill, which superficially resembles that of a hawk, proved very effective. One could say that the kea was pre-adapted for killing sheep.

Probably the usual course of evolution is for structure and habits to develop together. At the same time that a bird continues to share in a generalized diet, it may also become specialized little by little for a particular one. In times of food abundance or of slight population pressure this food specialization may not be of much importance. Periodically its pre-eminence in securing a particular food may be extremely important in its ultimate survival, while at other times a versatility that enables it to exist on a variety of foods is equally important.

This versatility of birds is probably one of the keys to the success of the class Aves. Some little-specialized species may change readily from one type of food to another during a single day. A flock of grackles that was feeding on acorns in a Middle Western wood-lot came down and caught grasshoppers in a grassy field shortly thereafter, with no apparent reason for the change. Perhaps they just liked the variety.

The ability to change from one food to another is particularly important in temperate and arctic climates, where seasonal changes are extreme. The northern forest, prairie, and tundra in summer are inhabited by a host of living things that provide a varied range of abundant food to choose from. But in the frozen winter the birds must make adjustments. The raven that eats insects in summer and berries in the autumn goes to the edge of the sea in winter for whatever the ocean may wash up, and even follows the polar bears for scraps and the dog teams for their excrement. Even tyrant fly-catchers and tree swallows, most insectivorous of passerine birds, may turn to berries temporarily in the autumn, before they migrate.

The birds that migrate find quite different conditions in their summer and winter homes. The diving ducks, called scoter, that feed on a prairie lake all summer and have vegetation as a considerable part of their diet, in the winter dive for blue mussels off the New England coast. The birds that move into the tropics have a whole new set of conditions to meet. American robins that eat worms on lawns in the north-eastern United States in June live on palmetto berries in Florida in the winter. The warblers that seek small insects among the leaves of the trees in a Canadian summer spend their winters getting fat on berries in the tropics.

The food of a wide-ranging species may vary from place to place. In many parts of the Temperate Zone the barn owl is known to depend on small mammals, but in southern California one of its seasonal foods is a small fish from the sea beaches, and in the West Indies lizards take the place of mammals in its diet.

Seasonal changes in food have been mentioned; changes to new foods over the years have also been correlated with man-made alterations in the scene. The kea and its change to sheep feeding is a classic case. Another involves tits in Britain, which have recently developed the habit of opening milk bottles left by milkmen outside householders' doors, and drinking the cream, a wholly new food for these birds.

The fulmar of the North Atlantic has profited by man's activities on the sea and has increased and spread for the last two hundred years from Iceland to Britain. In the early part of the period the whaling in spring and summer provided waste material on which the fulmar fed. When the whaling declined, the ice-carrying fishing trawlers appeared and provided free food in the form of fish offal thrown into the sea. James Fisher, the outstanding student of Atlantic sea birds, suggests that further possible refinements in processing and utilization of fish offal may remove a source of food for fulmars and gulls and cause a decrease in their numbers.[4] Despite the many adjustments which birds have made to their environment, environments continue to change and birds change with them.

Before patterns discussed in this chapter were outlined, it was observed that not all the data would fit into them. After considering the many modifications and exceptions in diversity, one may feel that the reality of postulated patterns, or their usefulness, is questionable. But there are so many factors in nature, which may occur together or separately, that it is a wonder that the patterns emerge as clearly as they do.

CHAPTER 6

Social Feeding

BIRDS are social animals, and in their feeding behaviour one sees cooperation and competition very plainly. There are many different kinds of cooperation and competition which have been important in the whole evolutionary history of living things. Earlier, the role of ecological competition in evolution was discussed. The present chapter deals with both cooperation and competition in social feeding. First, however, we will briefly survey, more generally, the various ways in which these two kinds of behaviour have been regarded in the development of man's understanding of evolution.

When the great English biologist Thomas Henry Huxley was campaigning for the acceptance of Darwin's theory of evolution, the theory was symbolized by the 'struggle for existence', with 'Nature, red in tooth and claw'. This view was seized on by the expanding industry and trade of the nineteenth century as a justification for the most ruthless cut-throat competition at every level. The weakest 'went to the wall' according to a 'law of nature'. Then came a revulsion against such 'inhumane' beliefs. In the society in which the welfare state has come into being, cooperation, not competition, is stressed. Philosophers have taken another look at nature and have seen many examples of cooperation. Trees in a forest have ceased to struggle for space and light, and protect each other against the wind. Analysis of animal societies by biologists show the same change in viewpoint. In two recent textbooks by world-famous authorities, cooperation is mentioned as a topic in the table of contents, but competition is not. In the elaborate index of one of the books, 'cooperation' has thirteen page references, but 'competition' does not appear. But the pendulum has swung too far. Both competition and cooperation occur in nature, at a great many levels.

One of the best places to study one kind of cooperation, or mutual aid, and competition, or exploitation, is in the social-feeding habits of birds. Under the broad heading of cooperation will be discussed three main types of activity, and under competition, two. Both of these aspects of behaviour may also appear in a single complex situation or series of social activities.

Cooperation is seen when birds lead or guide each other to food or join together, or with other animals, in the flushing of prey. It is also seen when birds make food available by providing scraps and when they use scraps made available by other animals. Finally, some birds cooperate in catching or killing their prey. Competition is perhaps best observed in the pilfering and in the robbing that occasionally or regularly goes on among some birds.

Cooperation in finding food occurs when two birds, or a bird and another animal, act so that at least one of them profits. Ideally both partners should share equally or the benefits should alternate so that there is an equivalent benefit to each. But sometimes one of the partners does all the work without bene-fiting and may even seem unaware of the other's presence.

Both partners usually benefit when behaviour such as leading or guiding to food is involved. At its simplest, this type of co-operation occurs when one bird sees food and goes to it, and others follow. Kites, crows, and vultures practise such co-operation when gathering at a carcass.[1]

This kind of behaviour is especially common on the game fields of Africa and was described by Sir Frederick Jackson,[2] one of the early British administrators in Kenya and Uganda. The crows perch and fly from tree to tree; the kites perch and sail at no great height; while the vultures, of which six species occur in Kenya, spend much time on the wing and may soar widely at

great heights. Each bird is on the look-out for food, for even on
the game fields meals for these scavengers may be widely spaced.
The whole countryside is scanned by one bird or another, day
after day. When one of them locates a meal and flies or sails
down to it, other birds soar towards the spot. If it is not a false
alarm, and there really is a feast in the form of the carcass of
an antelope or some other large mammal, these birds descend to
it. Other birds beyond see them and follow. Soon there may
be scores of birds of half a dozen species at the carcass.

This guiding relationship in birds is, in the long run, of
mutual advantage to all the birds concerned. Besides being
understood and acted upon by various species of birds, this
behaviour is also understood by some mammals. Jackals are
said to follow the flights of vultures to carcasses, and Sir Frederick Jackson wrote that in the early days the Swahili believed
that the trail of a Masai raiding party was indicated from afar
by the stream of vultures following it for the sake of the slain.
Presumably the Swahili could take the appropriate evasive
action.

Quite a different type of activity appears when birds cooperate by flushing prey – for instance, by stirring up insects for
each other. This differs from guiding to prey, in which an
abundance of food in a limited area is involved. The flushing
or beating of prey usually involves such food as insects that are
so small that many are necessary for a meal and so scattered and
hidden that they are not easy to see until they move.

Such a method of hunting is well known in human sport
under the name of beating. Grouse shooters use a line of men to
drive the birds over the guns, and those who do rough shooting
may walk several abreast through likely habitats in order to
flush the pheasants in front of them.

This sort of cooperative hunting goes on continually in flocks
of forest birds. One of the pioneer naturalists of South America,
the Englishman H. W. Bates, has given us the classic account
of a mixed feeding flock of forest birds. This was published in
his *Naturalist on the River Amazon* in 1863.[3]

. . . one may pass several days without seeing many birds; but now and then the surrounding bushes and trees appear suddenly to swarm with them. There are scores, probably hundreds of birds, all moving about with the greatest activity – woodpeckers and Dendrocolaptidae (from species no larger than a sparrow to others the size of a crow) running up the tree trunks; tanagers, ant thrushes, humming-birds, fly-catchers and barbets flitting about the leaves and lower branches. The bustling crowd loses no time ... In a few minutes the host is gone and the forest path remains deserted and silent as before.

Since then, other naturalists have discovered and studied this phenomenon of mixed flocking in both the New and the Old World tropics.[4] The flocks often contain hundreds of individuals and dozens of species. All the smaller insect-eating birds of a wide area of the forest band together each morning and travel and feed together all day long. The winter flocks of woodland birds in the North Temperate Zone, composed of tits, nuthatches, goldcrests, and the like, are essentially similar, but smaller in size and simpler in organization.

There is little discord in these flocks. From forest floor to treetop each species has its own special food preference. The occasions for competition between species are thus limited. The individuals of each species tend to be spread out, scattered, and thus the chance is reduced that two individuals of the same species will look in the same place at the same time for the same insect. As the flock moves along at a man's walking pace, some birds hurrying ahead and some lagging behind, the insects on which the birds feed are continually being startled into activity. A warbler startles a moth into flight and misses it and a fly-catcher snaps it up. Now one bird, now another, benefits.

A similar effect arising out of unilateral behaviour, in which one of the partners benefits from the efforts of the other, often results when a bird associates with a mammal. For example, frigate birds know that dolphins, chasing fish near the surface, cause the flying fish to leap into flight, so the birds fly overhead to snatch the flying fish from the air.[5] Another example is the way cattle egrets accompany cows for the sake of the insects startled into activity.[6]

I was able to observe the effectiveness of this use of a cow as a beater by a quite different bird, the ani cuckoo of Central America, which feeds in the manner of the cattle egrets.[7] Some of the time the anis walked over the pasture by themselves, catching what grasshoppers they could. But when a herd of cows appeared several anis stationed themselves by the feet or the muzzles of the grazing animals. An ani feeding alone averaged a catch only once every two minutes, but when it used a cow as a beater, it averaged three insects for the same period. In this instance, feeding with the aid of the cow was three times as effective as hunting insects alone. Also, it took much less effort, much less walking about, for the bird.

Equally saving of effort for the bird is the practice of accompanying a mammal or one of man's machines for the sake of the scraps made available, another cooperative type of activity. For example, the Inca terns of the Peruvian coast hover about the head of a rising sea lion for the sake of the fish scraps dropped from its jaws.[8] The profits are of course unilateral. Though this behaviour might be called pilfering, the scraps are of no importance to the sea lion. This activity is most clearly akin to that of the gulls following a coasting ship for the scraps thrown overboard from the galley, and both are scavenging of a sort.[9] But it is also very like the behaviour of American robins, which follow a farmer's plough for the sake of the worms and grubs turned up in the furrow.[10] This of course reminds us of the way birds beat for food, as described previously.

The grouping of these three types of cooperation – the mutually advantageous guiding to food, the beating for food, and the unilaterally profitable association in which one partner makes food available to another or to others – helps to emphasize the fact that birds are always alert to take advantage of the occasionally profitable aspects of their environment. When such an opportunity occurs regularly, the birds may adjust their lives to it. For instance, the food provided by waste from whalers and

Figure 11. *Relationship between the honey guide and man:* (a) *bird locates bee tree;* (b) *bird locates men;* (c, d) *bird leads men to bee tree;* (e) *men remove honey;* (f) *bird eats honeycomb left for it.*

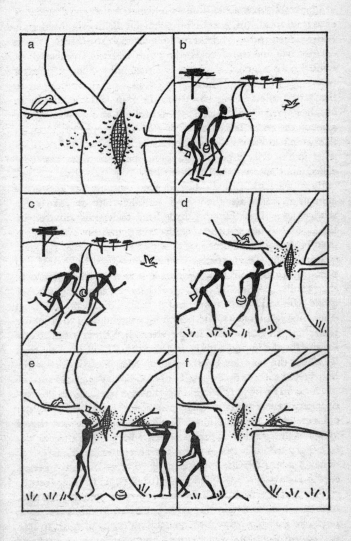

fishing vessels may actually affect the distribution and abundance of certain birds, as has been shown by British ornithologists James Fisher and R. M. Lockley in their book *Sea-Birds*.

Only two species of birds, the two tick-birds (*Buphagus*) of Africa, have adopted a way of life that links them completely to certain mammals, which provide all of their food.[11] These tick-birds' sole feeding habitat is the skin of large mammals, and here their food is almost entirely the ticks which infest the skin of the mammals. The birds hop about over the animals, like woodpeckers on the bark of a tree, and shear off the ticks. This is the only known instance in birds of what could be called an obligate social relationship. The tick-birds are not entirely parasitic. True, they depend entirely on the game animals or cattle for their food, but they also perform some services in return. The mammals have their ticks removed by the birds and are warned of approaching hunters by the keen-eyed birds' calls of alarm.

Two of the above types of cooperation – guiding to food and profiting from scraps made available – have been combined in the peculiar relationship that exists between the African honey guide (*Indicator indicator*) and man.[12] The story has been illustrated in Figure 11, and here it may be sufficient to point out that the bird has a taste for beeswax that it finds difficult to satisfy, for the honeycomb is well protected by the hollow trees in which the bees lay up their store. Man has a taste for the honey, and though he can easily open a hollow tree and rob the bees, he has difficulty in finding the bee trees. So in the co-operative relationship of man and honey guide, each partner contributes his special ability. The honey guide knows its home area and the location of the bee trees. Men passing through the forest are led to a bee tree by the special noisy flight of the honey guide. After the men open the hive and take the honey, the bird feeds on scraps of honeycomb left behind.

There has been much discussion about the amount of awareness and intelligence on the part of the bird in this association, but viewed in the light of the general tendency of birds to lead or guide to food and their equally common habit of profiting from the provision of food by another animal, the association between man and honey guide is seen as merely a situation in which both these common types of behaviour are involved. However, this honey guide–man relationship is specialization of a very peculiar kind, a special case involving two very different species of animals.

Cooperative behaviour in which prey is caught and killed has also developed to a high peak within certain species of birds; in activity of this sort both individuals share equally in the effort and in the benefit. At its simplest it is shown by the two bald eagles who singled out a lone swimming duck and took turns striking at it until the duck was too tired to dive any more and was easily picked up from the surface of the water.[13]

A similar practice, but one involving more birds, is the fishing of the white pelicans on an Oregon lake, seen by Dr Clarence Cottam of the United States Fish and Wildlife Service.[14] Twelve of these birds were swimming leisurely about on an arm of the lake when a school of fish approached. The pelicans spread out and surrounded the school. Then the birds began slowly and cautiously to narrow their circle, moving in perfect unison. Finally every pelican could reach the surrounded fish. Then, with rapid jabs of their bills, the birds began to feed, and every pelican got at least one fish. Here is an operation in which there was a synchronization of preliminary herding and corralling action by a group of individuals, until the critical moment when all could benefit.

Having examined the main ways in which social feeding of birds may be cooperative, one must turn to the other side of the subject and look at competition among birds feeding together. In this, of course, only one of the partners benefits; the association may involve birds of the same or of widely different species. Two main categories are recognizable – pilfering and robbing.

Pilfering occurs when one bird, peacefully feeding or perched near another, takes advantage of a chance to snatch food. This pilfering is a thing of the moment, an opportunity seized. Once the food has been swallowed, the episode is forgotten and the peaceful association goes on as before. Incidents of this sort are only minor in the day's normal activities for each species. A domestic hen, one of a flock scratching for worms, may have difficulty in swallowing its catch and other hens may try to snatch it away. A short chase may ensue. Once the worm has been swallowed by whatever bird, they all revert to their individual feeding. This behaviour is not restricted to birds of one species. In the United States both American robins and common starlings feed peacefully on a lawn. But at times a robin catches a worm and a starling may walk up and take it from the robin's bill without a protest from the latter.[15]

When pilfering has developed into an activity in which force or the threat of force is used by one bird to take food from another, the action can well be called robbery with violence, or brigandage. This relationship has been developed in a few robber species. Notable among them are the frigate birds, all of which get much of their food by taking fish from other sea birds, especially gannets; the skuas, which specialize in robbing terns of their catches; and the bald eagles, which make a practice of robbing the ospreys, or fish hawks.[16] All these robber species are quite capable of feeding themselves, and often do. But when opportunities for robbing are available they prefer to exploit their chosen victims. These robber birds are widespread, sometimes fairly common species, as also are the predatory birds, which actually eat other birds. There is evidently room in nature for a few of each, but the very nature of robbers and of predators is such that they must always be fewer than their victims.

So far, competition and cooperation have been discussed separately, as though they were unrelated types of behaviour. But low-level cooperation, such as one sees in mutual beating for insects in a mixed flock of insect-eating birds in the forest, is accompanied by continual pilfering within the same flock. For example, as was mentioned in the description of mutual beating, a fly-catcher may snap up the moth which a warbler startled into flight. This train of activity is sometimes carried

Figure 12. *Some social-feeding behaviour:* (a) *herons accompany a cow for the insects the latter flushes; a tick-bird is on the cow's back;* (b) *ravens cooperate in stealing a bone from a dog;* (c) *feeding pelicans surround and herd a school of fish.*

one step further. As the fly-catcher is about to grab the moth, a shrike may snatch it from in front of the fly-catcher's bill. Both beating and pilfering, both inter- and intra-specific, go on all the time.

Still more clear-cut instances of both cooperation and competition in the same situation are seen when individuals of one species combine to rob an individual of another species of its meal. Behaviour like this, at once social and antisocial, has been seen chiefly in members of the crow family, which are usually considered among the most intelligent birds. Three magpies came upon a golden eagle perched on the ground with a freshly caught ground squirrel it was about to eat.[17] The magpies gathered around the eagle, scolding and dashing towards it until the eagle dropped its prey, which one of the magpies carried away immediately. Later all three magpies shared the stolen squirrel quite amicably. A similar case involved three ravens and a dog with a bone.[18] While two of the ravens flew about the dog's head, croaking, the third bird came up behind the dog, unseen, and nipped its tail. The dog dropped its bone and turned round. At once one of the other ravens carried off the bone. Such activities as these indicate a shrewd awareness – the ability to contrive and take advantage of a situation in which a victim can be outwitted.

From this survey it appears that birds, being animals acute of vision and quick to respond, are ever ready to exploit any favourable element, however small and fleeting, in their environment. Opportunities for doing so continually arise when a bird associates with another, of whatever species, or with some other animal. Sometimes this association results in cooperation, either mutual or unilateral, and sometimes in competition; often both are inherent in the situation.

This is not the place to discuss the awareness by the bird of the social implications of its activity. Though some words used for descriptive purposes, such as 'exploitation' or 'robbery' may seem to hold moral overtones, none is implied. As must be stressed, birds are not immoral, but amoral. The purpose of this discussion has been simply to describe, in words at hand, the overt behaviour and its results.

Competition and cooperation are least in evidence when food is abundant, widespread, and easily available. They become more apparent when food is abundant only locally or is difficult to find or secure even when not scarce. Specialized cases of conspicuous competition or of cooperation are not common, even though in some instances such associations have become a regular way of life.

Within one bird species competition and cooperation tend to be more or less balanced, so that flocks exist in considerable harmony. The same is true of the association of many closely and even distantly related species with similar habitats and food preferences. Between quite different species with different food preferences, unilateral cooperation in social-feeding associations is sometimes found; between distantly related species with similar food preferences the fiercest, most outright competition for food occurs, though only occasionally.

The most widely applicable generalization to be drawn from these data seems to be that for the majority of birds a nice blending of cooperation and competition must prevail. Some few social-feeding relationships may become strongly cooperative and some few fiercely competitive. But most of the bird species stay near the middle of the road and are strongly opportunistic in their social-feeding behaviour.

CHAPTER 7

Food and Water

BIRDS are self-operating, self-repairing machines that need a supply of food as fuel for their continual operation.[1] The subject of nutrition can be considered from two points of view. One is that of the physiologist who works in the laboratory and regards food as carbohydrates, proteins, fats, water, mineral salts, and vitamins. He studies their use in metabolism – the rebuilding of tissues and the oxidation of food, especially of carbohydrates, to supply energy for the vital processes within the body, for heat, and for the overt activity of the whole bird.

A naturalist, on the other hand, regards food as the insects, mice, seeds, or fruit selected by the bird from its environment. Some of this food may have to be processed before being eaten, and some of it may be stored. Activities concerned with the availability and the types of organic food, water, and minerals in the bird's surroundings bulk large in a bird's life.

The two points of view are not mutually exclusive. Rather they are mutually interdependent. The naturalist can understand certain aspects of a bird's relation to its environment only by knowing something of its physiology, and the physiologist can understand some aspects of the internal economy of a bird he studies only by knowing the relevant parts of its natural history. This is well demonstrated by recent discoveries in relation to the drinking of sea-water by birds. Naturalists have known for a long time that some birds drink sea-water despite the fact that in certain others, like pigeons and domestic fowl, a high concentration of salt in the body may be lethal. How sea birds were able to excrete the excess salt in sea-water they drank remained a puzzle until a physiologist, Professor Knut Schmidt-Neilson, of Duke University, discovered the function of the nasal glands in birds.[2] These paired glands are located on the skull just above the eyes, as pointed out in Chapter 3. That they existed, and that they were well developed only in birds living by or on the sea, had been known previously. But it was Professor Knut Schmidt-Neilson who discovered that the glands had a special function in excreting salt from the body. The correlation of this physiological information with our knowledge of the sea birds' habit of drinking sea-water made it meaningful to the naturalist in his understanding of the lives of these birds.

The rate at which food is used, that is, the rate of metabolism, varies with the activity of the bird.[3] When the bird is active – running or flying – the rate is high; when the bird is quiet, with only its vital processes going on, such as breathing and digestion, the rate is low. Each species has its own rate. For comparing one species with another, a basic metabolic rate is calculated by measuring heat production of a bird under certain standard conditions of inactivity and converting it into calories of heat per kilogram of body weight per twenty-four hours.

A domestic fowl weighing 2,000 grammes has a basic metabolic rate of 50 calories; a mourning dove weighing 121 grammes, a rate of 127 calories; a wren weighing about 10 grammes, a rate of 589 calories; and a humming-bird weighing 4 grammes, a rate of 1,410 calories.

The main point is that smaller birds have a faster metabolic rate than larger ones; their body processes go on at a faster rate. This should be no surprise, for when lungs and heart were discussed earlier it was pointed out that the rate of breathing and the rate of heartbeat, both of them integral aspects of the metabolic process, are faster in small birds than in larger ones. Correlated with this is the need of small birds for relatively large amounts of food. Experiments have shown that the domestic fowl needs only 3 or 4 per cent of its body weight in food daily, while a mourning dove needs 11 to 12 per cent and a tit weighing little more than a wren needs 30 per cent. This whole complex of factors underlies the greater activity of small birds, which consequently require relatively more food to keep them going.

Certainly small birds must digest their food more quickly than larger ones. However, experimental work on the length of time food remains in the digestive system indicates that it is difficult to secure meaningful results because of the number of factors involved; these include the type of food, the treatment it receives, and the structure of the bird.[4] In the domestic fowl the hard grain eaten may be temporarily stored in the crop, and the contents of a full crop may take eighteen to twenty hours to disappear. Its next stop is in the gizzard, where it is given mechanical treatment; the average time spent here is about two

Figure 13. *Food specialists:* (a) *skimmer 'ploughs' the water for fish;* (b) *shrike impales a mouse on a thorn;* (c) *grackle soaks hard bread before eating;* (d) *Galápagos woodpecker finch uses a thorn to get a grub from a hole;* (e) *osprey seizes fish in its feet.*

hours. However, under certain conditions food marked with red dye has passed through the whole digestive system in about two and a half hours. In some small birds, like the flower-pecker (*Dicaeum*), the fruit eaten passes directly from gape and gullet to the intestines without going into the stomach, and food must pass through the system rapidly. When berries were fed experimentally to a number of species of small birds, the first traces of them in the excrement appeared in less than an hour.

Another aspect of metabolism, and one that comes to the attention of the field naturalist, is the length of time that birds can go without feeding. They do so, of course, all night when they are asleep and their metabolism is low. However, some small birds make night-long flights on migration, and then their metabolic rate must be near its maximum. For example, the ruby-throated humming-bird makes flights of more than five hundred miles across the Gulf of Mexico, and bobolinks and yellow-billed cuckoos fly equally far across the Caribbean Sea from Jamaica to Venezuela.[5] It has been suggested that they make these flights at night so that they can feed just before they leave and again on their arrival.

A bird's regular feeding is interrupted also during incubation. Many small birds, perhaps because of their high metabolic rate, leave the nest and feed several times an hour even during this period, but certain larger gallinaceous birds do so only once or twice a day. The record for this sort of fasting is held by the male emperor penguin of the Antarctic, which incubates its single egg by holding it on its feet for the whole of the two-month incubation period, and eats nothing during this time.

We also have some information from the experimental physiologist working with birds in a laboratory and concerned with the time birds can go without food: mallard ducks for three weeks, pheasants for over two weeks, and sparrows for only three days.[6] That still smaller birds would starve more quickly is indicated by their faster metabolism.

Birds have two notable adaptations to help reduce the strain of going for long periods without feeding. One is the storage of food in the crop as practised by gallinaceous birds, and the other is the storage of food as fat in the body and under the skin. The use of this body fat in night-long migration flights is proved by the pitifully emaciated condition in which some southbound passerine birds make their landfall in Venezuela after the sea crossing from Jamaica.

The carbohydrates, proteins and fats of the physiologist must be translated back into the insects, mice, seeds, and berries of the naturalist if metabolism is to be related to the life of the bird. Birds eat a range of animal food that covers most of the major groups of animals – worms, crustaceans and insects, molluscs, echinoderms, and all the vertebrate animal groups, including other birds and their eggs. The plant food of birds most typically consists of flower parts, fruits, and seeds. Some birds, such as crows, are nearly omnivorous and eat almost everything that any bird eats, but most birds are more selective, and are known as frugivorous, or fruit-eating; granivorous, or seed-eating; insectivorous, or insect-eating; carnivorous, or flesh-eating; and herbivorous, or feeding on green vegetation.

It is noteworthy that the most common and conspicuous organic matter in nature, the green vegetation of leaves and grasses which is the staple diet of many animals, such as rodents, and ungulates, is eaten relatively little by birds. Only a few, such as ducks and geese and some gallinaceous birds, feed commonly on it. It may be that the rapidly functioning system of the bird needs the more concentrated foods provided by animal matter and by the stored sugars, starches, and proteins of seeds and fruits.

It would be reasonable to expect that large birds would dine on large items of food and small birds on tiny ones, and to a certain extent this is true. But it does not always follow. The peregrine falcon may knock a duck out of the sky and make a meal of part of this bird, which is as large as itself. The kite, another diurnal bird of prey about the size of the falcon, may make a meal of a large number of locusts it catches out of a passing swarm, or it may come to a dead mule on the ground and consume bits of meat tugged from the carcass. One bird may swallow small fruits whole, while another may bite little pieces out of fruit as large as itself. The same individual bird may feed in both ways, depending on what kind of food is available.

Among the smallest food items used by birds are the blue-green algae cells sieved by flamingos from the waters of an East African lake, while among the largest, eaten piecemeal of course, are the dead floating whales over which petrels quarrel.

The size of a bird's meal is not necessarily limited by the size of its stomach. The gullet often is distensible – the whole gullet of a hawk, as well as its capacious thin-walled stomach, may be packed with chunks of meat until the bird looks misshapen; some fish- and snake-eating birds may hold the tail of their prey in their throat, in temporary storage as it were, while the front part of the prey is being digested down in the stomach. Some birds have crops, a special place for storing their food.

Birds often eat their food on the spot just as it is found. With a jerk of its head or a few movements of its mandibles and tongue, the bird transfers a bite-sized item from the bill to the gullet and quickly swallows it. Sometimes, however, some processing of the food is necessary. When a worm is too active to be swallowed at once, it may be run through the bill and nipped at intervals to quieten it, or a grasshopper may be beaten against the ground or the perch and nipped until the strong jumping legs come off and the body is crushed. A hawk may carry a dove to its perch and pluck off the feathers before it tears off pieces of flesh and swallows them.

Plants have evolved hard nutshells and seed coats to protect the stored foods intended for the sprouting of young plants, and turtles and clams and sea urchins have hard outer shells to guard their soft tissues against predators. An inevitable result is that predators have evolved ways for cracking nuts and seeds and for opening shells.

For example, sparrows and parrots have stout nutcracker-type bills. A hawfinch of Europe, related to the evening grosbeak of North America, can crack open olive pips and is said to exert a hundred pounds of pressure with its bill.[7] Nuts are hacked open by jays, which hold the nut in the feet and use the bill as a pick or hatchet, and by red-headed woodpeckers, which improvise a vice by wedging the nut into a crevice of a tree trunk. The grackle, or crow blackbird, has a special nut-opening device built into its bill.[8] There is a sharp, downward-projecting keel on the horny roof of the mouth, which works like a tin-opener. The grackle takes an acorn in its bill and rotates it so that the keel cuts the shell into two neat halves, freeing the kernel.

Turtles in their horny shells and the marrow left in the bones of a carcass after the kites, crows, and vultures have worried off the last fragments of meat would seem to be rather safe from birds. But the great bearded vulture, or lammergeier, found in the mountains from Spain and eastern Africa to India and Tibet, has solved that problem without any special equipment.[9] The bone or the turtle is repeatedly carried up into the air and dropped to the ground, until it splits open and the bird can get at its meal. This habit of the lammergeier was evidently known to the Greeks, for the death of the poet Aeschylus was attributed to a bird that mistook his bald head for a rock and dropped a turtle on it. Though the existence of this practice of dropping bones and turtles has been questioned, recent observations have substantiated the earlier accounts.

Clams and other shellfish from the mud flats exposed by low tide are handled in the same way by those omnivorous feeders, the crows and the gulls. They fly up and drop the shells onto a hard beach, a rocky outcrop, or even a hard road. The land snails of an English garden present a similar problem to the song-thrush, but the thrush has solved it in a different way.[10] It takes the snail in its bill and strikes it against a stone until the shell is broken and the snail's body is exposed. The frequency with which a favourite stone is used results in an accumulation of empty, broken snail shells around it, and the stone seems to merit the name 'anvil' which has been given it.

The grackles, which use their specialized 'nut-opener' on acorns and corn, have another approach for dry bread spread on a lawn near a bird-bath. When the grackles come they nip and bite at the bread and shake it with little effect. Sooner or later some of these birds carry pieces of the bread to the bird-bath and dip them into the water. Then the softened bread is easily eaten.

The diversity of methods by which these different, unrelated birds have solved similar problems is less interesting than the fact that sometimes a special structure has been evolved and sometimes not. In the latter cases specialization is to be found not in the bill, but in the behaviour pattern alone. In processing food, as in adaptation for finding food, diversity of behaviour far outruns diversity of structure.

This processing of food is a daily activity for many birds, but storage of food is exceptional in the bird world. In general, birds lead a 'hand-to-mouth' existence. When they are hungry they go out and find food. They adapt to seasons of scarcity mainly by changing to a different kind of food or by wandering or migrating to a place where food is more available.

As one would expect, the birds that do store food inhabit the temperate or boreal zones. The acorn woodpeckers of California are famous for their autumn storage of acorns in holes drilled in the bark of trees.[11] Thus when their summer diet of insects and fruits becomes scarce they have nuts available. Just how much awareness of the situation this habit implies is doubtful, for it has been recorded that in years when acorns are scarce, the woodpeckers store pebbles of a similar size, a quite useless activity. The storage of food also seems carried beyond the needs of the species by certain tits of northern Europe.[12] They store food most of the year – nuts in autumn, pine seeds in spring when the cones open, and caterpillars in summer.

In contrast, the thick-billed nutcrackers (*Nucifraga*) of Finland and northern Sweden feed most of the year on stored hazel nuts harvested during a limited period.[13] The nuts begin to ripen in August, and by late October they would all be carried away or eaten by mammals if the nutcrackers did not store their share. The birds bury the nuts in the ground, here and there, a few in each spot, and cover them smoothly. Then the winter snow, which may be as much as eighteen inches deep, puts a further concealing layer over the caches. Yet all winter the nutcrackers dig down through the snow and find them. They do not search at random, for a study of 351 excavations made through the snow by the birds showed that 86 per cent were successful. Amazing as it seems, they must remember the location of the nuts. The supply of stored food lasts through the spring to breeding time and provides some of the food for the young. Only for a short time in the summer is it necessary for these birds to turn to other foods.

The food ordinarily eaten by birds seems to contain minerals in adequate amounts. But just as certain herbivorous mammals go to salt licks, so do some seed- and fruit-eating birds. Frugivorous colies, or mouse-birds, of Africa have been reported gathering in some numbers to eat quantities of red earth from a small cave, red earth that was found to contain soluble inorganic salts.[14] Gambel's quail, of the arid parts of the United States, have been seen going directly from a night roost to a block of salt set out for cattle and pecking eagerly at it.[15]

Crossbills sometimes feed on the salt put on roads to melt snow.[16] While these birds seek out salt to eat, few individuals of the more northern species, such as these crossbills, would have it available regularly, and it has been found that in certain quantities salt can kill pigeons and chickens. On the other hand, some sea birds, such as albatrosses, become sick when kept in captivity and given only fresh water, and recover only when supplied with salt water.[17] Quite evidently the role of salt in body upkeep and the mode of its secretion vary from species to species and from time to time.

All birds need water in their diet. Some birds use salt water, some both salt and fresh, and some only fresh water. The role of the nasal glands in enabling birds to drink salt water was discussed at the beginning of this chapter. Most birds will come to drink when water is available. The bird-bath on the lawn or the dripping tap in the garden is always a source of attraction for them. In the arid country of Australia the seed-eating finches and parrots come long distances to water holes in such numbers as to be spectacular.[18] In arid parts of Africa and Asia live sandgrouse (*Pterocles*) peculiar to these areas; their main adaptation to the aridity is their habit of making daily flights to distant water holes.[19] In the nesting season the adult sandgrouse even carry water in their crops and regurgitate it for their young.

Under the arid conditions on the American deserts young quail must be hatched within walking distance of drinking water if they are to survive.[20] They can get some water from dewdrops and the adult quail can exist indefinitely without drinking if enough water-rich green vegetation and insects are available to supply their water needs. But no birds are as desert-adapted as some mammals, which can get along on a diet of dry seeds without drinking at all. The mammals do this by manufacturing their own water within the body, water of metabolism.

Drinking water is important not only in maintaining the water balance in the body tissues, but also in cooling the bird. A man pants when he is very active as part of his speeded-up metabolism, and when very hot he is cooled by the evaporation of water in the sweat on the surface of his skin. The bird is cooled by the evaporation of water from the inner surface of the air sacs (described in Chapter 3). The faster a bird breathes, the faster the cooling goes on. For this reason a bird standing in the hot sun will be observed to pant rapidly with open bill. The water lost must be replaced, and experiments have shown that mourning doves drink four times as much water at 100 degrees Fahrenheit as they do at 70 degrees.[21] At high temperatures a large proportion of the water intake evidently is used for cooling. These physiological needs for food and water all have their place in influencing the activity of birds, discussed in the next chapter.

CHAPTER 8

Activity and Rest

SOME of the ways birds differ from species to species are summed up when we say that birds have different personalities, and compare them to those of individual humans. For instance, jays are called saucy rascals; magpies are perky and confident; starlings are jaunty and garrulous; king-birds are quarrelsome and pugnacious; gnat-catchers, fidgety; cat-birds, lively and restless; wrens, excitable and always scolding; goldcrests, nervous and lively and always in incessant motion among the twigs and leaves; and tits are cheerful, acrobatic woodland sprites.

In contrast to the birds mentioned above, vireos are said to scan each leaf deliberately and carefully; waxwings are gentle and have refined ways; thrushes have serene repose; creepers patiently and ploddingly climb tree trunks, scanning the bark in a preoccupied, near-sighted way; and hoopoes have an undulating, lazy flight. Equally outstanding are the peregrine falcon, with a strength of wing and talon equalled by its courage; the little owl of Pallas Athene (*Athene noctua*), a veritable buffoon with grotesque bobbing actions; the wood-pewee flycatcher, peaceful and patient; and the golden eagle, which perches for hours in a majestic calm.

'Anthropomorphism', the mechanistic-minded behaviourists will scream, and of course they are partly right. Such personification can be carried too far or taken too seriously. But how else can one convey an impression of a certain kind of bird as easily or as quickly? To say that a bird seems excited, nervous, stolid, pugnacious, or indifferent serves the purpose admirably. Birds are not automatons, nor yet do they have all the mental attributes of humans. They lie somewhere in between and we can err by imputing too little as well as by imputing too much (see Chapter 21 on bird behaviour). The descriptive phrases give an idea of the tempo and the types of responses that are evident in many aspects of a bird's life, as any watcher at a bird-table can see.

Sex and family life, song and the defence of territory, may occupy much of a bird's time during the breeding season, but for the rest of the year top priority must be given to feeding. Seeing a tit moving about continually among twigs, leaves, and branches, one may think that the whole day must be spent searching for food, and wonder if all this activity is really necessary. When the tit comes to the bird-table, where there is an abundance of suet and sunflower seeds, it does not settle down and eat its fill. Rather there is a continual coming and going, a flitting here and there, and a peering at things. Such small insectivorous birds seem to be so constituted that they must be on the move all the time; when winter comes and food is really scarce, so that such ceaseless activity is necessary, they do not have to change their tempo. House sparrows that come to the same bird-table act quite differently. They eat their fill and then spend much time perching. Periods of rest alternate with periods of activity.

We are fortunate in having a quantitative study of just how much time of its day a small bird actually spends feeding. Dr Oliver Pearson, professor of zoology at the University of California, made such a study of an Anna's humming-bird which got all its food from the flowers of a single shrub, where it made its headquarters.[1] The bird spent only fifteen per cent, about two hours, of its thirteen-hour day feeding – hovering over and probing into the blossoms which yielded its main food of nectar and small insects. Most of the day it spent perching in the bush.

The activities of this humming-bird were more like those of

the sparrows at the bird-table than like those of the restless
tits. Presumably when food is scarce, the humming-bird
must spend more of its time foraging; it would then have to
speed up the tempo of its activity. Like the humming-bird, the
vulture may spend only a part of its time feeding. It can eat
enough from a carcass in a short time to last for a day or more.
One California condor has been recorded at its perch from
noon one day to mid-morning the next, more than twenty-one
out of twenty-four hours.[2] Sometimes vultures will leave their
perches to soar. This activity may be an alternative to perching,
but who can tell whether a soaring vulture is simply passing the
time until it is hungry again or is watching the ground for a
meal to be used immediately or to be remembered and used
later?

Many small and medium-sized birds probably feed intermittently during the day, with a longer pause during the midday
hours, but some larger ones have a well-defined daily pattern
of activity. This regularity is well illustrated by the movements
of the wood stork on a fine morning in southern Florida. It leaves
its night roost in a clump of cypress trees and flies to a prairie
pond, where it feeds actively on fish and aquatic invertebrates
until about eight o'clock. Then it gathers with its fellows on
some dry bank and dozes in the sun. In an hour or two, when
the sun begins to heat the land and to cause rising up-draughts
of warm air, the storks spread their long broad wings and begin
to climb, up and up, to join the soaring vultures until they are
only specks in the sky. In the afternoon it may either descend
and feed again or fly directly to its roost.

Perching, hopping, flitting, exploring and soaring, these are
the free-time activities of a bird. There is also time available for
the bird's toilet: for grooming, stretching, sunning, and bathing.
To some degree these activities are undoubtedly necessary for
the bird's well-being, but the extent to which they are indulged
in tempts one to think of them as leisure activities.

In the first chilly days of autumn a party of swallows, partly
numbed from the unaccustomed cold, may gather on a roof
warmed by the rising sun or on a stretch of paved road and
ruffle their feathers and half spread their wings so that the sun

can reach their skin. Even during the summer's heat the American robin searching for worms on the lawn may pause in the sunshine, and sun itself. In the same way, a tame meadowlark has been seen to enjoy the rush of hot air from a heater.[3]

A domestic fowl or turkey is likely to combine sunbathing with a dust bath. It scratches in a dry, sandy place, sprawls on its breast or side with its feathers ruffled and its wings partly spread, and kicks and pecks and shakes itself so that the dirt is worked well into its feathers. Periodically it is quiet in the sun's rays. Dust-bathing may change the appearance of the sparrows along a city railway track, where they scratch out little hollows in the cinders. There they sunbathe and dust themselves and finally hop up with their feathers impregnated with soot and coal dust. One would barely recognize those grimy birds as belonging to the same species as the fresh, clean ones that live in a suburban garden. If sun- and dust-bathing serve any function beyond that of giving pleasure, it may be the mechanical one of helping to arrange the plumage, just as sawdust is used by a taxidermist or a furrier to help renovate feathers or fur. Dust-bathing is particularly associated with birds of arid countries; in the plains and deserts some birds take only dust baths. But the house sparrow may alternate dust baths with water baths.

In the hot weather of midsummer a bird-bath is a popular place. Though birds may take a bath by fluttering through the raindrops of a shower or the artificial rain of a lawn sprinkler, or by flitting among the rain-drenched leaves of a tree, typically they hop into water to bathe. The bird squats down and flutters its partly opened wings, splashing water over itself and ducking its head so that water runs down its back. The plumage may become so water-soaked that the bird can barely fly up to its perch. Then comes a period of preening. The bird shakes itself and runs its feathers through its bill. This preening lines up the barbs and the barbules and unites the parts of the vane of the feather into the proper firm surface. It is now that the oil gland (see p. 20) at the base of the tail is used. The bird may nibble at it to promote secretion and may rub its head against it. The preen oil on bill or head is then spread over the feathers in further preening. Preening usually follows bathing, but is often carried on without it.

There are also a number of related activities that have been loosely grouped as 'comfort movements'. They are comparable to the scratching of a monkey, the stretching of a man, or the switching of a cow's tail. A bird cannot preen its head with its bill, but it can and does scratch its head with one foot. Sometimes the wings are raised and stretched over the back and the body depressed, or a leg and a wing are stretched together while a bird balances on the other leg. As a social activity, two parrots may preen each other's feathers.

A strange habit recorded occasionally for some birds – crows and ostriches, for instance – is that of acting as if they were bathing near burning straw and leaves. A rook is said to have tossed burning straw about as well. A few birds have even been reported as putting hot embers among their feathers.[4]

Another very curious phenomenon is 'anting'. This came to the attention of most bird students only in the 1930s, but so intriguing and so widespread and puzzling is the habit that in 1957, in a survey of the subject, Lovie M. Whitaker, of Norman, Oklahoma, was able to list 148 species, from pheasants to songbirds, from America and Europe to Australia, that 'anted'.[5] This is done in two ways: passively, when the bird may 'sit' among ants with its wings spread and its feathers raised, in a posture recalling certain aspects of sunbathing; or actively, when the bird may stand and place or dab the ants among the feathers of the posterior part of its body, especially under the wings and about the base of the tail. It is noteworthy that all the ants used are types that spray or exude repugnant substances, such as those that cause a burning sensation when placed on a human tongue.

Similar actions are carried out with various other objects that have a strong odour. It is possible to watch anting by putting out moth-balls for grackles to use, and grackles scavenging in the litter-bins of a city park have been seen anting with orange peel. A striking thing about all these kinds of anting is the intensity with which they are performed, an intensity which has led observers to speak of the forcefulness of the activity, of the ecstasy of the birds, and of the apparent satisfaction derived.

Evidently anting, smoke-bathing, dust-bathing (which is often associated with direct sunlight) and water-bathing are all related activities which produce a presumably pleasant sensation in the skin. The response may be the same basic one varied by the position and the type of the stimulus.

Since sight is the best-developed sense in most birds, they usually start their daily activities when it gets light in the morning. In Ohio, whether the sun rises at about five o'clock, as in June, or eight o'clock, as in December, the song sparrows give their first calls or songs about half an hour before sunrise, according to Mrs Margaret Nice, the naturalist housewife who has written the biography of the species.[6] It seems the increasing light awakens them, for they start their day when the intensity is about 0·25 footcandles. At this time the last bright stars are being dimmed by the coming light, but it is not yet quite possible, according to Mrs Nice, to read a watch without a torch.

Light of about this intensity marks the beginning of the morning period, and the end of the evening period, of civil twilight – the time before sunrise or after sunset when, as the encyclopedia says, the sun is six degrees or less below the horizon and there is enough natural light to perform any outdoor activities. Like sunrise and sunset, civil twilight is a useful reference point for recording time without a clock. It has a meaning for song sparrows and used to have a meaning for rural outdoor workers – the farmer used to say he worked from starshine to starshine.

Each species has its special time of awakening. A study of fifty-seven species of woodland and field in New England found a spread of one hour forty minutes between the awakening time of the earliest riser, the wood pewee, whose first song began, on average, eighty-two minutes before sunrise, and the latest, the downy woodpecker, whose first calls began, on average, nineteen minutes after sunrise.[7] Subsequent studies have given somewhat different results, but, more important, they have shown that the correlation between light intensity and awakening varies with the season in some species as well as varying from species to species.

While the song sparrow wakes at the start of civil twilight throughout the year, the American robin is less consistent.[8] In March and August it does start to sing or call at civil twilight, but at the height of the breeding season in May and June, it may sing as much as an hour earlier, the chorus beginning when there is only a hint of light in the sky. Evidently the changes in the bird's physiological condition, the endocrine changes connected with reproducion, make the robin – but not the song sparrow – much more responsive to small increases in the amount of light in the morning.

The song of the mockingbird has inspired scientists to a modest flight of fancy in calling the bird *Mimus polyglottos*, the 'many-tongued mimic', and the night singing of both the European nightingale and the mocking-bird of the southern United States has inspired poets. But the habit of night singing, common to many species, is a practical problem to the bird student who is studying birds' awakening times. He must separate the sporadic singing of a species in the night, which has no obvious function, from the beginning of the dawn chorus in which all the songsters join and sing continuously for a time, marking the start of their day's activity.

Dawn begins the day for the sparrows, but it ends the day for the owls and a few other birds which hunt during the hours of darkness and sleep away the daylight hours. Though owls and other night-birds have night vision, they cannot see in complete darkness. Then they are aided by their marvellous hearing – hearing so acute that owls can locate and capture moving prey by ear alone. But the faint light of the moon must be a help to these birds when they fly about.

The moon affects the activities of birds of coastal waters, ocean beach, and mud flat in quite a different way, not through its light but through its influence on the tides, which have two peaks every twenty-four hours and fifty-one minutes. Plover and sandpiper garner the invertebrates of the mud flat and beach at low tide, when the flats and bars are exposed. When

Figure 14. *Leisure activities:* (a) *anting,* (b) *stretching,* (c) *sunning,* (d) *bathing,* (e) *soaring,* (f) *preening,* (g) *drying wings,* (h) *yawning.*

the rising tide covers them, the birds gather above high water
to rest. Their main active periods may be during the midday
hours or in the morning and evening, but apparently they sleep
during the night.

Not so that aberrant wader, the woodcock, which has become
adapted to life in the uplands, sleeping on a dry hillside during
the day and at dusk moving to a damper situation, where it probes
for worms in the soft earth of a marshy hollow or thicket. This
method of feeding is made possible by tactile sensitivity in the
tip of the bill. Vision is of little help to the bird in actual feeding, but it is essential in guiding its flight and guarding against
its enemies. Accordingly, the eyes are as large as those of many
night-birds. In the course of evolution the eyes have moved
towards the top and back of the head, where they are out of the
way of mud and dirt and are well placed to watch for enemies.

Dabbling ducks and geese also have tactile sensitivity in their
bills. They may sleep far out on open water during the day to
avoid the wildfowl gunner, and come in to the grain and potato
fields at night. With their sensitive bills they sort food from
mud, clods, and stones. Though not usually thought of as particularly intelligent, these birds are an adaptable lot. While daytime seems to be their usual time of activity, not only do some
feed at night to escape enemies, but others have adapted to feeding when the tides have made the water level just right for pulling up eel-grass, as brent geese do, or for diving for mussels, as
scoter ducks do.

Humans who get up early go to bed early, and those who get
up late go to bed late. But this is not true of birds. The order in
which diurnal birds go to their sleeping places is the reverse of
the order of awakening. The late-risers go to roost earliest and
the early risers retire latest. Usually it is somewhat lighter when
birds retire than it was when they awoke.

Many birds sleep in the habitat in which they spend the day.
Ground birds may crouch on their feet on the ground, water
birds float on the water, creepers and woodpeckers cling to the
upright trunk of a tree, and tree birds perch on a branch or a
twig. A perching bird's grip is automatic with the bending of
its legs – the weight of the bird tightens the leg muscles and

the tendons that run to the toes. The reverse is also true, as those who have handled live hawks and owls know. To loosen the grip of a bird of prey on one's hand it is only necessary to straighten the bird's legs.

However, some birds sleep not in their feeding habitat, but in the niche in which they nest. Some of the long-legged wading birds, such as the herons, may roost in the treetops. Chimney swifts, which spend the day feeding on the wing, funnel into chimneys or hollow trees and sleep clinging to the interior walls. Many birds of the coastal waters come ashore to roost for the night, terns on sand-bars, cormorants on rocks or other perches, and frigate birds in trees. Some birds, perhaps only a few, sleep in nests all the year round, and woodpeckers and wrens may actually make nests for sleeping. Some of these may later be used for eggs and young during the breeding season.

In the usual sleeping pose the bird puts 'head under wing', as popular parlance has it – actually, the head is turned over the back and the bill is thrust among the feathers of the back. Some birds that sleep in holes, such as toucans, relatives of woodpeckers, may cock up their tails to get into the space. But in sleeping poses, as in other aspects of bird life, we get variety. A stork or pigeon may sleep with its head sunk between its shoulders, with its bill pointed forwards, and may sometimes sleep resting on its heels, the tarsus straight out in front. One leg is often enough to support a sleeping bird's weight, and the one-legged stance is especially noticeable in the long-legged flamingo.

Perhaps the strangest pose of all is that of the bat lorikeets of the Orient. These are tree birds which spend their days climbing about among the branches of flowering and fruiting trees. When they go to sleep, they hang from a branch, head down.

It doesn't seem credible, but there is some evidence that a European swift (*Apus apus*) may spend the night on the wing.[9] Presumably the bird sleeps in a series of short naps: sleeping while sailing on steady wings, losing altitude as it sails, then awakening to gain altitude by flying up, and so on. A comparable practice occurs in some marine animals, whales and seals, which nap between breaths as they float near the surface. One

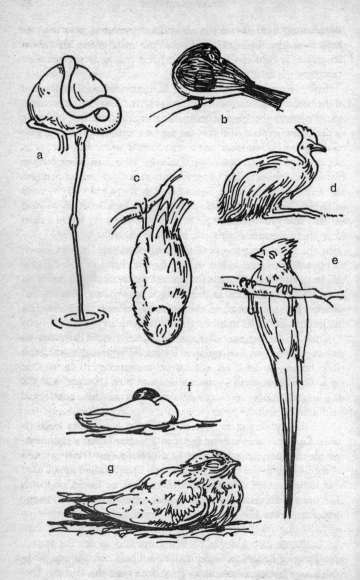

wonders whether soaring birds such as vultures, pelicans, and storks may not also catch a few winks as they glide high above the earth, but this would be very difficult to demonstrate. Certainly they commonly sleep perched, as some swifts do also.

The life of each sort of bird, from the lethargic vulture to the sprightly tit, has its own special rhythm. The rhythm of each is adapted to or is compatible with its own way of living. The tempo of a bird's life can be interrupted or changed by many things. A feeding snipe may find a worm big enough to fill its stomach and then run into the grass, crouch down, and go to sleep. The approach of night may speed up the feeding rate of a pigeon that is still hungry. The screaming of a jay that has discovered an owl may bring other jays from a wide area to join in the excitement of mobbing it. A spell of hot weather may make a falconer's hawks lethargic, while a spell of cold may cause humming-birds to become torpid. An approaching thunderstorm bringing wind with it may cause soaring pelicans to indulge in an amazing variety of aerial evolutions. Some of the bird's reactions to changed circumstances are purely physiological responses, but some of them are voluntary, based on information received by the bird's brain through its ear or its eye.

Perhaps the biggest changes of all in the bird's daily rhythm come with the turn of the seasons in temperate and polar latitudes. Social and habitat relationships are affected. At the start of migration a well-fed diurnal bird may, instead of going to sleep, set off in the evening on a flight that will take it all night, and next morning it may be several hundred miles away. In a spring migration the bird may move in a few weeks from the tropics with a twelve-hour day and a twelve-hour night, to the Arctic where the day is twenty-four hours long.[10] To meet these changed conditions it must make quite drastic adjustments to its daily rhythm. A little later, when it starts to breed, courtship and family demands may take more of its time than feeding which up to this time has been most important.

Figure 15. *Sleeping poses: (a) flamingo; (b) robin; (c) bat lorikeet; (d) cassowary; (e) coly, or mousebird; (f) duck; (g) nightjar.*

CHAPTER 9

Start of the Breeding Cycle

RAISING a family of young is a yearly occupation for most adult birds. Whether they lay one egg or twenty to a clutch, whether they live and breed one year or twenty, the biological aim is ultimately to replace each old adult with a young one.

There is difficulty in pin-pointing the start of the series of events that culminates in raising a brood to independence; this is illustrated by the extreme case of the white-rumped sandpiper (*Erolia fuscicollis*).[1] The adults leave the breeding grounds in Arctic Canada in August and arrive at the wintering grounds in the Argentine in September, when they are moulting into their dull winter plumage. The behaviour of the birds is now non-sexual, and the quiet flocks alternate between feeding and resting. By the following March a change has come. The birds are moulting from dull winter plumage into bright breeding plumage and the flocks are no longer quiet. They divide into small feeding groups that burst into choruses of soft song and twittering; fights are continually breaking out, the birds running at each other with open bills and spread wings, each trying to out-bluff the other; and flocks fly up to cut patterns in the sky. It is now autumn in the Argentine, and the birds are seven thousand miles or so from their breeding grounds, but they are displaying spring breeding behaviour.

Some time in May most of these birds, now in full breeding plumage, pass through the northern United States. By early June the birds reach the Arctic islands, to find them still snow-covered. Some of the birds have already paired off, but they must wait another week or so, feeding along bare sea beaches, until the rapidly advancing spring wipes the snow from the tundra. The birds then can move inland to take up nesting areas and quickly carry out their breeding activities, which must begin at once if they are to meet their schedule of leaving for the Argentine in August. The physiological changes and the behavioural patterns of breeding certainly become evident several months before the breeding time and several thousand miles from the breeding area. The whole spring migration is a movement to the breeding grounds. But it seems more practical to consider migration in a later chapter and for the present to consider the breeding cycle as started with the arrival on the breeding site.

A brief synopsis of the course of the breeding cycle for an 'average' bird is as follows: the pair forms, often with considerable courtship behaviour; a nest is built and actual mating takes place; the eggs are laid; incubation occurs, with the female taking the major role; the eggs hatch; the young are raised to independence; and the family breaks up. Of course, there is no such thing as an 'average' bird, so variations in the pattern are many and diverse.

However much the breeding cycles differ from species to species, they tend to be in tune with the local seasons, so that the young birds leave the nest and go out into the world for the first time to practise their untried skills when the climate is most favourable and food most plentiful. In the north-eastern United States this period is in summer, when the growth of vegetation has reached its peak and insects are most abundant.

Accordingly, most of the birds in this area nest in the spring. Typically, eggs are laid in May. In many species about six weeks are required for the development from freshly laid egg to independent youth, so the young can begin their independent lives at the proper time, in the summer, when the climate is beneficent and nature bountiful. Some species have special seasonal needs which affect the timing of their cycle. The great horned owl (*Bubo*) nests in March, its young hatch in April, fly in July, and may still be partly dependent on their parents in mid-autumn. The length of the breeding cycle dictates an early start if it is to be completed before winter begins.

The need of the young birds for special foods may affect the timing too. A few birds do not lay until early summer. The cedar waxwing and the goldfinch are the latest of these; they are unusual in feeding their quick-growing young on berries and weed seeds instead of insects or other animal food, and the emergence of these young birds coincides with the greatest abundance of this food in late summer.

Biologically, the essence of timing is the synchronization of the latter part of the breeding cycle with the maximum food supply. But if this is to be accomplished, the actual effective timing must come with the start of the breeding cycle, weeks or months before.

To those of us brought up in the North Temperate Zone, it seems natural that the returning sun, melting the snow and warming the earth, brings the migrating birds back to their breeding grounds and with its warmth starts the birds nesting. It was only in the 1920s that we began to understand some of the actual factors that time the breeding cycles, and with them the closely linked phenomenon of migration, which each spring brings birds hundreds and thousands of miles to their breeding grounds.[2]

Professor William Rowan was the pioneer in the study of photoperiodism.[3] At the University of Alberta he caught and experimented with wild juncos and crows. He found that artificially increasing the amount of light his birds received in autumn and winter caused their sex organs to emerge from the resting state and enlarge as they normally did in the spring, and this change, as part of the alteration in the hormone system, profoundly affected the birds' activities.

This epoch-making discovery, that a change in the amount of light a bird experienced daily could transform the condition of its breeding organs from the winter, or resting, state to one of spring-like activity, and the reverse, sparked much further experimentation that corroborated and elaborated Rowan's findings. Here we had a constant, twelve-month timing device – the seasonal increase and decrease in light – that was clearly one of the important factors in the regulation of the breeding cycle. This work also provoked much speculation and criticism by naturalists who knew conditions in many parts of the world. Temperate-zone species ordinarily breed in the spring, whenever it reaches their latitudes. But this season can be much earlier in one place than in another in the same latitude. Again, local weather conditions may cause the birds of an area to nest earlier one spring than another, and certain species may breed in autumn or winter. Evidently the uniform change in the amount of daylight is not the whole story.

Leaving the birds of the Temperate Zone, with their four orderly seasons, and those of the Arctic, with their harsh, long winter and short summer schedule, we find species of birds in East Africa that breed in April and May, at the beginning of the long rains, and again in the short rainy season in October and November. In the deserts of western Australia and of coastal Ecuador, where it does not rain every year, some of the birds wait until the rains come. These rains bring a flush of new vegetation and flowers and emerging insects, and the birds breed then, whatever the time of year. Completely free of the tyranny of regularly changing seasons are many of the tropical forests near the equator, where the climate and the length of daylight are uniform all year and the birds may breed at any time.

Evidently the timing of the breeding season is complex, not just a simple timing by the sun. Fortunately, the experiments in photoperiodism provided a further clue. It was found that in birds there is an innate cycle of rest: a refractory period exists during which the resting reproductive organs will not respond to any stimulus. This may last several months. It was also found that when this refractory period is over, a number of external factors can influence the regeneration of the gonads and the initiation of breeding. Besides light itself, these include warmth, rainfall, food, and the presence of a mate and of nest sites, all of which can act as accelerators. Other factors, such as cold, aridity, and lack of food, nest sites, or social stimulation, can retard or inhibit the onset of breeding.

These observations give us a working hypothesis of how the nesting season is timed all over the world. There is an innate time of rest, less than a year long. The recovery from this refractory period can be speeded up by favourable factors or arrested by inhibiting ones. Physiological changes occur automatically until the bird is almost ready to breed, and the reproductive system then awaits the final conditions that trigger breeding. Several factors may contribute; nowhere is the triggering action of a single factor seen more dramatically than in a tropical dry country at the end of the dry season. One day the rains come, and the next day the birds are building their nests.

One sex, usually the male, is ready to mate before the other. Courtship then plays an important part in raising the physiological and psychological condition of the other partner, usually the female, to the same condition of readiness. This need for courtship may have been one of the most important causes for the evolution of a pronounced sexual dimorphism in such birds as the plumed birds of paradise.[4]

The male magnificent bird of paradise seems to spend a considerable part of the year maintaining a solitary-display area amid the forest undergrowth, showing off his gaudy plumes sporadically in isolation. All the birds in the forest know where he is, for his loud ringing cries announce his location. Occasionally a female visits the area and the male displays to her, but she may not tolerate his advances. Finally comes a day when the female hops towards the displaying male and he goes into his most elaborate performance, flashing the brilliance of his glittering plumes. Then mating ensues. The female now goes her way alone, to occupy herself with nest, eggs, and young, while the male, his biological function fulfilled, stays at the bower, presumably ready to mate with another female.

Figure 16. *Preliminary breeding activities:* (a) *migrating* (*cranes*), (b) *singing* (*robin*), (c) *males fighting* (*cardinals*), (d) *mutual display* (*albatrosses*), (e) *male displaying to female* (*magnificent birds of paradise*).

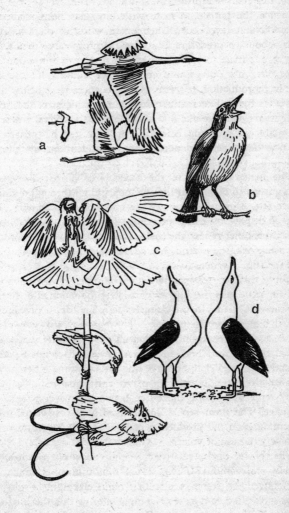

The female bird of paradise is dull, protectively coloured, as befits her role in reproduction. But the male, whose role is to influence the female to mate with him, has been shaped by selection that favoured a conspicuous, effective display. He is conspicuous to predators as well as to prospective mates. The loss of one male to a predator would not be too important, for these birds are polygamous and another would fulfil his short role in reproduction. It seems as if no chances were being taken, however, for unlike many perching birds his size, the young male wears plumage like that of the female for several years, and is capable of breeding before he has acquired his ornamental plumes. Thus reproduction is not dependent on the plumed males, though most of it is carried on by them.

The males of some of the other birds of paradise gather into groups to display in the treetops and go through a kind of dance which greatly enhances the effect of their activity. This sort of display by males in groups has evolved in birds of at least three other types: the cock-of-the-rock, one of the cotingas; the blackcock, the prairie chicken, and other gallinaceous birds; and the ruff, a wader.

While this type of mating display correlates with polygamy, and the male takes no further part in reproduction after fertilizing the egg, it may or may not be associated with pronounced sexual dimorphism in plumage. The plumed bird of paradise, the cock-of-the-rock, and the ruff all show striking, unexcelled sexual dimorphism both in coloration and in elongated ornamental plumes. Yet the prairie chicken and some other grouse, equally dramatic in their displays, and equally polygamous, show remarkably little difference between male and female in plumage. The great sexual dimorphism is in behaviour, in the dancing and in the production of loud sounds by wings or inflatable gular sac or voice.

The bower-birds, relatives of the birds of paradise, are equally polygamous. Their sexual dimorphism is much less pronounced. In some species that build elaborate bowers, the sexes look alike, and as if to compensate for this the bird uses coloured objects in its bower. One of these species, the gardener bower-bird of western New Guinea, builds a hut-like structure and clears a space in front of it. Here decorations are placed, including freshly picked flowers which are renewed daily. Dr E. T. Gilliard, of the American Museum of Natural History in New York, has made a special study of bower-birds, and has pointed out that this is a functional replacement of brilliant plumage by bright objects.[5] Presumably, when the female comes to the bower to mate, the male holds a flower in his bill while displaying to her, thus adding to the effectiveness of the display.

This behaviour may remind us of a young man giving flowers to his best girl for a somewhat similar reason. The effect of the flowers may be reinforced by presentation of a box of chocolates, and here we have courtship feeding practised by humans. Furthermore, the girl may open the box, pick out a chocolate, and hold it for the man to take a bite. In the same way, waxwings pass berries back and forth in their courtship feeding.[6] In this passing of food the purpose is not to provide nourishment. The activity can be interpreted as symbolic in several ways, but its immediate use is to heighten and maintain an emotional state between two individuals. Whatever the deficiencies of birds in intelligence, they seem to be extremely well endowed with emotional responses.

The holding of material in the bill during display is common in the courtship of some birds. Usually food or nesting material is held, and it may be passed back and forth as though it were symbolic of nest building and of the feeding of the young to come. This is common among the birds which form monogamous pairs and in which the male and female look alike. These have mutual displays, and both sexes share equally in nest building, incubation, and care of the young. In some grebes and herons, both sexes have ornamental plumes and use them in mutual displays and ritualistic dances, not only during the early days of courtship, but later in the breeding cycle. In the herons the displays have become conventionalized into nest-relief ceremonies, and in grebes, into various dances.

These displays now serve not only to synchronize breeding cycles and to promote mating, but also, in a further social function, to reinforce the pair bond and hold the two birds together

during the long, relatively inactive period of incubation. Among
these birds the same place serves as the display area of the male
and the nest site of the female, and each sex shares in part in
the activities of the other.

Other monogamous birds, notably most of the song-bird
assemblage, have a pattern of breeding which can well be called
the 'territory system'.[7] The territory plays an important role
throughout the breeding season. The sequence of events is best
seen in a migrating species. The males arrive at the breeding
ground before the females, and each male selects, establishes,
and defends a territory, which may be an acre or so in extent for
a warbler or a song sparrow. Each male warns off other males
by singing. At the territorial boundaries the males may dispute
with each other by song, or display – which takes the place of
fighting – or by actual scrimmaging.

The female then arrives. The male's song now serves a second function, to tell her that here is a male with a territory,
ready to mate. She selects a mate – or a territory. In any event,
she ends up with both, so it is difficult and perhaps immaterial
to determine which she chooses. Courtship goes on in the territory; the song and the display of the male again serve two
purposes: to warn off other males and to establish the pair
bond with the female and bring the physiological sexual cycles
of male and female into harmony. Mating (copulation) occurs,
and the nest is built in the territory. While the female incubates,
the male may or may not take turns with her, but his song and
display continue, still serving both to defend the territory and
to maintain the pair bond. Once the young have been hatched
the male often helps with their care and does less singing. The
territory still provides the food for the pair and now for the
young as well. But soon the territory defence weakens, and with
the growing up of the young the territory is abandoned and the
birds drift away.

This is the classical concept of territory which an Englishman, H. Eliot Howard, elaborated so successfully in 1920 in his
book *Territory in Bird Life*. It was hailed as a revolutionary
advance in the understanding of why birds fight and sing in the
spring, and provided a tremendous impetus to further field

study of birds. Its popularity as an idea is evident in Mrs Margaret Nice's 1941 review of the subject of territory. She points out that she found only 34 papers published before 1920, but 344 appearing in the next twenty years.

Naturally enough, over-enthusiastic students saw territories everywhere, and one extreme definition was put forward that 'Territory is any defended area.' This so falsifies the concept of territory that it comes to mean little beyond the fact that birds display aggressiveness in many situations, at many times of the year, even in defence of a roosting area or a feeding area in winter.

In holding a territory to which activities are restricted as outlined above, the bird gives up one of its typical avian traits, mobility. But it is capitalizing on another characteristic of animal life – the dominance of the individual on its home grounds over invaders. The bird holding a territory is also at an advantage in seeking food and avoiding predators, because it knows the area so well. Also, the bird avoids many disturbances from others of its own kind in mating, nesting, and raising its young. Thus reproduction is made easier.

There are also certain other advantages, some of which may have importance at times. For example, the territory provides a supply of food near at hand for the pair's exclusive use. And the spacing out of pairs ensures a uniform distribution of individuals over the suitable habitat area, and a uniform use of its resources. Consequently the level of the breeding population tends to be stable and the young have a relatively high chance of surviving.

Like many other aspects of bird life, the problem of space for the breeding season has provoked many responses. The true or typical song-bird territory, as outlined above for a migratory species, is only one of the solutions.

In certain species of birds, among them some of Mrs Nice's song sparrows, the young males may take up territories in the autumn and remain on them for the rest of their lives, but the females join the males on these territories in the spring and drift away in the autumn. It is probable that many species remain paired and on territories all the year round, especially in warmer countries. But where big, mixed flocks of birds are the rule, as in the tropical forests, one encounters a peculiar situation. Limited observation indicates that some birds may hold individual territories but periodically join the mixed flock for feeding. It has even been suggested that breeding birds that feed with army ants, following them for the sake of the other insects the ants stir up, may go a mile or so through the forest, maintain a moving feeding area there for the duration of the feeding period, and then return to the nesting area, where territories are maintained.

This recalls the modified type of territory, common among many song-birds, which the birds leave to seek food elsewhere. For instance, when I was studying the phainopepla in the desert of southern Arizona, I found that all the birds held small nest territories in the mesquite country but went to feed together on the mistletoe berries in a near-by cottonwood grove.

Territory of either type is often compressible, and a late-arriving male, by reason of his vigour, may be able to usurp enough of an area that appeared completely saturated to establish a territory between two others, taking part of each. In some territorial species the female may help defend part or all of the territory of the male, but in others, perhaps in many, several females may join the male and make nests in his territory, each defending her subsection of the territory against the other females.

Another type of modified territory is seen in the canvas-back duck in a prairie marsh. The birds arrive mated, or mate in the flock on the open water. Then, when ready to nest, each pair takes possession of a small area of water as its territory. This has been chosen by the female and is defended by the drake. The nest may be in the territory but is usually outside it, and when the female begins laying, the male accompanies her and waits near the nest until she rejoins him. After the female begins to incubate, the male usually abandons the territory as well as his mate and goes off with others of his own sex.

Unusual situations are seen in such birds as the phalarope, in which the larger, brighter female is the more aggressive sex partner and chooses and defends the territory, and in the communal-nesting ani. Among the ani, the whole flock defends an area against strangers of the same species; this behaviour is one aspect of a type of social nesting to be taken up in a later chapter.

CHAPTER 10

Nests and
Eggs

To put birds' nests in their proper perspective, one should consider them as cradles for the eggs and, in many cases, nurseries for the young. They are comparable to the nests of leaves squirrels make in the treetops, the pebble nests sunfish make in the bottom of a pond, and the elaborate nests of ants and wasps.

As birds evolved from reptiles, a development for which we have fossil evidence, the elaborate nest building of birds also evolved. Presumably it came from such early beginnings as the reptiles' habit of burying their eggs in the earth, though on this point we do not have fossil evidence. When birds became warm-blooded and their eggs needed continuous incubation, nests became necessary. Nest building and the warm-blooded condition probably evolved together.[1]

From species to species the nesting habits of present-day birds vary, ranging from the simple, approximating those of reptiles, to the very complex.[2] In most cases it is possible to find connecting types to form a series of intermediate stages. These series from simple to complex, while helping to understand how birds' nests could have evolved, do not indicate blood relationships, that is, actual phylogeny. It is true that certain groups of birds tend to make similar types of nests, the neat cup of different species of humming-birds, for example, and the inverted, retort-shaped nests of many kinds of weaver-birds. But in certain other groups nests are very diversified, and the same types of nests have evolved time after time in widely separated species. The sand martin and some petrels and kingfishers make burrows in the ground, and some parrots, woodpeckers, and tits dig nest cavities in tree trunks, but the relationship of these birds is remote.

As the English biologist Julian Huxley once remarked of species characters in another connection, the specific characters of nests seem to be frills on the evolutionary process.

A nest can be considered as a tangible, concrete record of a complicated behaviour pattern. Most activities must be recorded subjectively in words or captured on photographic film. But it is possible to put nests side by side and compare them as actual specimens. They show that each species makes a nest peculiar to itself. The extensive species differences that are evident in the bird's structure, its feeding habits, and its courtship patterns are also apparent in its nest-building practices as recorded in the completed nests.

The cup-shaped nest of twigs or grass built by so many birds is an admirable basic design. It can be adapted to fit into a great many places, from a burrow in the ground to a fork in the top of a tree, on a raft of floating vegetation, or against the sheer face of a cliff (Figure 17). This adaptability enables many birds to nest in their usual feeding habitats: the quail in the grass, the wren in the shrubbery, the vireo in the treetop – each where it is quite at home. Even the grebe in the pond can remain in its habitual surroundings. It makes a raft for its nest so that it can slide off in any direction into the water. Most species of birds build their nests in their feeding habitats.

The sea birds are an exception, for they must leave their feeding habitat and come on to land to nest, and the aerial birds must come to earth – to a cliff or a tree – to build their nests. Sometimes, of course, we get a surprise when trying to correlate habitat and nest site, a warning that evolution has not always proceeded along the course that seems most logical to us. It would seem very reasonable that the most aerial birds of all, the swifts, would make tiny nests on high branches whence they could easily glide off into flight. The crested swifts do just this. But some of the true swifts, even more aerial, may nest in caves

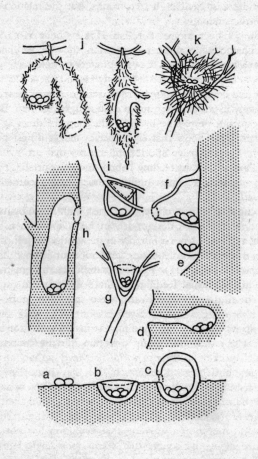

beneath the forest floor; to reach their nests these birds must fly down through the forest above which they feed. Some of the small auks that are so common in the Bering Sea, where they swim and dive for their food, nest in crevices among the rocks of the sea beaches, as one would expect, but one species flies far inland to lay its eggs in open nests above the treeline in the mountains.

The desirability of having the nest in the feeding territory or adjacent to it seems to be only one factor in the evolution of nests. Another, evidently, is the need of protection from predators – birds, mammals, or reptiles that might eat the eggs or young or even the incubating adult. The distribution of nests at scattered intervals all through the habitat, which is a function of territory, makes it difficult for any one predator to find many of them. As an additional protection many nests are hidden among the grasses or leaves, or match the surroundings. For instance, the chaffinch's nest, saddled on a branch, is ornamented with lichens that match the bark, effectively camouflaging it.

On the other hand, concealment has been abandoned by an oven-bird of South America in favour of a fortress type of nest. This bird often puts its nest on the top of a fence post. This is a peculiar place for a nest, and the nest itself is a strange one too. It is roofed over, made entirely of mud, and has only a small side entrance, which leads by a roundabout way to the nest chamber. The birds are only eight to nine inches long, but the nest may weigh nine pounds. It is baked hard and so provides the birds with protection similar to that enjoyed by those nesting in holes, in trees, or in the ground.

Some of the relatives of the oven-bird, the spine-tails, make their domed nests of sticks which should give some protection especially when, as sometimes happens, thorny sticks are used and a tubular entrance is added, bristling with thorns and just

Figure 17. *Some types of nests:* (a) *none made,* (b) *cup nest on the ground,* (c) *domed nest on the ground,* (d) *in a burrow in a bank,* (e) *shelf glued to a wall,* (f) *'retort' glued to a wall,* (g) *neat cup in a fork,* (h) *cavity excavated in a tree trunk,* (i) *basket slung by its edges,* (j) *pendant nests,* (k) *large bulky platform in a tree.*

large enough for the bird to creep through. Some small sea
birds, such as petrels, nest in burrows and go to and from their
nests by night to escape predation by gulls that would otherwise eat them.

Effective as these fortifications may be, birds like oropendolas
and weaver-birds have chosen instead to sling their nests from
the tips of slender twigs high in the trees and get protection by
their isolation. This location seems more in character for such
aerial animals as birds. The nests are in full view, but even the
most agile cat or monkey would have difficulty reaching them.
In its adaptation for this safety by isolation the cup nest is made
sack-like and attached by its edges, or it is turned into a covered
basket, as it were, with a side entrance and a strand of fibres
from which it dangles below its support. A long, tube-like entrance is often added, which helps foil a predatory hawk that
might alight on the nest and try to reach in with its feet.

Protection from mammal and reptile predators is also secured
by nesting on cliffs, on small islands, and over the water in
marshes and swamps. It is only in such predator-free situations
that birds can successfully nest in colonies. Some species of
colony-nesting herons have several alternative methods for protecting their nests. In some places they nest on the ground on
islands; in others, on matted reeds over water in marshes; and in
still others, in tall trees growing in water.

The complexity of such arrangements is indicated by some of
the results of the studies that the late Dr Robert P. Allen, of the
National Audubon Society, made on the American spoonbill.
He found that in Florida Bay the spoonbill nested regularly
only in the mangrove trees on islands on which there were no
raccoons. These climbing carnivores have a taste for eggs. One
year spoonbills started a colony on a mangrove island where
there were raccoons and all the eggs were destroyed by these
mammals.

A related occurrence involved a well-established colony of
herons in the low trees on an island in Orange Lake, in northern
Florida.[3] Raccoons were plentiful on the mainland and alligators
in the lake. After the slaughter of thirty-six large alligators, raccoons swam to the island and caused considerable damage to the

heron colony. Apparently the alligators had kept the raccoons away. Similar decimation has also followed when foxes have gained access to islands where colonies of water-birds nested.

Nest adaptations may reflect not only habitat characteristics and predator pressure, but also special incubation habits. The emperor penguin holds its single egg on its feet to protect it from the Antarctic ice on which it 'nests', and a flap of skin on the adult bird's stomach covers the egg to shield it from the mid-winter cold of the breeding season. Some of the megapodes, the only birds that do not incubate their eggs, scrape together an immense heap of leaf litter and soil from the forest floor and bury the eggs in this mound, where they are incubated by the heat generated by the decaying vegetable matter.

Just why each species should make a nest different from all others, and why the diversity in form, size, and materials should be so great, greater than in the structure of the birds themselves, is only partly explicable on functional grounds. There are nests so small and neat that they are hidden when the bird sits on them, and there are domed nests so large that the bird disappears inside to incubate the eggs. Twigs, sticks, leaves, grass, and feathers are the usual materials, but some birds have specialized in plant down, some in stones, some in mud, and certain swifts use only their saliva, which hardens upon exposure to air, for their nests. Often stems and fibres are simply laid in the nest and pushed, felted, and moulded with movements of breast, feet, and bill. However, the flamingo scrapes up mud into a heap with its bill to form the truncate cone that serves as its nest on a mud flat. The weaver-bird may make crude knots in the strands it weaves into its nest, and the tailor-bird 'sews' or 'rivets' leaves together to support and hide its downy cup nest. Of all the strange behaviour associated with nesting, none is stranger than the manner in which African love-birds carry nest material. They tuck it among their rump feathers, which hold it in place while they fly with it to their nests.

The manner in which the sexes share in nest building correlates with the mating patterns of the species.[4] In polygamous species, where the female meets the male only for mating, all the subsequent responsibilities of nest, eggs, and young are hers.

In some monogamous pairs both sexes share the nest building tasks and the care of eggs and young. Sometimes there is a division of labour in the nest building, the male bringing the material and the female incorporating it into the structure. However, in many territorial species the female alone works at the nest, while the male continues to guard the territory until the eggs hatch. Then he may help to feed the young.

A simple cup nest may take only a day or two to construct when the female is in a hurry to lay, especially in northern latitudes, where the season is short. But when the favourable season is longer, nest building may be a leisurely affair, taking weeks, and the male may even begin the nest as part of his courtship before he gets the mate who will complete it. The cactus wren, which makes nests all year for sleeping places and sometimes converts one of them to a breeding nest, may continue to add to the lining until the eggs hatch. Prolonged nest building may also be a mutual activity of a permanent resident pair, as it is among South American oven-birds, which start their nest in the autumn and carry the work on intermittently all winter and spring, whenever the weather is damp enough to provide mud. Under such circumstances nest building partakes of the nature of a leisure activity and serves, like mutual display, to help keep the pair together.

The eggshell, like the nest, has a passive role. It is the container for the fertilized cell that will produce the new young and for the stored food that will nourish the embryo until hatching. Its anatomy is described on page 26, and only the natural history of the egg is considered here.[5] The oval-shaped or round egg is produced completely within the body of the female. Consequently, the size of the mother bird limits and determines the size of the egg. The egg of the humming-bird is pea-sized, in some cases less than half an inch long, and weighs less than half a gramme; while that of the ostrich may be six and a half inches long and weigh 1,400 grammes. In comparison, the egg of a hen may be two and a half inches long and weigh about 60 grammes (just over two ounces). The relationship between size of egg and size of parent changes with the dimensions of the bird. Among small birds the egg may weigh from 10 to 20 per cent as much as the parent, while among large birds the egg may weigh only 2 to 4 per cent as much as the parent.

However, there is also another factor influencing egg size. Birds which hatch in a more advanced state, down-covered and ready to run about, like the young plover, need more food for their development in the egg, and consequently require larger eggs, than do birds of the same size which hatch in an undeveloped state and need to be cared for in the nest, like the young robin.

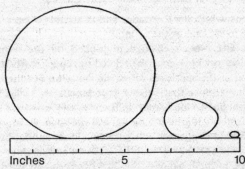

Figure 18. *Eggs, extremes in size (left to right): ostrich, hen, humming-bird.*

Eggs are laid at daily or longer intervals until the clutch is complete.[6] By contrast, some reptiles lay scores of eggs at one time. This spreading out of egg laying is a specialization for a flying animal so that the bird will not be heavily burdened with a whole clutch at one time. The complete clutch may consist of as few as one egg or as many as twenty, depending upon the species.[7] Those laying small clutches may lay a constant number of eggs; the size of the larger clutches may be more variable (Table II).

The small clutch size in birds agrees well with litter size in mammals. In both cases the small number of offspring correlates with the increased amount of parental care given the young. On the other hand, reptiles, which lay scores of eggs, and

TABLE II

Clutch Size among Birds

Size	Species
1 egg	albatrosses and other petrels, some auks and penguins
2 eggs	divers, many pigeons, humming-birds, etc.
3 eggs	many northern gulls
4 eggs	many northern sandpipers
3–6 eggs	many North Temperate song-birds (thrushes, etc.)
6–12 eggs	some North Temperate song-birds (tits, wrens, etc.)
6–15 eggs	some northern ducks and game-birds
10–20 eggs	grey partridge, some ducks and rails

amphibians, which lay thousands and thousands of eggs, give no care at all to the eggs or the young.

Clutch size, or clutch size multiplied by the number of clutches laid per year, must be related to annual mortality if the population of the species is to remain constant, but there are so many other factors that further correlations are difficult.[8] For example, a small clutch may indicate a safe existence for the bird, or it may indicate a long natural life-span. A large clutch may indicate a dangerous existence or a short natural life-span.

The role of clutch size, with its variation and its inter-specific differences, in the biology of the bird has been discussed above. Now let us look at the factors that influence egg production within a species.

As one would expect, the egg production of the domestic hen has been the most intensively studied. The aspects of the environment that influence this egg production are many; variations in light, temperature, humidity, and diet all play a part. The health of the bird, its age, and its ancestry (i.e., whether it comes from a line of good layers) are also important for maximum production.[9] There are records of 361 eggs laid by one hen in one year and 1,515 eggs by one hen in eight years.[10] Basic to this continued productivity is the fact that in some species (but not all) if an egg is removed from the nest, another will be laid to replace it. In the wild this has been demonstrated with the flicker that was induced to lay seventy-one eggs in seventy-three days.[11] In species like the flicker the bird apparently continues to lay until the 'right' number of eggs produces a tactile stimulus on the skin of the abdomen. This influences the endocrine system to secrete certain hormones which act on the ovary to terminate egg production. Such birds, called indeterminate layers, include also such groups as ducks and gallinaceous birds.

In some other species the number of eggs to be laid in a clutch seems to be genetically determined. The removal or addition of an egg makes no difference in the number the bird lays. These birds, called determinate layers, include many common song-birds and waders.

Many species will replace a clutch that has been destroyed, usually building a new nest for the replacement.[12] A single brood a year completes the reproductive activity of most birds. However, in the North Temperate Zone some song-birds and doves raise two or more broods in quick succession.

One of the best-known causes for variations in clutch size occurs in a change in latitude. The horned lark in the central United States lays three eggs; in southern Canada, usually four; and in the Arctic, usually five. The same may be true within a family. Sparrows and buntings native to Central America usually lay two eggs; those of the northern United States, four or five; and those of the Arctic, six. From these figures comes the generalization that many tropical birds tend to lay fewer eggs than do related temperate-zone or arctic species. The effect of another influence – diet – in changing clutch size is demonstrated in the hawks and owls that feed on mice and lemmings. When these small mammals become abundant, as they do every few years, the hawks and owls lay larger clutches.

The mechanism that determines the number of eggs laid is inadequately understood. Presumably the endocrine system is involved, and a variety of factors could trigger the increased laying: the sight of the abundant food, or the increase in the amount of food eaten, may have this effect; or perhaps some climatic factor that contributes to the larger food supply also affects the bird so that it lays more eggs.

Objects as palatable as birds' eggs are readily eaten by such keen-eyed predators as crows. It is perhaps to foil such predation that eggs of the ringed plover, laid in an open nest, are so

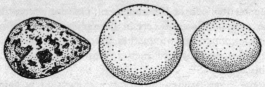

Figure 19. *Eggs, shapes and patterns (left to right): plover, owl, robin.*

mottled and blotched with various shades of grey and brown that they are very difficult to see against their background of pebbles. On the other hand, woodpeckers, nesting in egg-concealing holes, lay white eggs. But when we hypothesize that brown spots on a background of white, grey, olive, greenish, or blue eggs laid in open nests give protective coloration not needed by plain white or tinted eggs in covered nests or holes, we find many exceptions. We are forced to conclude that the colour and markings of its eggs are not of vital importance to the bird. The extent to which the incubating bird covers them from view may be a factor which reduces the necessity for concealing coloration. Perhaps, like some of the specific differences in nest building, variations in egg colour are simply expressions of the general tendency of birds towards diversity, the same diversity that is so important in feeding and mating.

The most meaningful generalization is that groups of birds usually lay certain types of eggs. For example, woodpeckers, parrots, pigeons, owls, and kingfishers lay white eggs; ducks and cormorants lay pale, pastel-shaded eggs; and many hawks, auks, and song-birds lay spotted eggs with markings that may form a wreath of colour around the larger end. Among the most unusual eggs are the handsome porcelain-like tinamou eggs, uniformly blue, yellow, or brown, and the guira cuckoo's egg, blue with white lines.

For the embryo to develop in the egg, heat must be supplied. The bird usually does this by fluffing out its feathers and sitting on the eggs so that they are right next to its skin. Certain local areas of the skin, called brood patches, become more highly vascularized and therefore warmer, and the feathers may be moulted from the patches, so that the eggs can be brought into close contact with them. These developments are brought about by the action of hormones, as has been demonstrated experimentally.

Incubation ordinarily is delayed until all the eggs, or all but one, are laid.[13] This insures that all the young will hatch at nearly the same time. But in some species, such as barn owls and some cuckoos, incubation may start with the first egg, and as a result the eggs hatch over a period of days. The resultant young are then of various sizes and ages. In times of scarcity the smaller young are at a disadvantage in being fed, but this may actually be an advantage to the species. When there is not enough food to go round, the weakest starve, the strongest survive, instead of all the young being half-starved.

The length of the incubation period is correlated in part with size. The extremes are found in small song-birds, which usually incubate for eleven to fourteen days, and in the albatross, whose eggs hatch in about twelve weeks. But the rate of development differs in different groups. The smallest eggs, those of the humming-birds, take only two and a half weeks to hatch, while the largest, those of the ostrich, take as much as six weeks.

The roles of the sexes in incubation are correlated with their roles in courtship and nest building, as we have mentioned earlier.[14] Where no pair is formed, the female does everything; where pairs are formed and both sexes share in the nest building and mutual courtship, both birds incubate; while in many strictly territorial birds, the male does not incubate, or does so only sporadically, though he may feed the incubating female or accompany her when she is off the nest searching for her own food, which she may do several times a day.

After watching a tit, continually active, gleaning through the branches after insects, one could confidently and correctly predict that its incubation, carried out by the female alone, would be interrupted by short spells of activity. This is just what is done. The female sits on the nest for a quarter or half an hour and then leaves it for five minutes or so. The more phlegmatic domestic hen sits quietly on her nest all day, leaving it only once or twice every twenty-four hours to feed. Doves alternate on the nest, dividing the twenty-four hours into two shifts, the male taking the day shift. Still larger birds, such as certain albatrosses, live at a slower tempo and can store enough food in their bodies to enable them to sit for periods of days or weeks before they are relieved by their mates. But the undisputed champion is the emperor penguin. The male penguin takes over the care of the egg shortly after it is laid and incubates continually for two months, without food, until the female returns to relieve him about the time the young bird hatches. Most birds would have starved in this length of time.

The female hornbill in Africa may sit on her nest, sealed in her nest cavity, throughout the whole incubation period of four to six weeks. But she is not foodless, for the male visits her regularly and passes food in to her through the narrow slit left in the sealed-up entrance hole.

The length of attentive and inattentive periods in incubation is governed by the length of time birds can go without food and by the nervous temperament of the birds. The same range of variation in activity and inactivity will be seen in the rates of feeding the young, taken up in the next chapter.

CHAPTER 11

Parents and Young

BIRDS have more family life than any other group of vertebrate animals except mammals. Concern for their young is practically absent in reptiles, amphibians, and fish, but in both birds and mammals it is important. With some exceptions, the parent bird feeds the growing young, warms them with heat from its body, supervises their leaving the nest and their entry into the world, and guides and protects them for a time thereafter.

The first part of the life of the young bird is spent in the egg as a growing embryo, living on the stored food of the yolk and interchanging oxygen and carbon dioxide with the outside air through the porous shell. After a period of from eleven days to twelve weeks, depending on the species, the young bird has used up all the food, fills the shell, and is ready to hatch. One can sometimes hear the cheeping of the chick through the shell during these last days in the egg.

Now the chick twists and turns and pushes with his bill until a series of punctures and cracks near the larger end of the egg allows the young bird to push the two halves apart and emerge.[1] During the few hours or days it takes to hatch, the bird uses two specialized structures. There is a calcareous projection, the 'egg tooth' on the tip of the upper mandible to help puncture the egg, and there is a special 'hatching muscle' on the back of the head and neck to give power to the egg tooth. Both egg tooth and hatching muscle quickly disappear after hatching.

The newly hatched young bird of the most precocious type is able to leave the nest in a few hours. In contrast, the least advanced may be helpless in the nest for days or weeks. The young birds that must stay in the nest and be cared for there by the parents are customarily called altricial or nidicolous, and those that are able to leave the nest shortly after hatching are called precocial or nidifugous.

Many species fall clearly into one category or the other, but there are, as one might expect, species with intermediate types of young. Some of these complexities are set forth in the following outline, adapted from one by Mrs Nice.[2]

TABLE III
Condition of Young Birds at Hatching

I Precocial – eyes open, down-covered, may or may not be fed by parents, leave nest first day or two
   A Independent of parents (e.g., megapodes)
   B Follow parents, find own food (e.g., ducks, waders)
   C Follow parents, shown food by them (e.g., quail, chickens)
   D Follow parents, are fed by them (e.g., grebes, rails)
II Semi-precocial – eyes open, down-covered, stay at or near nest though able to walk some way; fed by parents (e.g., gulls, terns, nightjars)
III Altricial – eyes open or closed, may or may not be down-covered, unable to leave nest, fed by parents there
   A Eyes open, down-covered (e.g., hawks, ibis)
   B Eyes closed, down-covered (e.g., owls, tropic birds)
   C Eyes closed, little or no down (e.g., perching birds, kingfishers, cormorants)

The type of care given by the parents obviously varies greatly with the type of young.[3] With altricial young, at first the care consists mainly of brooding and of bringing food to the nestlings, later mainly of feeding, and finally of guiding the fledglings in the habitat and helping to repel or distract predators. With precocial young, the parents' activities involve chiefly guiding the active young, brooding, and helping them escape predators.

The share of the sexes in the care of the young follows in part the pattern we have seen in nest building and in incubation and is correlated with that of pair formation. If no pair is

Figure 20. *A chick hatches.*

formed, the female alone feeds; if male and female share in nest building and incubation, both feed and brood.

But in territory-holding song-birds, where the male's role has been to defend the territory and he has taken no part in nest building or incubation, he largely abandons this defence when the offspring hatch and helps bring food for them. In the altricial song-birds in which a second brood is started so quickly that the cycles overlap, the male's aid is absolutely essential. He may carry the main load of caring for the growing young while the female starts her second clutch of eggs. The male's help is required in the domestic economy of the precocial coot, too. In this case hatching is not simultaneous, but is spread over a number of days. The male incubates the late-hatching eggs while the female seeks food for the first young. There is also a division of labour here when danger threatens. The female swims away with the older young while the male defends the nest and its remaining contents.

In a few species as distantly related as jays and rails, the parents are helped in their nest duties by unmated birds that join in the feeding of the young and in the brooding. In 1935 the American naturalist Dr Alexander Skutch, who is the authority on Central American birds, found that a Mexican brown jay's nest with its rightful pair in attendance had five such 'helpers' at the nest.[4] They were all full-grown but could be identified as immature, and could be distinguished individually, by the varying amounts of pale juvenile coloration

remaining on their bills, feet, and eye rings. These helpers not
only brought food to the nestlings, but also helped the parents
defend the nest against intruders. Several species of young rails,
only partly grown, have been seen to feed smaller young.[5] In
one case in the Dresden Zoo, recorded by the German ornithologist Dr W. Meise, an eight-week-old chick of the Argentine
crake (*Laterallus*), that was still being fed by its parents, presented food to a newly hatched chick of its parents' second
brood and shared in brooding it. However, the records of such
behaviour are few and scattered and their overall importance is
in question.

The detailed description of the different patterns of development of young birds, and of the related parental behaviour, can
begin with an examination of the altricial young.

A typical altricial song-bird takes a month or two to develop
from hatching to independence.[6] During about half of this time
the bird stays in the nest, completely dependent on the parent;
thereafter it is out of the nest in the grass, shrubbery, or trees,
becoming independent. The nestling hatches in a naked or
near-naked, embryo-like condition, with a translucent skin and
a relatively huge abdomen. It has stubby wings and legs, a long,
skinny neck, and a large head with closed eyes, a wide gape,
and a short bill. At rest, it balances on its abdomen with its
head turned under its breast, resting on its crown in an embryo-
like pose. It is not too particular about being right side up and
can right itself only with difficulty. At this stage the chick,
lacking temperature control, is cold-blooded, and must be

a   b   c

Figure 21. *Young birds:* (a) *altricial song-bird, first day;* (b) *altricial
song-bird, tenth day;* (c) *precocial chick, first day.*

brooded by the parent as much as the egg was. When not brooded, it will respond to sounds and to a jarring of the nest, as it does to the arrival of the parent, by thrusting up its head and opening its mouth wide, begging to be fed. Into this gaping maw the parent thrusts its beakful of insects or other food, and then it waits to perform its nest-sanitation duties. The young song-bird defecates after feeding, raising the hind part of its body and extruding the excrement in a mucus-covered pellet that the adult either eats or carries away and drops elsewhere. Among some other species, such as hawks and herons, the young birds back to the rim of the nest and void forcefully over the edge, thus keeping the nest clean. Nest sanitation is disregarded by some altricial species – the nest cavity of the hole-nesting hoopoe becomes foul and fetid, and in the latter part of the nest life of the northern finches the rim of the nest becomes encrusted with faeces.

There is little change in the bird's appearance during the first third of the nest life. During the second third, the nestling becomes more bird-like, even if somewhat scrawny. The eyes open, the pin-feathers grow rapidly, and their blue-grey sheaths burst at the tip so that the nestling becomes partly covered with feathers. The feet grow large and strong enough for the bird to grasp the nest material and to right itself easily into its new nestling pose – its bill pointed ahead and up over the rim of the nest. It responds now to the sight of its parent by begging, but the sight of a large, strange object, such as a man, causes the young bird to crouch motionless in the nest. Its temperature has become stabilized; the nestling is now warm-blooded and needs less brooding. Larger food items may now be fed to it.

The common method of feeding altricial young is for the parent to bring food in beak or gullet and to thrust it into the wide-open gape of the begging young. Only one bird, the rosy finch, has a special structural adaptation for carrying food to the young – cheek pouches opening from the mouth, a type of structure much more common in mammals than in birds. The humming-bird does not simply thrust the food into the nestling's gape, but inserts its long, slender bill into the gullet of the

young bird and injects the food, as it were. The pelican does just the opposite. It opens its wide gape and the young bird thrusts its head and neck, shoulder deep, into its parent's gullet, where it gets its meal of partly digested fish. Gulls, terns, and herons, which also feed partly digested fish, do so by regurgitating it into the mouths of the young birds, or on to the floor of the nest or the ground, where the older young pick it up.

Another type of food transportation is common with hawks and owls, which carry their prey in their feet. The young of these birds are fed in a special way, too. The parent stands on the carcass and pulls off pieces, and the young nibble them from the parent's bill. Later, carcasses are left in the nest; the well-grown young may pull off pieces for themselves.

Raw food, sometimes beaten or nipped, sometimes partly pre-digested, is the standard food for young birds. But one group is an exception. Pigeons feed 'pigeons' milk' to their small young. This is a soft, white, fatty material produced by the walls of the crop for just this purpose. Perhaps it is necessary because the diet of pigeons is predominantly vegetable and their growing young need the protein which is provided for many species by their animal diet.

The frequency with which young birds are fed varies. It depends on a number of factors, some of which are difficult to evaluate. The interaction of some of these factors is illustrated in the feeding behaviour of two species of African hornbill, as pointed out by the English naturalist R. E. Moreau when he was studying the habits of these birds in Africa.[7] One species brings a single food item in its bill to its nest, and may make thirty or forty trips an hour. Another species brings as many as twenty-five items in its gullet and regurgitates them one after another for its young. This bird makes infrequent trips, but

Figure 22. *Parental care: (a) robin carrying food to the young; (b) duck leading her young, which find their own food; (c) young pelican getting food from the gullet of its parent; (d) hen leading her young and showing them food; (e) humming-bird injecting food into the gullet of a young bird; (f) grebe carrying young bird on its back.*

presumably brings as much food as the first bird, with much less effort. The rate of feeding, the amount of food brought on each trip, and the number of young have all evolved together, and the combination that a species has evolved is not the only one possible.[8]

In looking for correlations we find the shortest interval between feedings in the small species, with their high metabolism. The longest intervals occur in large species. However, in certain small species – the storm petrels, for example – there are long intervals between feedings. The age of the young and the nature of the food provided may also make a difference. Very small young birds may be given small items at frequent intervals; when they are older, they may be given larger items at longer intervals (Table IV).

TABLE IV
Some Feeding Rates

Group or Species	Range of Frequencies
Song-birds	1–40 times per hour
Humming-birds	1–4　　,,　　,,　　,,
Pigeons	5–10　,,　　,, day
Gulls and terns	6–80　,,　　,, ,,
Hawks	6–50　,,　　,, ,,
Ibis and herons	6–30　,,　　,, ,,
Pelicans and relatives	1–3　　,,　　,, ,,
Storm petrels	1–2　　,,　　,, ,,
Albatrosses	2–5　　,,　　,, week

During the last third of its nest life, the altricial bird continues to develop its feathers, especially the wing quills. It preens itself, exercises, watches what goes on about it, and pecks at the edge of the nest or at ants and flies that come near it. Its response to parents and to humans remains the same except in one particular. At any time during the last third of its nest life, if it is frightened enough, it may leave the nest, a short-tailed, weak-flying bird. If not frightened, it may stay a few days longer in the nest, but then the parents themselves may take over. I have seen house wrens do this, in a garden near

New York City. The old ones flutter about and call excitedly
and this mood may be communicated to the young so that they
hop out of the nest. If they do not, the parents may coax them
out. They present food, then withdraw it, then move a little way
off, until the young ones hop out. The parents move off; the
young birds follow and are gradually lured into places of
safety.

Just when the young song-birds leave the nest seems not very
important, for their life is not very different for the next few
days from what it was in the nest. Perhaps the move helps them
to escape predation. Since the near-helpless young birds are
scattered rather than remaining in one place, they cannot all be
caught at once. Gradually the young one grows its tail, becomes
active, accompanies the parents, and feeds itself. Soon it is
independent and the family breaks up.

Outside the nest, the change from infantile begging to self-
supporting independence is ordinarily a gradual one. It is partly
a fixed thing determined by instinct. It may be hastened by the
waning interest of the parent or by the young bird's changing to
self-feeding. If the bird is very hungry it may still beg to be
fed; if only moderately hungry it may feed itself. Young thrash-
ers and young doves may change from self-feeding to begging
when an adult approaches them. Young sparrows, picking up
bread crumbs, may encounter a big piece of bread and beg at
the food itself. The two patterns, self-feeding and begging, may
alternate in response to both internal and external stimuli. In
captive birds hand-fed continually with no free food available,
the begging period has been indefinitely prolonged, and a cedar
waxwing has been reported which never learnt to feed itself.

A striking contrast to the ordinary gradual change from begging to self-feeding is seen in certain shearwaters. These young
are hatched in a burrow and fed there by their parents until
they are well grown and fat. Then the parents desert them,
sometimes even leaving on migration. The young complete their
growth by using their stored fat, and finally set out to fly, swim,
and feed by themselves without parental care or guidance. This
sudden change from a subterranean, dependent existence to an
unsupervised one at sea is as dramatic in its way as the indepen-

dent emergence of the megapode into the world. The complete-
ness of the instinctive behaviour patterns of both these birds
recalls the power of instinct in the social parasites, cow-birds
and cuckoos, which are brought up by foster parents but upon
fledging adopt the ways of the parents, uninfluenced by their
early environment.

The length of nest life, which varies from eight days to eight
months, is correlated with a number of other factors in the
biology of the bird, a few of which will be mentioned. The
period of nest life tends to be about as long as the incubation
period or somewhat longer, sometimes considerably longer.
This is presumably due to a somewhat similar growth rate before and after hatching, a growth rate that may vary from one
order of birds to another. The longest nestling periods occur
only in large birds (e.g., albatrosses), and the shortest ones occur
only in small birds (e.g., sparrows, wood warblers). This may
be due in part to the fact that the larger birds lay relatively
smaller eggs, so the young have more growing to do after they
hatch. Young birds that leave the nest before they can fly (e.g.,
sparrows) have a shorter nest life than their near relatives that
delay leaving the nest until they can fly (e.g., swallows).

The length of nestling life may be influenced by food and
temperature. This is especially true of swifts. The English
ornithologist Dr David Lack made a special study of swifts
(Apus apus) that nested in the tower of Oxford University
Museum.[9] He found that in summers when the weather was
good or moderate and flying insects were easily caught a few
young swifts grew up and fledged in as little as thirty-seven
days, but in summers with bad weather, which made it difficult for the parents to get food for the young, the fledgling
period averaged a week longer and one nestling did not fly until
it was fifty-six days old.

This great diversity is to be expected when we remember
that, after all, the altricial condition is not sharply separated
from the precocial one, but is one end of a gradual series (Table
V).[10]

How different is the growing up of the precocial chick of
quail or pheasant![11] It hatches, down-covered, with eyes open

TABLE V

Duration of Incubation and Nest Life of Some Altricial Birds[10]

Species	Incubation Period (days)	Nestling Stage (days)
Finches	11–14	8–17
Warblers	11–17	8–14
Nuthatches	12–16	22–24
Crows	16–20	15–38
Swallows	14–18	17–28
Woodpeckers	11–18	19–35
Swifts	17–21	20–42
Humming-birds	16–17	19–25
Parrots	17–31	28–36
Hawks	28–56	28–133
Pelicans and relatives	24–45	35–62
Storm petrels	36–50	56±
Albatrosses	63–80	150–251

and legs big enough to be useful. As soon as its down is dry it can yawn, preen, peck at things, and walk. Its stage of development at hatching is comparable to that of the altricial bird just before leaving the nest. In a few hours, the parent may lead the brood, which hatched almost simultaneously, from the nest. Eggs which have not hatched are abandoned in the nest. Periodically the hen calls her young to her for brooding, and she also calls their attention to food by pecking at it, calling, lifting it, dropping it, and calling again. Within a day or so the young are finding food for themselves. At a warning call they scatter, hide, and squat motionless, 'freezing', to reassemble later at rallying calls of the parent. The quail chick begins to show its body feathers through its down when two weeks old; by four weeks it is largely covered with the feathers of its first plumage, except for the head, which is still downy; by eight weeks the young bird is beginning to moult and is acquiring its adult plumage; at fifteen weeks it is practically indistinguishable from the adult.

The length of time the young precocial birds and their parents remain together varies with the species. The family may break up even before the birds are full-grown in some species, while in such birds as the bobwhite quail the covey may stay together and combine with other coveys, separating only with the approach of the next breeding season.

The young of the mound-building megapode are the most independent of all.[12] After hatching, the young birds dig out of the mound, and without any attention from the parent each goes its individual way, remaining solitary until the mating time. This absence of parental care recalls the situation among many reptiles from which birds have evolved. These young have some special adaptations. Notable ones are the large strong feet, which are useful to the adult in scratching together the mound and are useful to the young in digging its way out. Another adaptation is the degeneration of the egg tooth, which is represented at most by a vestige. The egg tooth is generally used by hatching birds to make a crack around the egg so that it can be pushed apart in two pieces. But to separate the pieces in this way would be impossible, obviously, in an egg buried in the earth. Instead, the eggshell becomes extraordinarily weak and brittle as hatching time approaches, and it breaks to pieces with the kicking and twisting of the young bird. Presumably the relic egg tooth is a heritage from surface-nesting ancestors that made more ordinary nests.

Some pheasants may fly at three days of age, but the megapode chick is even more precocial and has quills large enough to permit flight the first day of its life. And since it lacks any care or protection from the parent, maximum mobility is an advantage.

Attention has been focused on the megapode as extremely precocious, but ducklings are hardly less so.[13] Their down is so dense that they need little brooding, and they find their own food from the first. Though the young ducks usually accompany the female until well grown, ducklings can and have survived by themselves alone from their first day in the marsh.

Not all adaptations of precocial young are the expected ones. Just as we find some of the marsh- and water-adapted ducks perching in trees, so do we find a number of species, like the wood duck, that nest in holes in trees from which the young climb to the entrance and jump to the ground, floating down and landing lightly, unhurt. There is a minor but important adaptation for this type of nest – the long, sharp nails of the young wood ducks.

The German ornithologist Dr Oskar Heinroth, of the Berlin Zoo, discovered the importance of this adaptation when he put up nest boxes with openings near the top and smooth inside walls for the zoo's wood ducks.[14] Not only wood ducks but mallards used these nest boxes. The young wood ducks escaped safely, but the young mallards, which are ordinarily hatched on the ground and do not have sharp climbing claws, were unable to climb out and died in the nest boxes.

There is a striking dichotomy in the development of locomotion in the precocial young. The chicks of many pheasants and their relatives can fly in less than a week, a very useful ability for avoiding ground predators. But ducklings, which can swim and feed themselves in the watery marsh from the first day, are less threatened by such predators. Correspondingly, the wing quills develop slowly and the ducklings are not able to fly until they are six or seven weeks old. However, even before they can fly, the young ducks do use their wings in locomotion. They flap their stubby wings while paddling with their webbed feet as they flee over the water.

Though water birds, such as divers and ducks, have thick down, the parents do brood them at times on shore. However, grebes, the most aquatic of birds, have young with a thinner coat of down, needing more brooding.[15] This they get afloat by riding on the back of the parent and sometimes snuggling under the wings for warmth and dryness. When tired of this seclusion, young grebes may poke their heads up through the back feathers of the parent and look about as they ride along.

The precocial young, such as those of quail and ducks, are very different from the altricial young of song-birds, but there are birds, such as the terns, nightjars, and rails, with young that represent an intermediate condition (see outline on p. 114). It seems that here we have further expressions of those forces always acting in birds to produce diversity.

Judging by the precocial condition of hatchling reptiles and the general lack of care by the adults for the young in that group, precocial young birds are probably the more primitive type. The development of different types of young birds probably accompanied the evolution of different types of nests and specialization of the bird for different habitats. It seems difficult to imagine such tiny-footed, long-winged birds as hummingbirds, which do no walking, evolving without also evolving altricial young. The precocial condition of the young of quail and pheasants is quite practical in view of the ability of the parents and young to walk, and enables the parents to get the young away from the dangerous nest as soon as possible. It also enables them to scatter when an enemy approaches.

A special case of parental care is the injury feigning by the parents. This is well illustrated by the ringed plover, Figure 23. When a man or a dog approaches the young the parent may fly about, screaming, then drop to the ground and flutter away in a manner suggesting it is injured. The potential enemy is likely to follow and be led away.

It would seem that in the richly diversified class Aves, the specialization and diversity of the young ones was an essential

Figure 23. *Ringed plover feigning injury to lure an enemy away from the nest.*

element in the adaptation of the adults to various habitats and ways of life. The diversity of the ways in which different groups solved the same problems of nesting and nurturing reflects the diversity which we find time after time in other facets of the bird's life, facets as different as feeding and mating.

CHAPTER 12

Social Nesting

SOCIAL behaviour is important throughout life for many birds, and social behaviour is of necessity a critical factor in pairing, even where the meeting is a transient one for sexual union only. In monogamous species the pair is a social unit, the birds keeping together and the behaviour of each individual affecting the other. Later the young birds join the unit and for a time become part of a closed breeding society. In a wider sense the aggregation of displaying males, the colony of nesting birds, even the males that hold a series of contiguous territories, all form open social systems into which new individuals may become incorporated.

But there are more complicated situations, which can be compared with those of humans. There are the compound nests, reminiscent of apartment houses; there are mixed villages with several species nesting near each other; there are communal households occupied by more than one pair of a species; there are communal nurseries; and there are social parasites, who leave their offspring to be cared for entirely by strangers. It is these that are considered here, together with some reflections on how these patterns came into being.

The classic example of a compound nest is that of the sociable weaver-bird of South Africa, a veritable apartment house that has been called the greatest bird architecture in the world and that was well described by the great English naturalist Sir Andrew Smith more than a century ago.

This wonderful apartment house is built in a tall savanna tree and may be up to twenty-five feet across and five feet deep, with nearly a hundred apartments sheltered under a common roof.[1] Such a compound nest is the property of a flock of sociable weaver-birds. Monogamous pairing is the rule in this species, and each pair has its own nest. When a new compound nest is started, the roof is made first, as a joint project. It is in effect a thatched roof; the rain runs off it instead of soaking in. Then each pair hangs its typical retort-shaped weaver-bird nest to the underside of the roof. These are so close together that from below the collection of nests looks like a floor with many openings in it. The individual nests are not used a second year, but new ones are built and additions to the roof have been reported. Besides working at the nest during the breeding season, all the birds, male and female, do some repair work all the year round. An outstanding aspect of this sociable weaver-bird nesting is that, despite the communal nature of the nest building, there has been no breakdown in monogamous pairing within the flock.

A somewhat similar type of apartment house is seen in a few other species, including a buffalo weaver of eastern Africa, the palm chat of the West Indies, and the monk parrot of Argentina. In each of these species the colony builds a bulky mass of sticks high in a tree and in this each of the individual pairs has a separate apartment which is in effect a simple domed nest. That the central mass of sticks is a communal affair is deduced from the fact that all the palm chats work in close proximity in adding sticks. The buffalo weavers increase protection from predation by using thorns in the nest. Perhaps the whole structure is an adaptation for holding the simple domed nests high in a tree, where they are comparatively safe from predation, with the added protection of the strong nest structure.

Uninvited guests sometimes occupy a vacant nest chamber in a compound and lay their eggs there: the speckled duck (*Anas flavirostris*) in the nest of the monk parrot, or a pygmy falcon (*Poliohierax semitorquatus*) in a sociable weaver-bird's nest. This practice recalls the habits of certain other birds: such song-birds as wagtails and grackles occasionally placing their

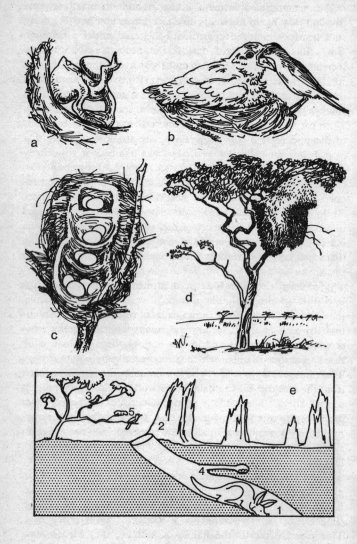

nests in the edge of the bulky stick nests of eagles and ospreys, the least bee eater (*Melittophagus pusillus*) excavating its nest burrow in the side of the aardvark's much larger burrow (Figure 24), and the house martin plastering its mud nest against the wall under the eaves of a man's house. These birds are simply taking advantage casually of a favourable nest site contributed by another bird or mammal and there is little of a social relationship between species and species.

However, there are times when such associations make life possible for a bird in an area where otherwise it could not find a suitable site for its nest. A snow finch of the Tibetan plateau lives in summer only where there are colonies of the mouse hare (*Ochotona*), in whose burrows it sleeps and nests. A similar situation exists in the level plains of Argentina, where a swallow nests only in the nest holes excavated and abandoned by wood-hewers in the side of the burrows of a large rodent, the viscacha. In New Guinea, Pacific swallows appear in new areas where settlers arrive and build frame houses, on which the swallows nest. In these instances the presence of a bird species depends on the prior presence of a species of animal that makes suitable nest sites available.

The pygmy falcon of South Africa that sometimes uses an old nest in the sociable weaver-bird colony raises some interesting speculations.[2] The falcon is a bird eater, but apparently does not eat the weaver-birds that are nesting all about it. Rather, it seeks its prey farther afield. As if in return for this immunity, the weaver-birds ignore the falcon and do not scold or 'mob' it.

Not infrequently, a weaker and less aggressive species nests near a strong or aggressive one, predator or not. The drongos

Figure 24. *Examples of social nesting:* (a) *newly hatched young European cuckoo ejecting the foster parent's egg from the nest;* (b) *foster parent feeding a well-grown European cuckoo;* (c) *many-storeyed yellow-warbler nest with cow-bird eggs buried with warbler eggs in the lower storeys;* (d) *sociable weaver-bird's apartment-house nest; and* (e) *aardvark* (1) *makes its burrow at the base of a termite mound* (2)*, and in the aardvark's burrow a bee eater* (3) *makes its nest burrow* (4)*; there the honey guide* (5) *lays its eggs, to be hatched along with those of the foster-parent bee eater.*

are pugnacious song-birds, and in India a bulbul, sun-bird, or fly-catcher may nest near a drongo nest. It would seem that these weaker birds find extra protection there because the drongo drives away intruders. This advantage is even more clearly present for the sun-bird which nests near a wasp's nest, as many do, particularly in Africa. Some day we may hope to have studies comparing the survival of young in nests protected by wasps with that of young birds in nests not so protected, to see just how much protection the wasps give.[3]

A notable related case is that of the mixed colonies of birds nesting in acacia trees in the drier parts of Central America, which I was fortunate enough to be able to see when I spent some time in El Salvador.[4] One acacia tree with numerous heavy curved thorns, each of which was hollow and contained swarms of extremely hostile ants, was occupied by a dove's nest and a single nest of each of six different species of passerine birds. This crowding together occurred in spite of the availability of a great many other trees near by that were without nests though apparently equally suitable. Though some of the species nesting in this tree are very pugnacious towards others of their own kind, there seemed to be complete tolerance for the individuals of other species. Here again we have protection by an aggressive insect. The sociability of the various species is unusual among song-birds and recalls the mixed colonies of herons and other marsh birds.

Another kind of social relationship occurs when the standard role of the female parent – or of both parents – as food provider for the young is eliminated or modified. In a previous chapter we mentioned helpers at the nest. Occasionally a bird lays an egg carelessly on the ground or in another bird's nest. Ducks are particularly prone to lay in one another's nests, irrespective of species, while in certain megapodes more than one female lays in one nest mound. Sometimes three to five individuals participate in the whole nest cycle of the acorn woodpecker of California. It is not uncommon for a song-bird carrying a beakful of food to its own young to encounter a begging young bird not its own, perhaps not even of its own species, and give it the food.

The best-documented replacement of the family system is the communal nesting of the ani cuckoos of the brushlands of the tropical Americas, studied by the American zoologist, Dr D. E. Davis, of Pennsylvania State University.[5] The anis live all year in flocks of a dozen or so birds and hold an area, which perhaps could be called a territory, that the whole band defends. Polygamy and promiscuity occur within the flock, and males and females help build a basin-shaped nest, in which several females lay eggs. Both sexes help in the care of the young. Further, when the young are full-grown, they may stay with the flock, help with the next brood, and breed with the colony the next season.

The young of certain precocial species sometimes escape from the care of their parents. Young ducks, which are, as we know, precocial, ordinarily accompany the parents from the time of hatching even though they need little or no actual feeding by the parent. In some species, such as eiders, the newly hatched duckling may join the brood of a female not its parent, and in this way compound broods of considerable size are sometimes formed. Several broods of green-winged teals, each with its parent, have been recorded as joining together in the face of human intrusion, the adults feigning injury over the water while the young escape in a single group.

A further development of social care after hatching is the crèche of flamingos and of penguins. The American ornithologist, Dr Robert Cushman Murphy, of the American Museum of Natural History in New York, summarized much of the earlier information on the penguins in his classic *Oceanic Birds of South America*.[6a] At a certain age the semi-altricial, down-covered young are left alone in the colony while the parents are at sea getting food. The young gather in dense groups, which serve to protect them from predation by skuas and from inclement weather. It was claimed that a few adult penguins are left as guards and custodians to drive off skuas. The returning parents, laden with food, were said to feed the first insistently begging young bird that presented itself. However, more recent studies, such as that of the British biologist Dr W. S. L. Sladen, now of Johns Hopkins University, have cast doubts on the latter part of this account.[6] Dr Sladen found that the 'guards' of the crèche did little to protect the young. Further, when he marked Adélie penguins so that he could identify individual birds, he found that each parent fed only its own young. In the same way, the well-studied common tern is known to learn to recognize its own young so that it is able to find them in a whole group of half-grown, hungry young terns.

On the other hand, Dr Robert P. Allen, who studied flamingos in the Caribbean islands for the National Audubon Society, found that communal feeding of these young birds is practised.[7] After a few days the single downy young bird of each nest is able to walk and run about, and the young of similar size herd together in great bands, or crèches. The returning parent feeds the 'nearest and most insistent' hungry chick that it meets.

It is interesting that these crèches have been reported from such extremes in climate – penguins in the frigid Antarctic and flamingos under the tropical sun.

While many of the irregularities just discussed are perhaps not in themselves of any great value to the species, they do indicate the diversity that can occur in such an instinct-dominated part of the bird's life as the reproductive cycle. It is this very diversity, epitomized in these variants, that provides the raw material on which natural selection can act to produce new patterns.

The cuckoo family that produced the communal nesting of the ani has also produced a number of social parasites, or brood parasites.[8] Both ways of deviating from the standard have been successful for certain cuckoo species, but the rather loose organization of the communal ani has not been adopted by other groups. By contrast, the social parasitism of the cuckoos finds parallels in four other groups: the cow-birds of the American song-bird family sometimes called icterid blackbirds,[9] honey guides of Africa,[10] weaver-birds of Africa,[11] and a duck of South America.[12] Each of these groups has some other striking peculiarities in the life histories of its members: the social-feeding behaviour of the honey guides, from which they get their name; the elaborate nest structure of the weaver-birds, unequalled in the bird world though approached by that of the icterid blackbirds; and the ducks' carelessness, not exceeded in any other group, in laying eggs outside the parents' nest. Thus each group that has developed social parasitism also exhibits some other extreme in behaviour. An extreme in reproductive or social behaviour in one direction may be accompanied by an extreme in another.

The breeding cycle of a social parasite in outline is as follows: the parasite lays its eggs in the nest of other species, which serve as hosts or foster parents; once the egg is laid, the role of the adult parasite in the reproductive cycle has been finished; the foster parent incubates the egg and raises the young, sometimes at the expense of its own young; the young parasite when fledged forsakes the foster-parent species and assumes the way of life of its own species, heredity triumphing completely over early environment.

This development of social parasitism involves the loss by the parasite of the instinct to build a nest, to incubate, to brood and feed the young. Also, it requires the parasite to regulate the time of its egg laying to match that of the host; to find a host that can and will accept the strange egg and raise the strange chick. The offspring of the parasite must adapt to cope with the competition of the rightful nestlings. The different parasite species have adjusted in different ways. For the most part the adaptations have been in behaviour, with only minor ones in structure.

We know in detail the life histories of only two species of parasites – the common cuckoo of Europe and the brown-headed cow-bird of North America. The data on the other species is more fragmentary, that on the parasitic duck being scant indeed. Thus the following elaboration of the patterns has many gaps, but it will serve to show some of the different ways that social parasites have used to solve problems.

The most primitive type of social parasitism is that of the black-headed duck of South America. It always lays its eggs in the nests of other marsh birds – rails, coots, ibis, gulls, and the like. Though its habits are comparatively little known, what we do know of ducks in general, including their tendency to lay in other ducks' nests and the extreme precocity of their young, suggests that the black-headed duck's parasitism calls for very little change in the bird's breeding cycle.

At the other extreme is the common cuckoo, which is the most specialized of social parasites. The female holds a territory to which she returns year after year, and she presumably mates with but a single male each season. Apparently each individual cuckoo selects for its eggs a host's nest of one species only. Thus there are tribes, or gentes, within the species: certain cuckoos parasitize only meadow pipits, others only tree pipits, or hedge sparrows, and so on. The eggs of each tribe of cuckoos match in colour and size those of the preferred host.[13] Since the cuckoo is larger than the host bird, this means that the cuckoo's eggs are relatively small; they weigh only about three per cent of the weight of the parent bird rather than nine per cent of the bird, as do the eggs of the host. The cuckoo's eggs differ from the host's in another important adaptive aspect – they have a thick shell to withstand the rough treatment they may get as they are laid.

At the beginning of the breeding season, the female cuckoo locates all the nest sites of her particular host in her territory and watches the nests being built. This sight appears to be the triggering mechanism that induces her to lay, comparable to the courtship activities and nest building which serve the same function for other birds. When her selected host has laid at least one egg and it is time for the cuckoo to lay, she sits up quietly for an hour or more while her egg is being readied for laying. Finally she flies to the nest and takes one of the host's eggs in her bill. Then, since the nest is too small for her to sit in, she crouches over it and lays her egg. The reason for the thick shell on the cuckoo's egg becomes apparent now. If the nest is domed, she may press her cloacal area against the entrance; her egg rolls into the nest and is safe from breaking only because of its thick shell. The cuckoo's egg laying is accomplished in a few seconds only, a remarkably short time, for speed is essential if the cuckoo is to avoid the scolding attention of the host species. The cuckoo then flies away with the host's egg in her bill and either eats or drops it.

The young cuckoo hatches at about the same time as do its

host's young, and then, naked and blind, it ejects its nest mates or the unhatched eggs one at a time, getting each one on to its back, which is especially flattened for the purpose, holding it there with its stubby wings, backing up to the edge of the nest, and with a sudden movement, throwing it out. This refinement of parasitism is important for two reasons. The young cuckoo has a much longer nestling life than the host's young, and it grows to a much larger size. Therefore it needs the full food supply its foster parents bring, for a longer period. And it gets it by this ejection of the rightful young.

The other social parasites – cow-birds, weaver-birds, and honey guides – have evolved the parasitic pattern independently and have solved certain problems in different ways. The scream-ing cow-bird of South America holds territory, forms pairs, and parasitizes only one species, the related bay-winged cow-bird, which raises its own young. The brown-headed cow-bird of North America holds no territory, is promiscuous in mating, and parasitizes a wide variety of hosts indiscriminately, escaping the attention of the host by laying in the twilight hours of the dawn, when the host is absent, and having its young grow up peacefully with the young of its host. The young weaver-birds, which mostly parasitize related weaver-birds, also grow up peacefully with the young of the host. Young honey guides, however, dispose of their nest mates. Their method is different from that of the young cuckoos. The young honey guides kill their nest mates by biting them with the needle-sharp hooks on the tips of their mandibles, hooks evolved for this special pur-pose, which are shed in a short time.

These differences help to emphasize the fact that this type of parasitism has evolved independently a number of times. Evidence drawn from observation of the various stages of social parasitism and of the behaviour of non-parasitic relatives of the birds concerned indicates that it may evolve in two ways – through nest parasitism or through egg parasitism.

The stages through which nest parasitism arises are illus-trated by the habits of different species of the cow-birds, still extant. One species, the bay-winged cow-bird, pairs but does not establish a territory or build a nest. Rather, it wanders

about looking for a suitable old disused nest or for an occupied
one from which it can oust the owners and in this it lays its eggs
and raises its young. Another species, the screaming cow-bird,
pairs and establishes a territory but, as has been mentioned, is
a social parasite on the bay-winged cow-bird. Territoriality and
nest-building habits have been lost in the brown-headed cow-
bird of North America, resulting in social parasitism arrived at
by nest parasitism.

In the cuckoos egg parasitism seems indicated as the route
by which, through natural selection, social parasitism has been
brought about, if we can judge by the behaviour of still extant,
related species. The American black-billed and yellow-billed
cuckoos have poorly developed nest-building instincts, judging
by the scant nests they make. Cuckoos generally may lay their
eggs at long and irregular intervals, and the yellow-billed and
black-billed species sometimes lay in one another's and in other
birds' nest. Finally eggs are laid only in other birds' nests. The
end stages are similar in cuckoos and cow-birds, but the roads to
them are different.

The very term social parasite conveys an implication of
moral judgement and anthropomorphic bias. But the animal
world is completely amoral (not immoral) and success rather
than virtue is the keynote in animals' lives. Social parasitism in
birds is just another way of life, one of the ways that birds have
adapted. It is a progressive modification of a pre-existing, free-
living form, and the adaptations have come about independently
a number of times.

CHAPTER 13

Wandering, Homing, and Orientation

IT is not surprising that birds wander widely. One would expect it, in view of their powers of flight. What is surprising is that far-wandering birds return home even over unfamiliar land and trackless seas. And it is surprising that many birds do not wander at random but have definite ranges, large and small. It appears that birds use their wings not only for wandering, but also for staying at home. Thus we frame two generalizations, each contradicting the other and each only partly true.

This paradox is illustrated by the short-eared owl, which in the Old World breeds in Europe and northern Asia and regularly winters south to northern Africa, India, and China. Occasional strays have been recorded in Micronesia, and there is an endemic sub-species restricted to the island of Ponape in the Caroline Islands, near the Equator. Presumably two far-wandering strays reached this tiny oceanic island and stayed there to breed, establishing a population that has been there long enough to develop peculiar characteristics. But despite the history of wandering in the species, this Ponape sub-species has never been recorded on any neighbouring island. We are forced to conclude that far-wandering occurs in some species but is less common for birds in general than is a settled way of life.

The swifts are among the most mobile of birds. Yet there is

a swiftlet (*Collocalia esculenta*), widespread over the mountain slopes of New Guinea, that is a most notable example of a sedentary species.[1] These New Guinea swifts feed in typical fashion, flying back and forth over forest and clearing, catching insects in the air. The birds' patterned routes must cover scores or even hundreds of miles in a day, yet when we collect these birds at different altitudes we find that the birds from each altitude are different in size, those from the higher altitudes being larger (Table VI).

TABLE VI

Wing Lengths of Swifts (*Collocalia esculenta*), at Different Altitudes on a Mountain Slope in New Guinea

Altitude (feet)	Wing Length (millimetres)
11,500	120
7,000	114–118
3,800	108–110
sea level	97–102

It seems almost incredible that these free-flying birds, on the wing all day long, should not move a few thousand feet up and down the mountain slopes. We know that some pigeons and certain parrots make daily flights to and from sleeping roosts that are several thousand feet above their feeding areas, but evidently these swifts confine their flying to a small area.

Certain migrating birds with restricted breeding ranges well illustrate the way a bird uses its wings to get back to its home range. Especially good examples are the island-nesting species of the southern oceans. The greater shearwaters (*Puffinus gravis*) migrate up into the North Atlantic, but at breeding time all of them return from this vast area to the tiny Tristan da Cunha group of islands in the South Atlantic. A small land bird, the Ipswich sparrow, is equally illustrative. Sable Island is a low sand-bar, twenty miles long and one mile wide, about a hundred miles out in the Atlantic Ocean off Nova Scotia. Ipswich sparrows winter along the eastern coast of the United States, but in spring they return to nest only on Sable Island.

It may sometimes be difficult to separate far-wandering from migrating, and one wonders whether the albatross of the far southern waters that, when not breeding, goes round the globe on the west winds south of the continents is wandering or migrating.[2] But there is no question that long-distance wandering has occurred when one or two birds turn up far outside their range. The South Trinidad petrel has a normal range in the South Atlantic, six hundred miles south of the Equator, but a single bird – the only one on record for North America – was once found in central New York State, far out of its normal range and in a quite different habitat.

If many stray birds are to be observed and recorded, there must be many bird observers – as there are in Britain. Perhaps that is why, over the years, so many examples of strays have been recorded in Britain. Many of these are straying land birds which have apparently made the trans-Atlantic passage. A recent survey of the records by the English ornithologists, W. B. Alexander and R. S. R. Fitter, indicates that aided by the

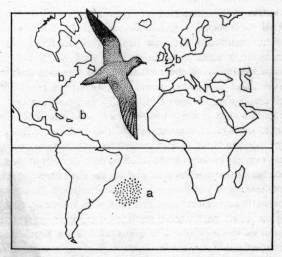

Figure 25. *Wandering of the South Trinidad petrel in the Atlantic area:* (a) *normal range,* (b) *recorded strays.*

autumn winds, more than a hundred American land birds, including such unlikely species of small song-birds as kinglets and vireos, have actually flown non-stop to Britain or western Europe across the Atlantic, a distance of two thousand miles or so.[3]

The presence of a particular species of stray and wandering bird in a specific locality is, by definition, unusual, but in an area that has received much study, the number of such species involved may bulk large in the 'local list' of species. The Chicago list contains 360 species, only 200 of which are of regular occurrence. The other 160 include strays such as a ruff from Europe, a western gull from the Pacific coast, a skimmer from the Atlantic or Gulf coast, a scissor-tailed fly-catcher and a wood stork from the southern United States, and an ivory gull from the Arctic.

Many of these strays are solitary birds, but sometimes unusual conditions may bring numbers of a species. In December 1927 European lapwings appeared in numbers in Newfoundland and eastern Canada. One of them had been ringed earlier in England. While estimates of the numbers varied, one observer alone reported seeing a thousand birds. A study of the attendant conditions led the English ornithologist H. F. Witherby to postulate that a sudden spell of cold weather started a migration of these birds.[4] As they passed from northern England to Ireland, they were blown off course by a fifty-five-mile-an-hour east wind, which carried them out over the Atlantic. Adding their forty-five-mile-an-hour flying speed to that of the wind, we conclude that they must have made the crossing to Newfoundland in just under twenty-four hours. In all the previous history of ornithology there have been only ten individuals of this species recorded on the American continent.

Some species of birds are noted for making periodic invasions beyond their habitual ranges. The little auks known as dovekies winter at sea in the Atlantic, feeding on plankton in waters as far south as those off the Carolina coast. When heavy storms of long duration occur, the birds are unable to get enough food, and great numbers of them drift before the wind, starving. Some are driven far out of their normal range and are washed up along the beaches or come ashore in hundreds or thousands as far south as Florida.[5]

The wandering or erratic movements, or periodic invasions, which are characteristic of certain species may apparently also be correlated with fluctuations in food supply unconnected with overwhelming storms. Every few winters, snowy owls visit the north-eastern United States in large numbers. These invasions evidently coincide with a periodic shortage of the small rodents that are the owls' food in their normal Arctic habitat.

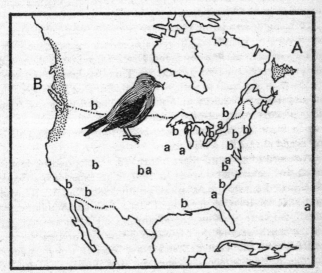

Figure 26. *Wandering of red crossbills* (Loxia curvirostra) *in America. Newfoundland red crossbill* (L. c. pusilla)*: (A) breeding range,* (a) *recorded wanderers; Sitka red crossbill* (L. c. sitkensis)*: (B) breeding range,* (b) *recorded wanderers.*

The crossbills of North America, close relatives of the finches, are also notorious for their wandering, erratic flocks which search for seed crops on the conifers that do not set seed in quantity every year. This nomadism seems an adaptation to local erratic abundance of food; the birds may breed in an area

one year and not return to it for many years following. In
America some flocks of a small-sized Pacific-coast sub-species
have wandered as far as the eastern United States (Figure 26).
Such movements of populations occur in many parts of the
world. On the edge of the wheat belt in western Australia, emus
often increase and spread into the wheat fields in such numbers
that they are a pest to farmers. At long intervals the sandgrouse
of the arid steppes of Asia, distant relatives of the pigeons, erupt
in great numbers and move into western Europe, reaching England, where the invasions of 1863 and 1888 still merit special
attention in bird literature.

Straying or wandering birds have been the usual colonizers of
such oceanic islands as the Galápagos, Madagascar, and the
islands of Hawaii, Polynesia, and New Zealand, as is discussed
in the chapter on bird geography. Thus we know that some
birds never get back to their homeland. But that birds are able
to travel long distances to reach their homes we know from
the regular patterns of migration, and also from experiments in
which birds have returned after being transported from their
nests and released at a distance.

A record long return flight of marked, transported birds was
made by Laysan albatrosses in 1957. The experimental work
was carried out by the American ornithologist Karl W. Kenyon
and Dale W. Rice, of the United States Fish and Wildlife Service, who were studying the albatrosses on Midway atoll, far
to the north-west of the Hawaiian Islands.[6] Through the cooperation of the United States Navy aircraft using Midway
Islands Naval Station as a refuelling stop during trans-Pacific
flights, albatrosses were sent to various points round the edge
of the North Pacific and released there. One bird was removed
from its nest, sent to the Philippine Islands, and released 4,120
airline miles from its nest, and outside the normal range of the
species. In thirty-two days it was back at Midway atoll. Several
birds were sent to the state of Washington, an airline distance of
3,200 miles in the opposite direction, and released there. One
returned to Midway atoll in ten, another in twelve days. The
most spectacular sea-bird homing flight previously recorded
had been that of a Manx shearwater, transported by aeroplane

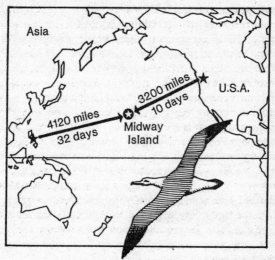

Figure 27. *Record long-distance homing flights of Laysan albatrosses removed from nests near Midway Island.*

3,200 miles to Boston, Massachusetts, which returned in twelve and a half days to its nest off Wales.[7]

There have been so many experiments with various types and species of birds, over long and short distances, that the principle of homing is well established. Here, in brief, are the results of experiments with a few species: house wren, 14 birds were transported half a mile to three miles from their nests and 9 returned; cow-bird, 130 were transported two to twenty-four miles from their breeding area and 78 returned; Leach's petrel, 64 were transported one to twenty-five miles and 46 returned; 160 were also transported sixty-five to 470 miles and 98 returned.[8]

In these experiments not only breeding birds, but also wintering chickadees of the eastern United States have been used; and of 32 chickadees transported one and a half to two miles 17 birds returned. Data such as the above establish the fact that both short- and long-distance homing do exist.

How birds actually find their way over the great distances has long been a matter for speculation. Sometimes they fly over routes that may be outside their personal experience, and sometimes over routes that certainly are outside the range of the species. Recent experimental approaches have thrown more light on the subject, removing it from the realm of speculation in some degree. This experimental work is necessarily difficult because of the nature of the problem, and for obvious reasons many of the experimenters have used homing pigeons.

Homing pigeons are derived from the common domestic-pigeon stock, which is itself descended from the wild rock dove of Europe.[9] For over a century homing pigeons have been selectively bred for their homing ability and used in the popular sport of pigeon racing. In racing in the United States, the birds are taken to a release point sometimes as much as a thousand miles from home, and the first bird that returns home wins. Usually the birds have had previous training, and some of the performances are remarkable. Sometimes, however, there are what pigeon racers call 'busts', when, for unknown reasons, hundreds of birds, including fine birds with splendid records, fail to return, and the few that do get back straggle in very late. While racing pigeons are not wild birds, it is probable that the sensory mechanisms of orientation are the same in both and the results from experiments with one will help us understand the other.

First we must understand that the homing ability of pigeons varies greatly from individual to individual; only birds selected for good homing ability, and in good physical condition, are used. These are then trained to give outstanding results.

Training sometimes includes releasing the birds at greater and greater distances from home, always in the same direction. In addition to watching the birds from the ground, observers have sometimes followed them by aeroplane, so we have a considerable volume of data for individual birds over many miles.

The experimental work on pigeon homing, summarized by Dr D. R. Griffin, of Harvard University, indicates that there are three levels, or types, of homing. In Type I, the birds, when released in a familiar area, orient by known landmarks, and, when released in unfamiliar territory, wander about searching for landmarks they recognize. In Type II, the birds fly in a definite direction. This is sometimes, but not always, the direction to which they have been trained. This aspect of the problem is little understood. In Type III, homing pigeons released in unfamiliar territory start off in the right direction for home very quickly. Here we have a phenomenon for which the most acceptable explanation is that in choosing their direction the birds use the sun's arc or other celestial navigation, even if we don't understand just how it works.

Among wild birds it seems evident that Type I orientation is commonly used. Birds become familiar with their home area, which for such large soaring birds as vultures, eagles, storks, and pelicans may cover scores of miles. There is a record of a flock of snow geese in Alaska which, having finished their migration, flew 120 miles along the coast in four hours, looking for a suitable place to settle. This behaviour well illustrates how birds can become acquainted with a wide area and can use landmarks, in this case the coastline.

In Griffin's classic experiments a light aeroplane was used to follow gannets taken from a colony in the Gulf of St Lawrence and released in the interior of Maine, a hundred miles from salt water and thus in unfamiliar territory. Individual birds were followed for distances varying from 25 to 230 miles, and their flight patterns indicated that several of them were flying in a gradually widening spiral which would ultimately bring them to the familiar coast. Theirs seemed to be not a random but a methodical search for familiar landmarks to use in Type I orientation.

Perhaps related to Type II is the directional flying of transported mallards described by Dr G. V. T. Matthews, of Cambridge University.[10] This was quite different from the spiral searching which Griffin reported for his gannets. On release, these birds showed a strong tendency to fly north-west at first for no obvious reason. Matthews consequently called this 'nonsense' orientation. It is possible to imagine that for terns, for instance, that nest along the Atlantic coast of America and might be transported or blown inland it would be an advantage to have an innate tendency to fly east when over land. This behaviour would get them to a favourable habitat where they could orient themselves by Type I homing.

To illustrate Type III orientation, we have the extreme case of the Laysan albatrosses, referred to earlier. On the return flight one bird averaged 317 miles of airline distance every day. Certainly we must postulate some long-distance orientation and navigation here.

Of course, more than one type of orientation could be used in the same flight. For instance, Type III could take the bird to the approximate location of its home and then Type I could enable it to complete the journey.

A number of theories, some speculative, some based on experimentation, have been proposed to explain how birds orient or navigate in Types II and III. Several of these continue to be so popular that a summary of them is advisable.

A theory proposed in 1946 by the physicist G. Ising, of Djursholm, Sweden, suggests that bird navigation uses Coriolis force, i.e., force related to the rotation of the earth, in which the speed at the Equator is a thousand miles an hour while at the poles it is zero.[11] The force has an actual physical existence, but its effects on a bird would be very slight. It seems impossible to devise experiments to check these effects. The receptors to perceive the force would have to be enormously more sensitive than anything known in animals. Also, the effects of the force could be swamped by other factors, such as air turbulence. Consequently the validity of the theory has not been demonstrated and acceptance is an act of faith. Today the weight of informed opinion is against accepting it.

Several other theories postulate that birds are sensitive to the magnetic field of the earth. Perhaps because man has used a compass in navigation for a long time, these theories have received and still maintain considerable popularity. But it seems physiologically impossible for birds to detect this magnetism. Furthermore, though some experiments convinced the men who made them, the results have been either capable of different interpretations or open to criticism, and careful repetitions of the experiments by others have provided no support for these magnetic-field theories.

Yet another idea was proposed in 1947 by Dr H. L. Yeagley, of Pennsylvania State University. Use of the Coriolis force was postulated for determining latitude and of the magnetic field for determining longitude.[12] The experimental techniques included the attachment of magnets to the birds. But the objections already mentioned apply to this theory also.

It has also been suggested that since the tropics are warmer than the temperate and polar areas, they have more infra-red light, and birds may guide their autumn migrations by this, simply flying towards the brighter infra-red of the warmer skies. But experiments have demonstrated that the range of vision in birds is about that of man; they cannot see infra-red light any better than we can.

The ability of bees to use a pattern of polarized light in the sky in orienting their travelling has been well demonstrated by Professor Karl von Frisch, of the University of Munich.[13] However, the results of similar experiments with birds have been entirely negative.

That the force and the direction of the wind affects the extent and direction of bird migration, and that birds often move greater or smaller distances with certain types of wind, is known. But winds seem a secondary modifying factor rather than an important orienting one.

The theory that birds use celestial navigation, taking visual clues from the sky and orienting by the sun and the stars, is receiving a great deal of support in the middle decades of the twentieth century. This view stems from the experimental work of such men as the late Dr Gustav Kramer, of the Max Planck Institute for Comparative Psychology, at Tübingen, Germany; Dr G. V. T. Matthews, of Cambridge University, in England; and Professor Frans Sauer, of the University of Florida, in the United States.

It has been demonstrated that starlings in experimental round cages can be trained to seek food in a definite compass direction, provided the sky is visible through windows at six equally spaced points. Evidently the starlings orient by the sun or by the brightest part of the sky.[14] Furthermore, the starlings continue to seek food in the same compass direction in the afternoon as in the morning. Evidently the birds also take into account the course of the sun across the sky.

When experimental techniques with mirrors and with an artificial 'sun' cause the sun to appear to be in the 'wrong' position in the sky, the trained starlings orient correctly to the artificial sun, that is, in the wrong compass direction. Therefore there seems no doubt that starlings and perhaps many other birds can orient themselves by the sun and compute its course in the sky from the small arc they see in a short time.

Some song-birds when held in cages show a 'migratory rest-lessness' (*Zugunruhe*) in the night at the periods during which they would normally migrate, in spring and autumn. Some recent experiments, well summarized by Dr Jean Dorst, of the Museum of Natural History in Paris, in his book *The Migrations of Birds*, take advantage of this phenomenon. Certain Old World warblers of the genus *Sylvia*, held in round cages and exposed to night skies and to various star patterns in the artificial skies of a planetarium, have shown by the direction of the movements in their migratory restlessness that they are orienting to star patterns – which stars, or groups of stars, remains to be determined.[15]

Experimental work also has been done with adult shearwaters taken from their nests on Skokholm Island, Wales, and released at Cambridge, England, some 240 miles away.[16] Cambridge is inland and is certainly in territory unfamiliar to these shear-waters. Yet when fifteen birds were released on a clear day they quickly started off in the right direction, and all returned to their nests, the quickest within twenty-four hours and all by the following night. By contrast, on two later occasions shearwaters were released at the same place when the sky was heavily over-cast, and the birds started off in all directions. The first to return to Skokholm took several days, and some never returned. Presumably these results corroborate the theory that these birds orient by the sun or the stars, for when they were unable to see them in cloudy weather their homing was less successful.

Basically, this is, of course, the method used by human nav-igators, but the men need equipment for observation, such as chronometers and tables of figures. A realization of the refinement of technique necessary for the bird to get its bearings by observing the sun has caused hesitation in accepting the sun-arc theory, even though some sort of celestial navigation seems involved, especially over long distances.

In accepting, as the most likely theory to date, the hypothesis that birds possess some sort of ability in celestial navigation, we must remember that we are discussing new discoveries in a field that is being very actively investigated. New findings will certainly modify and expand our understanding. Progress is being made in what seems to be the right direction, but it is well to remember that in 1961 Dr Gustav Kramer, who did so much in this field, wrote that indications are that '... there exist means of orientation still unknown to us'.

So far, we have been considering homing and related navigation. In the next chapter, after discussing the facts of migration, we will take up orientation in relation to migration.

CHAPTER 14

Migration and Hibernation

THE flying wedges of honking geese that pass overhead twice a year, across town and country, by day and by night, symbolize the drama and mystery of bird migration. Each spring these geese move north to take advantage of the Arctic summer for raising their families. Each autumn, as inclement weather arrives to make life there impossible for them, the geese and their young move south to spend the winter in a milder climate. As spring approaches they set out north again, and so the cycle goes on year after year.

These geese are only a small part of the host of migrating birds: birds as small as humming-birds and kinglets and as large as cranes, eagles, and pelicans; birds that fly from the Arctic to the Antarctic, like the Arctic tern; and birds that make only short journeys, like the mountain quail (*Oreortyx picta*) of California that walks just a few miles down the California mountains in autumn to escape the heavy winter snow. From the Equator nearly to the poles every continent and every ocean is affected by bird migration.

Outside the humid tropics the alternating seasons of wet and dry, hot and cold, plenty and scarcity, are major aspects of the environment. Some animals have adapted their lives so that they remain active through all the seasons; some pass the inclement season by hibernating, in a state of suspended animation; and some migrate, moving elsewhere to escape the unfavourable part of the year. Birds show all these adaptations. In all but the most severe climates, some birds are year-round, active residents; at least one species, the poorwill (*Phalaenoptilus nuttallii*), of California, hibernates; while many birds, taking advantage of their great mobility, have adapted by developing the habit of migration. The practice of migration is shared with a few insects and some fish and mammals, but it is especially characteristic of birds. It must have been an integral part of the adaptation of the evolving bird faunas as birds spread out over the temperate and arctic zones from their original home in the humid tropics.

The bird's adaptations for migration may include a longer, more pointed wing tip than is found in non-migratory species, but most of the adaptations are not structural but behavioural. They include the habit of making long journeys, the ability to correlate these with the seasons, or even to anticipate the seasons, and the ability to maintain the proper direction over great distances. The results are often spectacular. Let us look at some of these flights and the patterns they form.

The major world patterns of migration are correlated not only with the changing of the seasons, but also with the location of the great land masses. These are most extensive in the Northern Hemisphere, where the continents of North America and Eurasia converge and almost completely surround the Arctic Ocean; in striking contrast, only half of Australia and the attenuated tips of South America and Africa project into the South Temperate Zone towards Antarctica.

The main migration routes tend to run north and south, as one would expect.[1] They take birds from their breeding grounds in the Northern Hemisphere to winter in more clement latitudes near the Equator: from North America to South America; from Eurasia to Africa, southern Asia, and even Australia. In the Southern Hemisphere birds fly for the winter from southern South America to tropical South America, from southern Africa to tropical Africa, and from Australia to New Guinea and adjacent islands. Africa is especially known for some migration within the tropics, towards or crossing the Equator, and correlating with the alternation of wet and dry seasons.

The sea birds of the southern latitudes need to be mentioned

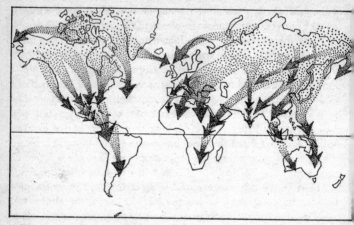

Figure 28. *Main post-breeding migration routes of some Northern Hemisphere breeding birds. Note the extent of east–west movements and penetration into the Southern Hemisphere.*

separately,[2] for they show two types of long-range movements from the tiny islets on which they nest; some seem to ride the prevailing westerly winds around and around the land-free waters of the sub-Antarctic latitudes, while others fly north and penetrate far into the North Temperate Zone waters of the Atlantic and the Pacific oceans in the austral winter that is the northern summer.

Though migration routes tend to run north and south, there may be a strong east-west component in a route, for a number of reasons. The triangular shape of North America funnels some migration routes in Central America. In the Old World the north-east–south-west direction of the Atlantic and the Pacific coast of Eurasia, the warmer winter climate given western Europe by the Gulf Stream, and the presence of the Himalayan Mountains, which constitute an east-west barrier deflecting southward migration, all help give a pronounced north-east–south-west direction to the Eurasian migration. Some birds from central Asia and Siberia even fly south-west to spend the winter in Africa.

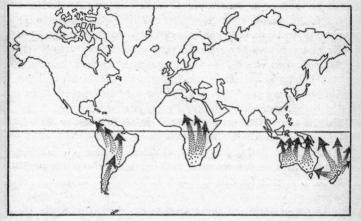

Figure 29. *Some post-breeding migration routes of Southern Hemisphere land birds. Note the slightness of penetration into the Northern Hemisphere.*

Sea birds nesting in the Canadian Arctic, such as eider ducks, may fly a thousand miles west along the coast before they turn south through Bering Strait to reach their wintering area in the Bering Sea. Many of the western sandpipers that nest in Alaska, winter in Florida, and Ross geese from the central Arctic winter in California, flying diagonally across the continent. The wheatears of Alaska and Siberia cross Asia to winter in tropical Africa. The migration of some water birds, like ducks and grebes, may be to the nearest coast, whatever the direction, and then south along the coast.

The width of water gaps may influence migration routes; European storks, for example, go round one or the other end of the Mediterranean on their way to Africa. But many species do cross the Mediterranean, and the crossing of five hundred miles of water by small land birds is common practice: they fly across the Gulf of Mexico, and across the Caribbean from Jamaica to Venezuela. The golden plover and wandering tattler of western Alaska make long water crossings on their way to Australia across the Pacific with its scattered islands.

The route of the golden plover of the Canadian Arctic forms one of the exceptions to the general rule that spring and autumn migrations follow the same course. On its southward flight the bird goes east to Nova Scotia, then over the ocean to South America, then over land to the pampas of Argentina. The return course is farther west; the bird crosses the Caribbean and the Gulf of Mexico, and then proceeds up the Mississippi valley to the breeding grounds, making a great circular route. A similar circular course is flown by the shearwaters that nest on islands off southern Australia. The birds fly up the west side of the Pacific to the Bering Sea area and down the east side to cross again to the breeding grounds. In doing this they take advantage of the prevailing winds and of favourable food conditions in the water.

The routes outlined above seem to be adaptations to climate and geography, enabling the birds to move most efficiently between the summer and the winter range. But sometimes a migration route has a historical imprint; it retraces the route by

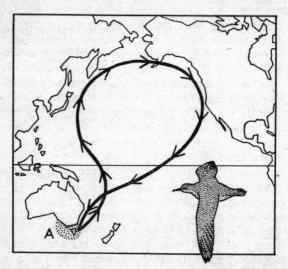

Figure 30. *Circular migration route of the slender-billed shearwater that nests in the south-eastern Australian area* (A).

which a species colonized an area. This is beautifully illustrated in the migrations of the Arctic warbler, a Eurasian species that has recently colonized Alaska, and of the grey-cheeked thrush, a North American species that has recently colonized Siberia. When they migrate after breeding, their routes cross as they fly over the Bering Sea, the warblers going to the ancestral wintering ground in tropical Asia, the thrushes heading for tropical America.

The long-distance migrants have been stressed, but there are probably more species that migrate short distances, just far enough to find adequate food, to winter in the mid-latitudes at least. Many ducks and sparrows, for instance, when they leave the Arctic, do not go half way to the tropics. In the length of their migrations, most species fall somewhere between the extremes.

In a single area in the North Temperate Zone it is possible to find four types of migrants. Examples of these from Indiana, in the central United States, and from the British Isles are as follows:

I. Winter visitors – birds that nest to the north but spend the winter here
British Isles: white-fronted goose, snow bunting
Indiana: old-squaw duck, tree sparrow

II. Summer visitors – birds that nest here but winter to the south
British Isles: swifts, swallows, warblers, flycatchers
Indiana: vireos, wood warblers

III. Passage migrants – birds that breed to the north and winter to the south, passing through twice a year
British Isles: jacksnipe, Greenland wheatear, black tern
Indiana: solitary sandpiper, certain warblers

IV. Permanent residents
British Isles: dipper, house sparrow, rook
Indiana: cardinal, blue jay

Indeed, the migratory status of individuals within some species, such as the song sparrow, is so variable that during the year, in one locality in the United States, one can find certain individuals within a single species that fit into each of the four categories. In England the lapwing as a species is present throughout the year, but in autumn many of the summering birds migrate south for the winter while birds from the north take their place.

Not all members of a species may leave the wintering grounds; this is particularly true, or perhaps particularly noticeable, for the waders that are conspicuous on tropical and South Temperate Zone beaches. None of them ordinarily breed in their wintering areas, but very rarely European storks have been reported breeding in their winter homes in South Africa, and it is probable that certain tropical populations of northern species originated when stray migrants were left behind, such as the Micronesian island short-eared owls mentioned earlier.

Not all related species have the same migration pattern. The purple sandpiper and Baird's sandpiper both breed in the New World Arctic, but the former winters on the temperate-zone coasts of North America, while the latter winters in the South Temperate Zone, in South America. The sanderling, which also has an Arctic breeding range, has a winter range that overlaps those of both the sandpipers just mentioned.

The relation between the size of wintering area and the size of the breeding area varies. Because of the shape of the continents, the widely distributed birds that breed across northern North America and winter in Central America or in southern South America are much more concentrated in their smaller wintering grounds. The same is true of some northern ducks and geese that do not go as far, but are concentrated for the winter in a few suitable areas of marsh, such as those of the Caspian Sea, the Carolina coasts, Louisiana, and interior California. It is noteworthy that these areas support a much larger population of birds in the non-breeding season than in the breeding season. On the other hand, the Ipswich sparrow, with a total breeding range of less than twenty square miles, winters along hundreds of miles of the eastern United States coast, and the greater shearwaters, which are widespread over the North Atlantic when not breeding, all gather at the tiny island group of Tristan da Cunha to nest.

The habitat preferences of migrants are adjusted to summer and winter ranges: many tundra-breeding waders go to the ocean beaches, and some warblers exchange coniferous forests for tropical forests in winter. But the most striking change is that of birds like the skuas and phalaropes, which are birds of tundra or marsh in summer, but pelagic birds in the southern latitudes in the winter.

Many small land birds migrate by night, as is shown by the night mortality at television towers and the observations of migrations through telescopes aimed at the moon. Presumably this practice enables them to feed at each end of each lap of their journey. This opportunity to feed is particularly important for land birds which must fly all night to make long water crossings. But some birds are daytime migrants – hawks and cranes, for example, and the swallows that feed as they migrate. Some, such as geese and waders, migrate by day or night.

The rate of migration of many small land birds seems leisurely. They fly for a few hours, then rest and feed for a day or so, then fly again. The rate is affected by a number of factors. The northward-moving cliff swallow averages twenty miles a day from California to British Columbia, but averages ninety miles a day from there to Alaska, increasing its speed as it nears its breeding grounds. The Canada goose is an early migrant, keeping pace with the spring. Geese going from the southern United States to central Mackenzie may average sixty miles a day. The late-migrating grey-cheeked thrush may average 130 miles a day from the Gulf of Mexico to Alaska.[3] The Arctic tern must travel at least twenty-five thousand miles in nine months. These rates of travel are only approximations, of course, based on average arrival dates rather than the flights of individual birds, but are perhaps more significant than particular flights would be in showing what the birds actually do.

However, there are records of individual long, non-stop migrations. There is one flight of blue geese that in 1952 went non-stop from Hudson Bay to Louisiana, a distance of some 1,700 miles.[4] This flight was not followed by an aeroplane, but the circumstantial evidence provided by observations at various points on the route seems conclusive. Geese are much sought

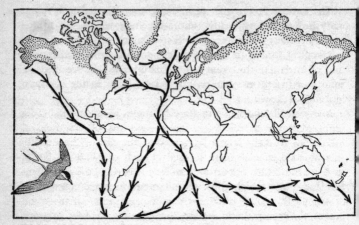

Figure 31. *Southward migration route of the Arctic tern, which nests in the far North.*

after by wildfowl gunners and the stopping places of the birds are well known, as is the fact that in some years the birds are not seen at any of them. In this instance the start of the migration was observed by the Canadian ornithologist Graham Cooch, who was studying waterfowl in the James Bay area at the south end of Hudson Bay for the Canadian Wild Life Service. In the evening of 16 October he reported the first big flight of blue geese leaving and flying south. The next day, at North Bay, 370 miles south in Ontario, and at Winnipeg, in southern Manitoba, aircraft were warned of many flocks of geese flying south at altitudes of six to eight thousand feet. One aeroplane actually collided with a goose near North Bay and had to return to the airfield, damaged. The goose flight was next reported over Iowa and Missouri, about eight hundred miles south-west of North Bay, on 18 October. The birds were flying south at an estimated altitude of three thousand feet. On the morning of the next day, 19 October, the birds arrived on their wintering grounds in Louisiana, where John L. Lynch, of the United States Fish and Wildlife Service, reported the first big flocks of the season. All through the Middle West wildfowlers asked what had become of the blue geese. There seems little doubt they had flown over without stopping, averaging nearly thirty miles an hour for some sixty hours of flying time.

Evidence of rapid, long-distance migration is also provided by bird-ringing.[5] An aluminium band with a serial number and address is put on a bird's leg, and when the bird is recovered the date and location of this recovery are reported, along with the identification number. Active ringing programmes are being carried out not only in Europe and North America, but also in Africa and Australia. One record flight by a ringed bird is that of a lesser yellow-legs that went a distance of 1,900 miles, from New England to the West Indies, in six days, averaging 316 miles a day.[6]

Radar has been a help in finding out how high migrating birds fly. In 1961 the British ornithologist I. C. T. Nisbet visited North America and with the cooperation of American colleagues used a radar height finder for the study of nocturnal migration at Cape Cod.[7] Most birds flew between 1,500 and 2,500 feet above sea level. Some were as high as 5,000 feet, but a very few were recorded at 20,000 feet. These last appeared to be waders that were starting or completing long sea crossings. Nisbet compared these data from Cape Cod with records made in England, which averaged higher, but this work is still in its preliminary stages.

The precision of a bird's navigation is evident from observations; for instance, as we know, each year millions of greater shearwaters return from their North Atlantic wintering grounds to breed on tiny islands in the middle of the South Atlantic. From bird-ringing records we learn that some long-range migrants breed in the same locality in which they nested the year before, and we have the classic case of white-throated sparrows returning from their Canadian breeding grounds to winter on the same Georgia lawn year after year.

Some of the many aspects of migration have been presented in this chapter. There is no doubt that migration is adaptive, a way of life that permits a part-time occupancy of more of the globe than birds could otherwise exploit. The diversity of patterns correlates in part with environmental conditions, but some of the diversity seems to be the result of interspecific factors that give different species different wintering grounds, just as they tend to give them different breeding ranges.

But there remain the whys and hows of navigation and timing.[8] Discussion of these is best broken into three parts, each considered separately: choice of direction,[9] navigation, and timing.[10]

Choice of Direction. The choice of direction is to a great extent an instinctive one, fixed by natural selection. This process of natural selection is still going on. Even today in certain species young birds, just able to travel, spread out in all directions after the nesting season. In the north-eastern United States, for example, some egrets come north on a post-breeding dispersal in July and August which also has sent the young birds in other directions. Here we have the material on which natural selection can operate. Those birds that choose the right direction have the best chance to survive.

There are also some experimental results which demonstrate both the instinctive choice of direction and modification of it. White storks of eastern Europe migrate south-east so that they can go round the eastern end of the Mediterranean to Africa; storks of western Europe migrate south-west so that they can go round the western end to reach their winter home in Africa.[11] Young storks transported from western to eastern Europe and released there after the adults had gone, headed south-west, in their ancestral direction, rather than in the direction appropriate for that area. But other young storks, moved before the local adults had migrated, accompanied the old birds when they left, flying in the right direction. These experiments demonstrate not only the existence of an innate sense of direction, but also the fact that the guidance of the experienced birds may override the instinctive pattern and be more important in guiding the young birds.

Navigation. Migrating birds may instinctively choose a direction, but there remains the question of how they know one direction from another and what stimuli they receive from their surroundings to navigate by.[12] Present evidence is that navigation in migration is similar in method to that used in long-range homing, as discussed in the preceding chapter. Local topography, coastlines, mountain ranges, cloud banks, ocean currents, all may play a part, but the most important guides for long-range migrations are probably the sun and the stars. These are the guides humans also turn to in long-distance travel, and birds may instinctively use them in determining their basic direction, modifying their course by reference to coastlines, mountains, or other landmarks. However, one must remember that the study of orientation is far from complete. Much that has been postulated must still be checked by further experimentation.

Timing. The nature of the mechanism that, for example, starts a bird from the Arctic on its way to the South Temperate Zone and sends it back to arrive in the Arctic again at the right time for breeding the following year, is difficult to determine by direct experimental study and checking.[13] Not all species migrate at the same time. The start and the rate of some migrations seem to be influenced by the weather, the birds moving to their breeding grounds as soon as weather permits and staying until the seasonal change in the weather forces them out. Others leave their breeding grounds well in advance of the inclement season, while food is still plentiful. Presumably there is an innate annual rhythm or cycle correlated with the breeding cycle. Perhaps this cycle needs setting only once a year, probably at the time the breeding cycle is started. This timing may be affected by both inhibiting and accelerating factors present in the bird's environment, as discussed in Chapter 9. Much of the current experimental laboratory work on this subject has concentrated on physiological changes in the bird, particularly those associated with photoperiodism, growth of the gonads, deposition of fat, and energy exchange and balance. The results, combined with those on the timing of the breeding cycle, furnish material on the background of bird migrations.

It seems certain that migration patterns have evolved, been lost, and re-evolved in many groups many times to fit a wide variety of changing local conditions. It is probable that numerous factors may be involved in navigation and in timing and these may not be the same for every species or in every part of the world.

As has been mentioned, only one species – a nightjar, the poorwill of California – is known to hibernate. This bird sleeps away the winter in rocky niches in the walls of canyons. This discovery of a hibernating bird was reported only in 1948, by the American naturalist Edmund C. Jaeger, of Riverside, California, and it came as a surprise to the scientific world.[14] Jaeger provided the first acceptable data, the first real evidence, that hibernation occurs in birds. It is true that Aristotle recorded the hibernation of birds, and many subsequent authors reported such things as swallows passing the winter in mud at the bottom of a pond and cuckoos shedding their feathers and creeping into crevices to sleep away the cold season.[15] But most of these stories are in the same class as such myths as the tale of the barnacle geese growing out of barnacles.

In December 1946 Jaeger found a poorwill in a state of profound torpor in a cavity in the rock wall of a canyon of the Colorado desert. The next winter he found a poorwill, perhaps the same bird, in the same place, and he checked it periodically from November to February. All this time it was in a state of profound hibernation, with a body temperature of about 66 degrees Fahrenheit instead of over 100, as is normal for the bird. He handled it, put a numbered ring on its leg for identification, and put it back in its roosting place without awakening it. The third winter the same bird was back again, hibernating in the same place; then it disappeared. Thus the fact of hibernation in this nightjar was established. Since then, physiologists have studied the poorwill and some other nightjars, and have corroborated and extended Jaeger's findings.

The temperature of most birds may drop a few degrees during the sleeping period. However, the humming-birds and their relatives the nightjars and swifts present some unusual characteristics. Sleeping humming-birds may have a body temperature much lower than it is in the daytime. As their temperature falls, the birds become torpid and incapable of flight. Metabolism may drop to a twentieth of its daytime resting rate. With the return of day the temperature rises, the body processes resume their normal rate, and the birds become active. It has been suggested that in such small birds, with their consequent very rapid metabolism, this conservation of fuel for the body may help the birds to live through the night without starving to death. Certain swifts, notably the European *Apus apus*, may become torpid when food is scarce in cold wet weather, and this reduction in activity enables them to survive limited lean periods. Probably more cases of torpor and hibernation will be found among the many species of swifts, humming-birds, and nightjars, and perhaps among some Old World birds, such as the colies of Africa which are said sometimes to be numb with cold in the early mornings. We must be prepared for other unexpected discoveries, which are most likely to occur in the biologically least-explored tropics.

CHAPTER 15

Predation and Parasites

PREDATORS are usually larger than their prey and parasites are usually smaller, often much smaller. But the differences between the two are more fundamental than that. Predator and prey are both units in a large habitat, a habitat of trees and grass and insects, or of water, fish, and crustaceans, and the predator usually kills its prey quickly and eats it. A bird parasite, on the other hand, is a unit in a habitat consisting of the body of the bird, and it eats pieces of this habitat, bit by bit, as a goose grazes in a field of sprouting wheat. If through over-population a parasite kills its host, it is as much a catastrophe for the parasite as for the host. The parallel to this event in the relationships between bird predators and prey is not easy to find because of the mobility of birds, but it is plain in many situations involving mammals – for instance, when deer become over-abundant, eat all their food, and starve in winter.

A list of all the kinds of animals that kill and eat birds would be a long one, including the fire ants that destroy hatching quail eggs, the spiders that catch small birds in their webs, the pike that take small birds fluttering over the surface of the water, the turtles that seize herons, the snakes that take eggs or young from nests, the cats that catch sparrows, the coyotes that eat duck's eggs, and the peregrines that kill teal.

Predation is often a spectacular action, and, though incidents involving it are rarely seen by humans, each such incident is remembered. The attitude towards this predation varies. A cat that catches song-birds in a garden may sadden a bird-loving gardener, and the hawk that kills a partridge that a sportsman wants to kill may enrage the gunner. A great horned owl that takes a pheasant from a game farm is a pest of the game farmer which he cannot tolerate, but a falcon striking a pigeon out of the sky may be a thrilling sight to a falconer, and a snake eating an egg out of a bird's nest or a marsh hawk surprising a wader can offer intriguing data to a naturalist.

The effect of predation on a bird species is difficult to measure. To calculate it, one needs to know the number of individual birds killed by the predator in a specified period of time, the size of the population from which the killed birds were taken, and the mortality rate from other factors. Even then, in a natural population, if one source of predation were removed, other factors might compensate.

Most of the existing data about predation concern the general feeding habits of the predator. In a few instances there is information about the number of individual birds an individual predator kills, or about the relative abundance of prey and predator. From the evidence on hand we get the impression that regular predation on adult birds is largely carried on by other birds.

A great many species of birds prey on adult birds. These include the great cormorants, which have been recorded snatching passing swallows from the air; skuas on their nesting grounds, which regularly eat small birds; roadrunners and some other cuckoos, which include small birds in their varied diet of insects and small vertebrates; frogmouths, which may not distinguish between large insects, mice, and small birds; nightjars, which occasionally snap up small birds; some kingfishers, hornbills, and crows, all of which take small birds infrequently; and certain shrikes, which do so regularly.

But with the exception of the sea leopard preying on penguins, discussed below, the most active predators on adult birds are probably the hawks and owls, and particularly a few bird specialists within these groups, such as the falcons which may overtake their prey in full flight, and the short-winged hawks of the genus *Accipiter* that skulk and surprise their prey and capture it with a quick dash.

An outstanding bird predator, whose life history has been modified by this specialization, is Eleanora's falcon, a medium-sized falcon that nests only on cliffs of coastal islands in the Mediterranean area.[1] Most hawks and falcons nest early but this species hatches its young in August, so that they leave the nest by early October. This late nesting correlates with the heavy southward migration of song-birds passing from Europe to Africa. Most of the year this falcon feeds on large insects, but its young are fed from the easily available stream of autumn migrants, which coincides with the falcon's breeding season.

Figure 32. *A specialist in bird predation. Eleanora's falcon nests on islets in the Mediterranean area and delays its nesting so that its young in the nest can be fed from the hordes of south-moving song-bird migrants in late summer and early autumn.*

In Holland the effects on bird population of predation by the sparrow hawk (*Accipiter nisus*) were studied by the Dutch ornithologist Dr L. Tinbergen.[2] He estimated the population of prey species from sample counts supplemented by other methods and the amount of the sparrow-hawk kill from sample counts of remains of kills at plucking posts or nests. He arrived at the conclusion (among others) that in May sparrow hawks killed 8 per cent of the house-sparrow population and 0·3 per cent of the wren population. While the apparent precision of these figures is attractive, it is difficult to relate them to the annual effect of mortality from all causes on the sparrow and wren populations.

The late Paul Errington, formerly professor of zoology at Iowa State College, based on his studies on bobwhite quail in the north-central United States the proposition that predation was ultimately correlated with the carrying capacity of the habitat.[3] When quail were common and ranged far from thick cover, many were taken by hawks; when quail were scarcer and because of harassment by hawks, kept closer to cover, hawks took a smaller percentage of them. He went even further and suggested that the birds taken by direct predation might well have perished from other causes during the winter.

These findings recall the relationship between Dall's sheep and wolves, observed by the American naturalist Adolph Murie when he was stationed in Alaska by the United States Fish and Wildlife Service.[4] The sheep are relatively safe from wolves as long as they stay on the more rugged parts of the mountains, but become vulnerable when they feed on the adjacent flat meadows. The wolves, in effect, help to keep this species of sheep a fleet-footed, nimble animal of the mountains. Hawk predation may be a factor in keeping the bobwhite an alert bird of the denser brush and its edges.

An intriguing paper on screech-owl predation on birds was given by the late Professor A. A. Allen, of Cornell University.[5] A pair of screech owls nested on his grounds in Ithaca in 1921, and he kept a record of the food brought to the nest for the young. This included 98 birds of 24 species. Obviously some were captured outside his grounds but many came from within it. Yet the total population of birds in the area was changed but little. In 1920 38 pairs of 19 species had nested in the area; in 1921 45 pairs of 15 species nested there, and in 1922 22 pairs of 17 species. When both of a nesting pair of birds were killed by the owls in the same night, their territory became vacant. But when only one of a pair was taken in a night, the survivor secured a new mate almost immediately. Though this pair of owls killed a number of birds slightly more than the total number of birds breeding on the area, their predation did not materially change the size of the breeding population. Evidently replacements were recruited from a reserve of unmated birds.

However, population reduction has been recorded for certain game species under special conditions. In the north-eastern United States during some winters there are invasions of goshawks from the north. Frequently the grouse population of the affected areas has been drastically depleted by these winter visitors. Goshawks are not bird specialists, but prey on mammals up to the size of rabbits as well as on birds up to the size of grouse, so grouse may be an alternative food that receives more attention when other prey is scarce.

In the pine country of southern Georgia there are great plantations maintained for quail shooting. Naturally a large harvest is desired and the proprietors are loath to share this harvest with predators. A study made by the American pioneer in game management H. L. Stoddard, then of the United States Bureau of Biological Survey, shows that only one species of hawk, Cooper's hawk, is an important predator there.[6] Other hawks may take an occasional quail, but not enough to matter. It is interesting, as Stoddard points out, that this conclusion based on field studies is in accord with earlier conclusions about the food habits of hawks based on examinations of the contents of their stomachs.

Not only is the Cooper's hawk the main avian predator of quail here, but it is probably the quail's worst enemy. Stoddard estimates that in a year the Cooper's hawks harvest as many quail as do sportsmen in their shooting season. The need for evading the hawk may have had an effect in the development of the quail into an ideal game bird, but as the hunting of man on these preserves now supplies the same selective factors, the hawk can be dispensed with.

Though the predation by mammals on adult birds seems of minor importance, it is possible that the activities of the Antarctic seal called the sea leopard form an exception.[7] Its normal food is squid, fish, penguins, a few other swimming sea birds taken in the water, and other seals. Seen in motion pictures, the sea leopard seems to hold the penguin in its teeth and tear or shake the body out of its skin. Though some penguins are eaten by killer whales, the main enemy of the adults is this seal.

Penguins ashore are sometimes hesitant about going into the water, for it is at the foot of the ice that the sea leopard lies in wait for them.

According to the theory of selection, the weak and the unfit will be taken first by predation, and we have some direct evidence that this does occur. Dr David Lack of Oxford University describes eight cases in which the sparrow hawk's prey was abnormal: these included one blind, one lame, and one weak bird;[8] another set of observations showed that three out of nineteen wild birds caught by peregrine falcons were abnormal in some way. In Vermont there is a record of a weak, emaciated crow being taken by a red-shouldered hawk, a bird that usually does not take such prey.

Adult, non-breeding birds, with their mobility, are relatively immune to most predation. But the eggs and the young lack this immunity, and a sizeable toll is taken by many predators, including foxes, cats, raccoons, skunks, civets, squirrels, rats, snakes, and such birds as gulls and crows. Ants which invade hatching eggs and kill the emerging chick can also take a substantial toll. In northern climates eggs are available as food only during the short breeding season, and during that time the predation pressure may be severe. It may be that such pressure from predatory foxes and coyotes has caused eider ducks and auks to prefer nesting on islets off the coast where these predators cannot reach them.[9]

In more temperate climates, where the egg season is often longer even if still partly seasonal, the effort to escape predation is perhaps responsible for the placing of the nest in extreme situations – pendent from the tip of a long branch, near a wasp's nest, or glued to the wall of a cave.

In the tropics two egg specialists have developed. One is the egg-eating snake (*Dasypeltis scaber*) of Africa, about one and a half to two feet long, which is known to eat nothing but eggs.[10] It evidently must gorge and grow fat during one bird-nesting season and then fast until the next. Its adaptations for this diet include a reduction in the number of teeth and the development of a series of spines projecting from the vertebrae into the gullet. Pressure of the throat muscles breaks the egg open against

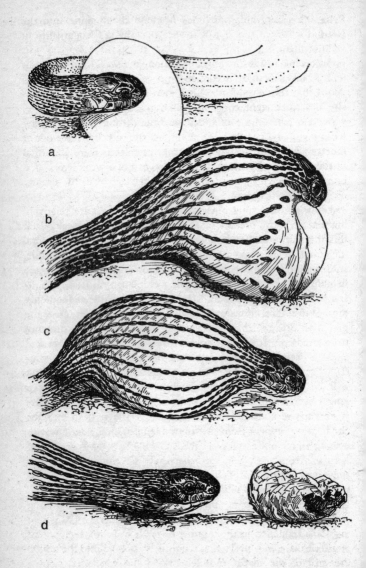

a

b

c

d

these. The contents are then sucked out and the shell regurgitated.

The other important egg eater is the harrier hawk (*Gymnogenys typicus*), also of Africa, which eats a variety of small food items which it may remove from cavities in trees, and eggs and young from the retort-shaped nests of weaver-birds, to which it may cling upside down.

Parasites are naturally inconspicuous and seldom seen. Their presence is often noted only when a dead bird is examined. It is therefore not surprising that parasites are usually discussed as causes of disease and death. This matter will be touched on in the following chapter on vital statistics, but here let us consider these organisms for their own sake, as members of ecological communities.

Consider a pigeon, flying by. It may seem to be all alone, but the chances are that what we see is really a whole community.[11] The bird is like an island with its own flora and fauna, carrying some at least of the seventy or so plants and animals that have been recorded as living in or on the domestic pigeon. These include two species of ticks, eight of mites, one fly, one bug, six lice, nine roundworms, eighteen tapeworms, three flukes, eight protozoans, two fungi, nine bacteria, and four viruses, and this is doubtless far from complete.

Some of these parasites are microscopic; others, such as the flies and ticks, may be as large as a housefly; and tapeworms may be several feet long.[12] Impressive numbers of even larger parasites have been found in a single bird – a thousand tapeworms in the intestines of one pigeon, thirty pigeon flies among the feathers of one bird, and twenty bird lice on just one feather.

Just as the animals on an island divide up the living space among themselves – birds in the trees, rabbits on the ground, moles burrowing under the earth, and fish in the streams – so

Figure 33. *An African snake,* Dasypeltis scaber, *not known to eat anything but eggs. This snake is nearly toothless, but spines project from the vertebrae into the gullet and help crush the egg. The contents are swallowed and shell ejected.* (After Shaw, C. E., Zoonooz, Vol. XXXIV, No. 1 (1961), pp. 1–7.)

do the animals and plants on a pigeon divide up the living space. Among the feathers are flies and lice; on the skin, ticks and mites; burrowing into and under the skin, other mites; under the eyelids, roundworms (eye worms); in air passages, mites, roundworms, and fungi; in the intestines, tapeworms, roundworms, protozoans, and bacteria; in the bloodstream, roundworms, protozoans, and viruses; in the tissues, roundworms; and in the brain, viruses.[13]

Furthermore, some of the animals living among the feathers on birds occupy special habitats within this area. Some broad, round lice live on body feathers; some longer, more slender ones prefer the head or wings. Some mites prefer to live on the quills, and some very small lice and mites drill holes in the shafts and live inside them.

Some roundworm members of a bird community do not spend their whole life in the same part of the bird.[14] Their peregrinations are probably something like this: the egg, swallowed by the bird, hatches in the intestines, where the adult life of the worm is to be spent. However, the young worm travels during its first ten days. It penetrates the wall of the intestines, is caught up in the bloodstream and swept into the liver, thence goes to the heart and lungs. Then it burrows from the lungs to the windpipe and finally to the gullet, whence the route is prosaic, by way of the alimentary tract to its adult habitat, the intestines.

The food of the different members of this community is as various as their form. Flies and ticks, some mites, and some lice suck blood; some lice eat downy parts of the feathers; some mites, living inside quills, feed on the pith found there, while other mites eat scurf and skin debris; worms in the intestines lie in a bath of partly digested food and absorb it through their body wall; some roundworms and protozoans feed on the blood.

Probably all birds support sizeable communities of other animals, and of course there is the question of how these organisms arrive on the 'bird island'. Some, like lice, undoubtedly are handed down by parent to offspring through contact when the adults are breeding. The antiquity of some of these chains of transmission may be judged by the fact that a species of louse may be found on only one species of bird. The passenger pigeon, for example, had an endemic louse, and when the last passenger pigeon died the last of this species of louse died with it.

There are strange and complicated life histories tied up with colonizing. Some roundworms simply lay great numbers of eggs, as many as twelve thousand a day, which are voided by the bird. Continuation of the life cycle depends upon their being swallowed by the right kind of bird. But in some flukes the life cycle is very complicated.[15] Male and female organs may be present in the same individual and self-fertilization the rule, so it is not necessary for two animals to find each other in the dark labyrinth of the bird's insides, where they live. The eggs, voided by the bird with its faeces, in some species are eaten by a snail in which the young live part of their life. Then the snail is eaten by a fish, and finally the fish is eaten by a bird, in whose body the worms pass their adult life.

Yet other organisms, like the one-celled animals that cause malaria, some roundworms, and some viruses, are carried by hosts, such as mosquitoes, which become infected when they bite one bird, and pass on the parasites to the next bird they bite.

The consideration of this chain of events brings our pigeon back into perspective. As the filaria in the bloodstream is a tiny unit in a 'bird island' community, so the pigeon is a small unit in a larger community. In this community it eats grain and in its turn adds to the supply of poultry on the market and, in some cities, provides the main food for wintering peregrines. The pigeon also gives pleasure to some people, who like to scatter peanuts or bread for it, and annoys others with its messy habits. Its swift flight and its homing abilities have been used in developing the sport of pigeon racing. In the Egyptian delta the pigeon is one of the reservoirs of the virus which causes 'West Nile fever'.[16]

Communities such as that outlined for a pigeon of a city street are not restricted to birds, of course. Mammals, fish, snails, worms, all may have other smaller animals living on or in them. Each animal is a community in itself. Even the pigeon fly may have a mite on it, and the mite in its turn may carry bacteria.

An ideal balanced community may exist happily, with no species interfering unduly with any other, though individuals perish. But the constant adjustments within a population are better compared to the movements of a pendulum than to the static equilibrium of a balance, and even so, when one takes the long view, it is apparent that there are always species that lose out, though they may be as big as dinosaurs or have teeth as long as a sabre-toothed cat's. There is always something getting out of balance. Often the disruptive element is an invading animal or plant, such as the chestnut blight from Asia that wiped out the American chestnut trees,[17] and the Dutch elm disease that is killing the American elm. The rabbits that were introduced on Laysan Island disrupted the whole community of nesting birds by eating up all the vegetation.[18]

When the herbivorous African giant snail was introduced into the Pacific islands, it became a major agricultural pest.[19] The accidental introduction of African malaria-carrying mosquitoes into Brazil in 1923 caused an epidemic of malaria that killed an estimated twenty thousand people.[20] The Rockefeller Foundation and the Brazilian government conducted a campaign against the mosquito that resulted in its extermination in South America, a campaign that involved the work of over three thousand persons and cost over two million dollars.

Such widespread destruction by one animal or plant kills 'the goose that lays the golden egg', for the invader finally suffers from a shortage of food. That natural checks and controls may develop is nowhere better illustrated than by the fate of the Australian cottony-cushion scale that was introduced into California about 1868. It threatened the citrus industry, but was brought under control by the introduction of its counter-pest, an Australian ladybird.[21]

The study of such intricacies, showing the interdependence of living things, is fascinating. But no one biologist can be expected to know how to classify and name all these diverse organisms, which must be done before they can be talked about, and certainly no one man has the time to work out all their life histories. Thus the investigations are cooperative and piece-meal. The bird specialist sends the lice from a bird to a louse specialist; the specialist in ticks sends the birds from which his ticks came to an ornithologist for identification. With the recognition of the role that some of the organisms of these communities play in spreading and causing human disease, public-health and tropical-medicine units have developed pro-grammes for studying them. In addition to the main results, there is a cross-fertilization of ideas that is stimulating and productive.

CHAPTER 16

Vital Statistics

IN the first half of 1964 the discovery of four new species of birds was announced in the scientific literature: a fly-catcher from an island near New Britain, a warbler from New Guinea, a tanager from South America, and a humming-bird from southern Mexico. A recent Field Museum of Natural History expedition to Angola brought back three new bird species: a fly-catcher, a thrush, and a helmet shrike.[1] Since discoveries such as these continue to be made, we can assume that there are still other bird species to be discovered in the lesser-known parts of the tropics. How many more are yet to be found can only be estimated. There may be several hundred to be added to the list of ten thousand or so known species.

The count of the number of bird species in existence can never be precise and definite, for not all ornithologists agree on the status of certain birds. For example, the yellow-shafted flicker (*Colaptes auratus*) of eastern North America and the red-shafted flicker of western North America hybridize extensively in areas where the two meet. Are they to be called species or sub-species? The black-capped chickadee (*Parus atricapillus*) of North America is rather similar to the willow tit (*Parus montanus*) of Eurasia except that it has a different-sounding voice. Some ornithologists think both form one species; others, that each is a species.[2] Perhaps 5 to 10 per cent of living birds present such problems in classification.

The present widely quoted figure of 8,600 known species comes from a calculation made in 1946 by Dr Ernst Mayr, director of the Museum of Comparative Zoology at Harvard University, and can best be accepted as a minimum estimate.[3] Probably a more realistic, though less precise figure is that of ten thousand bird species, give or take a thousand or so, extant at the present time.

Accurate counts of the number of individuals in a species are possible only under special conditions. The plight of the nearly extinct whooping crane has caught the imagination of the American public, and the species is claimed to be the best-known rare bird in the world.[4] All existing individuals winter in a carefully preserved small area on the Texas coast, and each year the birds make the long round trip to and from their nesting grounds in central Canada. Bird watchers, conservation societies, and government wildlife officers eagerly keep track of them, and accounts of their status are published in the big-city dailies. Since 1922 the whooping-crane population has varied between twenty and forty birds; a newspaper account in March 1964 reported only thirty-two wild birds alive at that time.

The Harvard ornithologist James C. Greenway in 1958 summarized the status and numbers of many species with small populations.[5] A few examples may be quoted. The California condor had only an estimated fifty to a hundred individuals alive at that time, all in the mountains of one part of California. In Bermuda a petrel called the cahow, that was thought to be extinct, was rediscovered, and the breeding population was estimated at about a hundred individuals. The shore plover of New Zealand, now with a limited distribution only on offshore Southeast Island, had a population of seventy individuals.

A few fairly accurate counts have been made of conspicuously larger populations of birds. Gannets nest on cliffs on both sides of the North Atlantic, and two English ornithologists, James Fisher and H. G. Vevers, have made surveys of the world gannet population.[6] In 1939 they calculated that there were 166,000 adults; the number was revised in 1951, because of known increases of the species in parts of its range, to 200,000 adult birds. A fairly accurate count has also been made of the emperor penguin, which nests on the edges of the Antarctic continent. Dr G. M. Budd, who was medical officer to the Australian Antarctic

Research Expedition of 1959–60, used data he gathered person-ally from his land travel, along with aerial photographs of colonies and published accounts, and estimated that there were at least 120,000 pairs of breeding birds in at least twenty-one rookeries.[7]

But most of the time in recording bird populations such terms as 'rare', 'common', and 'abundant' are used instead of figures. Even these terms are not adequate in some cases. 'Rare' does not do justice to the status of the obscure New Guinea flower-pecker (*Melanocharis arfakiana*).[8] The first found was a single specimen secured by the Dutch bird collector A. A. Bruijn in western New Guinea in 1876. Despite the many bird expeditions to New Guinea in succeeding decades, the species was not found again until 1933. Then, on 22 November, in the mid-mountain forest of eastern New Guinea, a Papuan native brought me what proved to be the second known specimen. No further specimen has been found.

Nor would 'abundant' adequately indicate the numbers of Antarctic whale-birds seen by Dr Robert Cushman Murphy of the American Museum of Natural History. This authority on oceanic birds wrote that in November 1921, when he was travelling near South Georgia on the brig *Daisy*, the ship was always in the midst of these birds, and they sometimes 'filled the air like snowflakes for hours on end'.[9]

There have been estimates of the local concentrations of cer-tain birds which give an idea of the impressive total numbers that must exist. The American blackbirds, especially the cow-bird, grackle, and red-winged blackbird, nest widely over the North American continent and in winter withdraw southwards, where they gather to sleep in great mixed roosts. The United States wildlife biologists J. A. Neff and B. Meanley found that, in the Mississippi valley from Louisiana to Missouri, great roosts occurred about every fifty miles.[10] The number of birds in many of them ranged between one and fifteen million. Com-parable winter roosts of a finch called the brambling have been recorded in Switzerland by the Swiss ornithologist E. Gueniat.[11] The flocks and colonies of a weaver-bird, the quelea, in Africa seem to rival the locusts in their depredations on grain. One colony covering ninety-three acres contained about two and a half million nests according to a 1958 survey made by the English ornithologist D. Vesey Fitzgerald.[12]

For more precise population data we have censuses, actual counts of breeding birds from unit areas. The number of pairs of a species nesting in an area may depend on their tolerance for each other, among other things. Herons and gannets, colonial nesters, may nest just far enough apart so they cannot reach each other with their bills. There may be several thousand nests in a single tree in a heron colony. But many land birds, as we know, hold territory around the nest. The territory may be an acre or so in extent for many small song-birds; with other birds it may be much larger. The veteran British ornithologist Col. Richard Meinertzhagen writes of a pair of Verreaux's eagles that held a territory of four hundred square miles, from which they excluded all other eagles.[13]

As one would expect, the density of the total population of nesting land birds in a particular area varies with the habitat. According to the chart presented by the American ornithologist Dr J. C. Welty, habitats with sparse populations include the Alpine Zone in Finland, with nine adult birds per hundred acres, and the desert steppe of Colorado, with ten birds.[14] Near the other extreme the natural mature deciduous forests of West Virginia have as many as 724 birds per hundred acres, and the mixed forests of Holland, 896 birds. Some cultivated lands, such as gardens, villages, and golf courses, have still higher counts.

Data such as these form the basis for the estimates that there are 120 million birds in England and Wales and 5 billion birds in the United States, and for the calculation by the American ornithologist Dr L. W. Wing that a total world population of 100 billion birds may exist.[15]

Population densities vary not only from place to place but from time to time. In Saxony, according to a twelve-year survey of hole-nesting birds published by the German ornithologist R. Berndt in 1949, the number of pairs of nesting starlings fluctuated irregularly between forty and one hundred.[16] In North America a survey of ruffed grouse made under the leadership of the ornithologist G. Bump indicated that the populations fluctuated between four and twenty-one birds per hundred acres in a nine-year cycle.[17] The activities of man may cause changes in population size. For example, species that thrive around settlements may increase, and predatory species persecuted by man may decrease. An important point is that many populations, without obvious cause, seem to fluctuate around a certain density.

The first basic element in maintaining a population density is the production of eggs. The number of eggs laid has already been discussed; here it is sufficient to point out that this number varies from one in the albatross, some pigeons, and some auks to twenty or so in some of the gallinaceous birds and the rails. Species laying only a few eggs at one time usually lay a fixed number, while birds with larger clutches lay a more variable number, which may change with the food supply and with geography.

Many small land birds breed in their second calendar year, when they are not quite a year old.[18] The short life-span of many of them makes this quick breeding a necessity for carrying on the species. The actual period necessary to reach sexual maturity may be less than a year. Indeed, some captive birds have laid eggs at three to six months of age. This capacity for early laying is most likely to be used in the seasonless part of the tropics or in areas with irregular seasons, but even in the Temperate Zone in Florida, where most breeding is seasonal, Dr R. F. Johnston of the University of Kansas found a wild ground dove (*Columbigallina passerina*) in breeding condition at six months of age.[19]

Some birds with longer life-spans may not breed until they are two years old, like some of the gulls, hawks, and divers, while some large hawks and storks may be six years old, and some large albatrosses eight years old, when they first breed. Since their life-span is long, they can have enough offspring, over the years, to maintain the population level, even though each clutch is small. In these species fluctuations in numbers are slow.

The significance of an unbalanced sex ratio as a population factor is as obscure as its actual existence.[20] A common impression is that males are in a slight to a considerable majority, but this impression may result from the fact that the bright-coloured and singing males are more conspicuous. The extent to which male birds predominate in duck hunters' bags and in traps operated for duck ringing,[21] the predominance of males in collections of some New Guinea honey eaters (twenty males to one female in one case), and the predominance of females in some breeding colonies of polygamous American blackbirds have given rise to speculations concerning actual sex ratios at different ages and their correlation with different breeding patterns.

An approximation to the expected 50:50 ratio has been demonstrated in domestic fowl, some quail, and the boat-tailed grackle. The widely quoted report of an unbalanced sex ratio in this grackle seems to have been an error, according to the investigations of Dr R. K. Selander, of the University of Texas.[22] In laboratory experiments drakes are reported to succumb more quickly to stress than ducks; a similar vulnerability is displayed by the males of some other animals.[23] In the wild, males seem more numerous than females, perhaps because the females, with the additional stress of a major share in nest duties, are more open to predation. But the determining of an actual sex ratio for a population of significant size, a sample free from bias, is difficult.

Whatever the sex ratio in the whole population, there is no doubt that units of a population may have an unbalanced sex ratio. In nesting colonies of the blackbirds and grackles mentioned above, there may be two or three females to one male. One explanation for the proportion among grackles, according to Dr Selander, may be that the first-year females are present and breeding but not the first-year males. In some species of ducks, after the females start incubating, the drakes desert the breeding grounds and gather in large numbers elsewhere. In some species, outside the breeding season, the sexes may segregate into flocks in which one sex or the other predominates, and their patterns of roosting, feeding, and migrating may not be the same. In the south-eastern United States, as Dr Selander has also recorded, flocks of male grackles often feed in city parks, but the females keep to the rural areas. In the Temperate Zone the males of migrant species often arrive ahead of the females in the spring. This is especially noticeable in the flocks of red-winged blackbirds.

One of the advances in biological economy evolved by both birds and mammals is a reduction of the number of young, correlated with a great increase in the amount of parental care the young get as they start out in life. Even the ten to twenty eggs of the duck or partridge, and the several clutches of four or five eggs laid by the American robin in one season, contrast strikingly with the many thousands of eggs that fish and frogs may produce.

Despite the parental care, a large percentage of birds' eggs never produce flying young. The many studies that have been made give diverse results, but a general statement can be made that only about half the eggs of song-birds are successful.[24] In many water birds, ducks, and gallinaceous birds the young survive from only about a third of the eggs.[25] Some of the studies show that mortality can correlate with nest site. In those sites that are best protected, such as those of birds that nest in holes, like woodpeckers, the birds may fledge young from about two thirds of the eggs.

The first few months are the most hazardous of the bird's life, as is illustrated by the data of Dr John Emlen, of the University of Wisconsin, on the California quail.[26] The over-winter mortality of the adults he studied was 50 per cent, while that of the young, inexperienced birds was 70 per cent. A similar situation probably exists for many other species.

The age that birds reach can be estimated in several ways. The most significant for population studies is the calculation of adult mortality and expected longevity based on an analysis of ringed birds. This is a complicated process, and only a few of the results are presented here, from a paper by the American zoologist Dr D. S. Farner, of the University of Washington.[27] The mortality rate varies from group to group, but in some species the adult rate seems relatively stable. The adult annual mortality rate is highest in gallinaceous birds (60 to 80 per cent), ducks (40 to 65 per cent), passerine birds (40 to 68 per cent), and in pigeons (55 to 58 per cent); lower in gulls (18 to 30 per cent), herons (30 per cent), cormorants (12 to 30 per cent) and in swifts (19 per cent).

Correspondingly the expected average life-span as given by Dr Farner is shortest in gallinaceous birds (a year or less) and in ducks and passerine birds (one to two years), and longest in the swift and penguin (about five years).[28] These figures are rounded, and they are, of course, based on only a few species.

This average life-span of course does not tell us how long individual birds have lived. Some direct data on the age of individuals are obtained from the recovery of ringed birds, where we have both the ringing and recovery date. Some record old ages discovered in this way are those of a Canada goose, twenty-three years old; an osprey, twenty-one years; a swallow, sixteen years; a blue jay, fifteen years; a black-capped chickadee, nine years old. The record ages known for wild birds may be those of a herring gull of twenty-eight years, an Arctic tern of twenty-seven years, and a European oyster-catcher that reached the age of thirty-two years and is said to have been the oldest known wild bird.[29]

In captivity – in zoos and as pets – birds of much greater age have been reported. Some of the accounts are so inadequately documented that they may be considered folklore. Such a tale was told by the great German explorer Alexander von Humboldt of a parrot in South America.[30] It had been the pet of a tribe of Indians, who taught it to talk. These Indians became extinct, but the parrot lived on as a pet in other hands and was the sole possessor of the extinct language.

But there are many well-documented old-age records. The English naturalist Major S. S. Flower made a survey of them in 1938, from which a few examples may be cited.[31] The greatest age is recorded for an eagle owl (*Bubo bubo*) that reached sixty-eight years. A sulphur-crested cockatoo reached fifty-six; a bateleur eagle, fifty-five; an Andean condor (*Vultur gryphus*), fifty-two; and a white pelican (*Pelicanus onocrotalus*), fifty-one years. All these are fairly large birds. Among the smaller birds, several weaver-birds reached nineteen years; a cardinal, twenty-two years; and a canary, twenty-two years.

One can easily point out various causes for the death of birds, either singly or in large numbers. A bird is caught by a cat, hawk, or snake; dashes into a window or an overhead wire; is hit by an automobile; is killed by hailstones; or is shot. Large numbers of birds are killed by hitting television towers or are stricken by botulism, the result of ingesting the toxin produced by an anaerobic bacterium that flourishes in some prairie ponds at a certain water level. A coyote that gets on to an island where ducks are nesting can create havoc. A storm during migration may sweep large numbers of birds out to sea to perish. Starvation and disease may play a part. Since bird populations tend to remain constant, despite varying conditions, one must conclude that the various factors promoting and limiting survival interact and balance each other. This is well illustrated by the figures for two different years on the death of young emperor penguins in an Antarctic colony, quoted by Dr G. M. Budd (Table VII).[32]

TABLE VII
Death among Emperor Penguins

Year	Cause of Death		Total
	Predation	Undernourishment	
1952	5 per cent	80 per cent	85 per cent
1956	34 per cent	52 per cent	86 per cent

We can summarize by saying that complex food, social, and shelter needs are balanced against weather, predation, disease, and habitat factors. For instance, when an unusually large number of birds have survived, there may not be room enough for territories for all, so some may be unable to reproduce. Probably the reproductive potential of the bird and the mortality-rate factors have both been adapted to the survival of the species.

Extinction, the death of a species, has played as essential a role in evolution as the death of the individual has played in the survival of the species. Theoretically, if all types of birds that had ever lived were represented today, we would have all the intermediate stages between *Archaeopteryx*, sparrow, and ostrich, all one inter-grading species. The avian palaeontologist Dr Pierce Brodkorb, of the University of Florida, has calculated that in the 150 million years or so that birds have existed, about a million and a half species have evolved.[33] Of these, all but the ten thousand species living today have become extinct. These figures are of course highly speculative, as all such figures must be. But they do emphasize the truth that the birds now living are but a small fraction of the birds that have existed. In the far-distant future some species now known will have disappeared and new ones will have evolved.

In the last 270 years, since ornithologists have been keeping track of the birds, some species have been brought to an untimely end. A recent survey made by James C. Greenway lists forty-five species and forty-three sub-species (eighty-eight in all) known to ornithologists that have become extinct.[34] A further twelve species and seven sub-species (nineteen forms) are probably extinct. Among these extinct and near-extinct birds are such diverse kinds as emus, parrots, and sparrows. A few lived on continents, but most of them lived on islands. Only five lived in North America proper: the Labrador duck (extinct in 1875), the heath hen (1932), the Eskimo curlew (last specimen, 1932, but sight records made since indicate that it may still survive), the passenger pigeon (1914), and the Carolina parakeet (a sub-species, 1914). The great auk, which lived in the North Atlantic, was last recorded in 1844.

We have no records of recent extinctions in Africa, South America, or Europe. In Asia the crested sheldrake was last recorded in 1916, and in Australia a green-wren was last recorded in 1875. The situation on some islands is very different: twelve species and sub-species have become extinct in the West Indies; thirteen species and thirteen sub-species in the Hawaiian Islands; and fourteen species and twelve sub-species in the central and western Pacific islands.

In a few cases, like that of the great auk, the immediate cause of extinction has been direct killing by man. But in the main extinction has resulted from the changes that European man made in the countries he colonized: the destruction of the habitat and the introduction of foreign predators, diseases, and competitors. In Europe and especially in western Asia, where great changes in the countryside were made before records of birds were kept, there were probably living during the Christian era species, of which we have no record, that have since disappeared. An indication of what may have occurred is given by the discovery in Oriental gardens of Père David's deer and the ginkgo tree, neither of which is known to exist in a wild state.

It was formerly said that the axe and the plough were the most important destroyers of bird life. Now these have been joined by the bulldozer and the dragline, which also eliminate birds by obliterating their habitats. Once their habitat is gone the birds disappear even though not a single individual has been killed outright. In recent years the pesticides used against both insects and plants have loomed large as a possible wholesale threat to wild life. They are essential in maintaining modern man's standard of living, but there is a need for careful scrutiny and evaluation of their side effects.

CHAPTER 17

Colour and Coloration

COLORATION in birds has a range of variation and reaches a brilliance not equalled elsewhere in vertebrate animals, although perhaps rivalled by that of insects. Birds' colours run through the whole spectrum – red, orange, yellow, green, blue and violet – and include white, black, and grey as well. Also present are the mixed tones, characteristic of birds' feathers, notably the earth colours: the browns and related buffs – ochraceous, ferruginous, and rufous – and the leaf-matching greens, olives, and brownish greens. Some birds are uniformly brilliant, like the scarlet ibis; some are dull, like the cat-bird and the dipper; some are brightly and boldly patterned, like blue and red macaws; and some are finely and intricately patterned in bars, vermiculations, spots and streaks of soft brown, grey and black, like nightjars and woodcock.

The repetition in quite unrelated birds of some patterns, such as the white outer-tail feathers, pale rump, and pale eye rings of so many species, and the black bib of the male house sparrow and the chickadee, may simply reflect the common ancestry of birds. It is extremely probable that the reptile ancestry of birds had useful colour patterns and that these patterns, originally inherited from reptiles, have subsequently evolved along with the rest of the bird.

There are three ways in which coloration can aid a bird: by helping it in relation to its inanimate environment, by helping it escape enemies, and in social communication.

Relation to Inanimate Environment. It is well known that the unpigmented parts of the feathers wear more quickly than the heavily pigmented parts. This is easily seen in the way white 'mirrors' in the tips of a gull's wings wear and disappear, and in the way in which the pale, wedge-shaped marks on the inner-wing quills of waders and woodpeckers wear away, giving saw-tooth edges to the feathers. Perhaps for this reason the flight feathers of birds are usually the most heavily pigmented part of the plumage, and some, though not all, white birds have black primaries.

It is possible that the Arctic ptarmigan's all-white winter plumage, since it lacks pigment, has more empty air spaces in the cells and thus may provide better insulation against the cold than pigmented plumage could give. The absence of pigment may function in the same way for wolves, caribou, Arctic hares, and polar bears. The prevalence of white in the plumage of tropical sea birds may also aid as insulation, keeping the heat out instead of in. The black caps of many pale-grey and white terns may protect the brain against the actinic (violet and ultraviolet) rays of the direct sunlight. However, when we try to apply such suggestions to whole faunas, we quickly find that they have been framed for special cases only, and exceptions are many. The raven in the Arctic is all black, and the little auk has a black back; the fairy tern of the tropics has all-white plumage and a dark skin, and the tropical noddy tern has dark plumage with a pale crown and a pale skin.

We do find certain general relationships between coloration and habitat. Many, though not all, sea birds are grey above and white below, black above and white below, or mostly white – whatever group they belong to, and whether they live in polar seas or in tropical ones. Birds of the grasslands tend to be brownish, and often they exhibit a fine pattern which har-monizes with dead grass (though not with green grass). Birds of the treetops often have much green in their plumage, but it is also in the treetops of the tropical forests that the largest percentage of brilliantly coloured and patterned birds are found.

These are general tendencies with many exceptions, but it

seems desirable to mention them, even without an attempt at explanation.

Escaping Enemies. In discussing colour as an aid to helping birds escape their enemies we are on surer ground, for we have the bird's behaviour in relation to colour as an aid to our deductions. There are two ways in which colour can help: by providing camouflage and thus helping the bird to escape observation, and by advertising that the bird has ill-tasting flesh.

The success of cryptic, or concealing, coloration as camouflage results from the fact that form can only be seen when it is made evident by differences of colour or tone, or of light and shadow. When these diminish, the shape of an animal becomes more and more difficult to recognize. Nature here works in a manner just opposite to that of the artist. The artist applies paint to create the illusion of a real, rounded object where there is only a flat surface. Nature, in camouflaging animals, uses colour and pattern to create the illusion that the background is uniform and that the animal is not there.

The most universal principle of concealing coloration is countershading, in which the upper parts, where most light falls, are darker than the under parts, where less light reaches the body.[1] This distribution of tones makes the bird appear uniformly coloured all over and therefore less conspicuous. Of course there are exceptions, such as the black-bellied plover, the eider duck, and some bustards.

Some birds match their backgrounds in colour and pattern.[2] This is well illustrated by the tan-brown, streaked, dead-grass pattern of the snipe that lives in grassy meadows and the red-brown, blotched, dead-leaf pattern of the woodcock that lives in thickets. Both are birds that crouch at the approach of an intruder and depend on their concealing coloration to escape observation.

Another principle of cryptic coloration is exemplified by disruptive patterns.[3] Young kill-deer and many other waders have a blotched pattern of dark and light on their upper parts; this breaks up the bird's outline and provides effective concealment when the young bird crouches motionless, or 'freezes', among the pebbles.

The effect of concealing coloration may be heightened by form and pose. We have mentioned the 'freezing' on the ground of a cryptically coloured species. But when a screech owl perches close to a tree trunk on a branch, not only does its variegated plumage repeat the mottled pattern of the bark, but the shape of its head, with its upward-pointing horns, makes the owl look like the end of a broken-off stub. Another example is furnished by the frogmouth of Australia. It may perch on a branch, point its head skyward, eyes partly closed, and sit motionless, again looking like the end of a broken-off stub. Similarly a bittern, with plumage the colour of dead reeds, may straighten up when alarmed, bill pointed skyward, and use shape as well as colour to achieve concealment among the reeds.

A combination of protective and advertising colours, cryptic and flash colours, displayed alternately, may be effective in confusing a predator. Imagine a falcon stooping at a flying turnstone, which shows a conspicuous black-and-white pattern on its lower back and rump in flight. The turnstone alights and folds its wings, and the black-and-white pattern disappears. Such sudden apparent changes in colour at a critical moment may conceivably startle or confuse the falcon, just as a sudden cry can startle a predator. The respite gained, even if only momentary, may make the difference between escape and capture for the intended victim.

Advertising colour which warns of bad-tasting flesh is more common among insects than among birds, but it does exist in some birds.[4] Hugh B. Cott, an English naturalist who wrote the definite *Adaptive Coloration in Animals* in 1940, has since conducted a series of experiments in the edibility of birds.[5] He used cats and hornets as the experimental tasters, and their choices were checked by human tasters. The preferences of these three tasters, indicating palatability in general, agreed. The results of these experiments indicate that there is a wide range of palatability in the flesh of different species of birds.

Figure 34. *Concealing coloration: in screech owl* (a) *and bittern* (b) *pattern, colour, and form are concealing; in ptarmigan* (c) *white plumage in winter matches the snow, brown in summer matches the ground.*

Further, it appears that the most conspicuously coloured birds
have the least palatable flesh and the most cryptically coloured
birds are most palatable. For instance, larks, which harmonize
so well with their background, taste much better than black-
and-white chats, which sit up conspicuously on exposed perches.
Cott suggests that selective pressure by predators has forced
vulnerable species along two divergent lines of specialization,
leading those that are more palatable towards concealment and
those that are more distasteful towards advertisement. This line
of reasoning is of course concerned with only one aspect of a
whole complex of factors, including the use of advertising colour
for display in sexually dimorphic species and for other intra-
specific communication.

Social Communication. Being animals with a strong sense
of sight, birds undoubtedly use the colours and patterns, which
differ from species to species, as guides to identification. Some
may learn their species characters from seeing their parents, but
most of this recognition is probably instinctive. Social parasites,
raised by foster parents, must have a completely instinctive
recognition of the members of their own species. Cues for this
recognition undoubtedly include not only colour and pattern,
but also size, shape, behaviour, and voice. The ease with which
dull-eyed man can recognize many bird species by the general
appearance and behaviour suggests that the fine details of pattern and colour are only reinforcing stimuli for sharp-eyed

Figure 35. *Disruptive patterns and flash colours: in young plover (a) the
pattern helps to conceal the birds; in the adult turnstone (b) the flash
pattern exposed in flight changes the appearance of the bird (compare with
the kill-deer, c).*

birds. An albino crow in a flock of normal black crows may be accepted as one of the flock despite its striking difference in colour, again indicating that instinctive recognition may be based on a wide range of characters, some of which can be considerably modified without disrupting the identification.

In social communication by movements, some flash colours add conspicuousness to the movements and thus increase their effect. The display of white rump feathers by a brambling as it flies off emphasizes the fact that one bird of the flock is on the wing. The others may either follow quickly or look about to see if flight is needed. Of course, the same flash colour may have a dual effect at times, also confusing a would-be predator.

In some species the individuals are all alike in colour, in others, they are not. Colour differences within a species are correlated with a variety of factors:

I. No dimorphism. Colour is the same for all sexes and ages; generally found in species with dull, cryptic coloration (e.g., song-thrush, wren, many other song-birds).

II. Species dimorphism. Various colour phases exist, independent of sex, age, or season (e.g., greyish and reddish phases of female cuckoos, dark and light forms of Arctic skua, and the very variable neck colour of the ruff's neck adornment).

III. Sexual dimorphism.
   A. Male brighter than the female. A common condition, with varying degrees of difference, correlated with the male's being the more aggressive sex partner (e.g., blackcock, pheasant, many duck species).
   B. Female brighter than the male. A rare condition, correlated with the female's being the more aggressive sex partner and the male's caring for the eggs (e.g., phalarope, bustard quail, painted snipe).

IV. Seasonal dimorphism. Two quite different plumages are worn in a year – a summer and a winter plumage or a breeding and a non-breeding plumage.
   A. Both sexes (e.g., ptarmigan are brown in summer, white in winter, correlating with changes in the landscape; divers, grebes, and many waders change from a more or less

ornamental breeding plumage to a duller or plainer off-season plumage).

   B. Males only. The male changes from a highly ornamental breeding plumage to a duller plumage, resembling that of the female (e.g., ducks, ruff, reed bunting).

v. Age dimorphism. The young are more vulnerable to predation, and correspondingly the plumage may be duller and more cryptic.

   A. Young different from both bright-coloured parents (e.g., robin, American robin, most gulls, night heron).

   B. Young like the duller parent (e.g., blackbird, kestrel, linnet).

vi. Aberrations. Unusually black (melanism), white (albinism), red (erythrism), or yellow (xanthochroism) individuals occasionally occur in many species as a result of physiological changes in colour deposition; these birds are considered freaks. Melanism and albinism are most widely known; erythrism and xanthochroism occur less commonly, in parrots and some finches.

The range of colour in birds is great, but that of the pigments is small and most of them belong to one of two groups.[6] Diversity is added by what are known as structural colours, which occur when the fine structure of the outer layer of the feathers reflects and scatters the light in different ways. Bright colours are usually found only on the exposed parts of the feathers; the concealed bases are often neutral or white. The longer quills of the wings and tail tend to be heavily but more plainly coloured than the contour feathers. This distribution of pigment is correlated with the greater amount of wear they get.

The two main pigments are the melanins, the more common, which give yellows, browns, and blacks, and the carotenoids, which give yellows and reds. White is a structural colour without pigment occurring when the structure reflects all light. There is no blue pigment, and blue is always due to a certain structure's overlaying a melanin pigment. There is a green pigment, turacoverdin, known only from the turacos of Africa, but most green colour has the same origin as blue, except that the structure has carotenoid pigments below it instead of a melanin.

A special red pigment containing copper is also found in the wing feathers of some turacos. Earlier accounts spoke of the red's being so water soluble that turacos out in the rain had the colour washed out of their feathers. This is not true.

Different microscopic surface structures of the feathers produce metallic and iridescent effects that can be amazingly brilliant, including all the colours of the rainbow as the birds turn in the light.[7] Among the most brilliantly iridescent birds are humming-birds and sun-birds.

Melanins are synthesized in the body of the bird, but carotenoids must be secured directly or indirectly from plants, though they may be altered before being deposited in the feathers. An understanding of this has enabled zoo keepers to exhibit pink flamingos; when fed a carotenoid-free diet, the birds grow only white feathers.[8]

Freak individuals of many species, even crows, may lack all pigment in their feathers, feet, and bill; these parts are white, and the iris, being without pigment, looks pink because the red in the blood vessels shows through. Incomplete albinos may have many or few white feathers, but often the albinistic pattern repeats itself symmetrically on the right and left sides of the bird.

Yet another type of colour sometimes seen in birds is adventitious. Examples are the rusty-brown stain on the feathers of the heads and necks of snow geese that have been feeding in water that is rich in iron, and the yellow or red dusting of pollen on the foreheads of Oriental white-eyes that have been feeding at flowers.

Luminous birds have been reported intermittently since the time of the Roman Pliny, whose *Natural History* appeared about A.D. 77. Yet scientists have been unable to find living light, or bioluminescence, in birds, or in their closest relatives, the mammals and reptiles. Bioluminescence does occur in other living organisms, for example in the flesh of the beetles called fireflies, in marine fishes, in the one-celled animals that give the sea when disturbed its phosphorescence, and in the lowly bacteria and the mycelia of fungi that cause rotten wood to glow with the light called fox fire.[9]

The last two of these examples give clues as to why birds at times appear luminous.[10] The barn owl in Europe is one of the birds most often said to give off light at night. It sometimes lives in hollow trees and it is possible that the fox fire of rotten wood rubs off on to its plumage.

Sea birds do not figure in the early accounts, but one night in September 1957 the American naturalist J. Y. Christmas, of the Gulf Coast Research Laboratory, Ocean Springs, Mississippi, saw luminous terns.[11] He was on the research vessel *Hermes*, riding at anchor near shore in the Gulf of Mexico, and a violent storm came up. The turbulence, the rain, and the wind caused the surface of the water to become a sheet of phosphorescence, and the white caps were lines of racing luminescence. Soon there appeared pale spots of light, at first recalling sailors' stories of St Elmo's fire playing about the rigging. As they came nearer, it was seen that they were the luminous shapes of flying birds, presumably terns that had been roosting on near-by sandbars. Evidently the waves that had disturbed the terns in the night had splashed them with phosphorescent water and the tiny light-emitting organisms had stuck to their feathers.

There still remains the oft-reported observation of the luminous breasts of fishing night herons. It has been claimed that the light is produced by the patches of powder-down which these birds have on their breasts. But experiments and examinations to verify this claim have all had negative results. The phenomenon, if it exists, has not been explained.

In general, colour change in a bird's plumage is a matter of feather replacement by moult. The possibility of colour change in an adult, grown feather is limited, because the feather, like the hair and nails of mammals, essentially consists of dead material. Its colour is determined while it is growing, and is thereafter unaffected by physiological factors. But considerable change in feathers may result from contact with the environment. The tips, especially pale ones, may break off with wear. The snow bunting is a classic example of this. In winter it is a pale rusty-brown bird, but in summer it is a black-and-white bird because the rusty-brown tips of its feathers have worn off.

Sometimes the barbs do not break off, but the fine barbules wear off; then the shape of the feather remains unchanged, but the colour alters. The male purple finch becomes a deeper red, and an African goshawk a deeper black, through changes of this sort.

Fading of the browns of the plumage of a desert bird exposed to fierce sunlight may make it much paler, a change accompanied by wear. But there are also most striking changes from fading which are not accompanied by wear – for example, the manner in which the salmon-pink tinge of the American merganser's plumage disappears, and the vivid yellow of the flank plumes of the twelve-wired bird of paradise becomes quite white.

A related colour change is seen in the green hunting jay of southern Asia, which may become a blue bird even during the time it wears one coat of feathers.[12] Specimens of this bird, bright green when collected, turn blue within a few years in a museum. The red colour of a turaco's wings may darken in specimens, and in other species the browns in plumage frequently turn more red-brown and the olives become more brownish in museum specimens.

In discussing colours of birds, we are ordinarily referring to the appearance of the feathers. The skin usually has little colour in it beyond a pinkish or yellowish tinge unless it is exposed, as in wattles or the bare heads of vultures and cassowaries; then it may be bright red, yellow, or blue.

The bill and feet may harmonize with the plumage or may contrast, and the inside of the mouth may be brightly coloured and used in display, as in some birds of paradise. The young of some small weaver-birds have patterns in the inside of the mouth. In some birds the colours of bill, mouth, and feet may serve the same functions as the colours of the plumage (in display or in courtship, for example).

CHAPTER 18

Skin, Feathers,
and Moult

BIRDS, like mammals and reptiles, are covered with skin. Bird skin is soft, flexible, and usually tender, though ostrich skin is tough enough to tan and use for fancy handbags and shoes. Most of a bird's skin is covered with feathers, which are horny structures produced by the skin.[1] Each grows from a small papilla, easily seen in a plucked chicken or goose (whence comes the expression 'goose-flesh', used for the roughness on human skin caused by the erection of its papillae, due to cold or fear).

Only birds have feathers, and all birds have feathers. So much are they a part of a bird's make-up that if the fossil *Archaeopteryx* had not been accompanied by prints in the rock of its wing and tail feathers, it might have been called a reptile rather than a bird.

Feathers evolved along with flight and with the warm-blooded condition of birds. They provide a light, flexible insulating coat that is essential for maintaining the warm-bloodedness,[2] and at the same time they smooth the angular shape of the body into streamlined contours that promote the bird's efficiency as a flying animal. Feathers also provide most of the flying surface of the wing, which is very light and flexible and can be repaired by the moulting and replacement of worn or broken feathers. In this respect the bird's wing is more advanced than that of any other animal.

Just as birds can be considered modified reptiles, so feathers can be considered modified reptile scales. They are more than scales with a fringe along the edge, however, and have a definite and complicated structure. The individual feathers are of various sizes and shapes, but basically a feather consists of a stiff, tough, tapering shaft with a flexible vane, or web, along each side for most of its length. The short basal part of the feather, the calamus, is round, has no vane, and is nearly hollow. At the bottom there is an opening, the lower umbilicus, through which the blood supply entered the feather when it was growing. The angular, solid rachis is the part of the shaft which bears the vane. This vane provides most of the area of the feather. Each vane is composed of a row of barbs lying side by side and held together by smaller branches, the barbules with their hooklets. Sometimes there are fifty barbs on one side of an inch of shaft and five hundred to a thousand barbules on one side of an inch of barb. When the vane is forcibly disrupted, stroking it with the fingers, in imitation of the bird's preening, can realign the barbs and re-engage the hooklets, so that the vane is like new again.

The feathers of some birds, such as the emu, are double, with an after-shaft which branches off at the base of the rachis and is about as long as the main part of the feather and much like it in appearance. As we move up in the evolutionary scale, the after-shaft diminishes. In gallinaceous birds it is about half

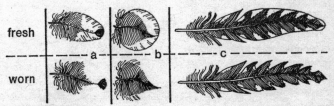

Figure 36. *Effects of wear on the colours of birds:* (a) *pale edges wear off the breast feathers of the African groundscraper thrush, leaving dark spots at tips;* (b) *pale tips wear off the contour feathers of the snow bunting, making the bird darker;* (c) *pale notches wear off the inner quills of the yellow-legs, making the back more uniform in colour.*

the size of the main part of the feather. In song-birds, regarded as the most advanced in this respect, the after-shaft is very small or lacking.

The basic type of feather has been modified in two directions, which reach their extremes in hair-like filoplumes, in bristles, and in down feathers which lack a rachis and have barbs that lack barbules and hooklets and are often crinkled.

The feathers that overlap to form the coat of feathers, the plumage, are mostly of the basic type. These contour feathers clothe the head and body of the bird; the rows of elongated, stiffer feathers that form most of the wings and tail are called quills. Scattered among the contour feathers, or occurring in special areas, may be filoplumes with no obvious function. Bristles may be present in eyelashes, as in the hornbills, and they occur about the gape in some fly-catching birds, as if to provide a net to help catch their active prey or to guide insects into the gape, or perhaps to perform some tactile function, like the whiskers of a cat.

The down feathers are important for insulation. The contour feathers are spaced a little way apart at the base, but their overlapping tips touch. Consequently, air is trapped all through the plumage, in dead-air spaces that provide the very best insulation, comparable to that obtained in houses by means of double windows. The bird can make some adjustments in this insulation, in response to the outside temperature. When it is hot the chickadee presses its feathers close to its body, thus

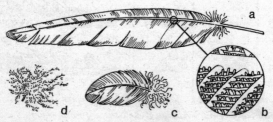

Figure 37. *Feather types and feather structure:* (a) *wing quill;* (b) *inset showing the structure of the shaft, parallel barbs, and overlapping, inter-locking barbules;* (c) *contour feather of the body;* (d) *down feather.*

reducing the air spaces in its plumage and speeding up the dissipation of heat. When it is cold the bird fluffs out its feathers until it looks nearly twice as big, and the plumage then has much more trapped air in it, which adds to its insulating effect.

The down feathers form a second layer, a sort of underwear, next to the bird's skin. The effectiveness of this light, elastic, air-filled material is recognized by man in his use of eiderdown. He prizes this down, gathered from the nests of eider ducks, as material for sleeping bags, quilts, jackets, and the like.

Feathers must not only protect the body of the bird against the cold, but in some species must also protect it against the wet. Evidently this function is not so important for tropical land birds, such as the coucal cuckoo. That veteran ornithologist of East Africa, Dr V. G. L. van Someren, found that after a heavy rain coucals became so wet and bedraggled from creeping through brush and grass that they could be run down and captured by hand.[3] Left to themselves, they climbed to the tops of bushes and spread their wings and tails to dry in the sun.

The extent to which the plumage of many song-birds becomes water-soaked can be seen in birds that become wet from bathing in a bird-bath. Their plumage is only shower-proof, and they hunt shelter when it rains hard.

With swimming and diving birds of northern and southern latitudes, birds that may spend months at sea, as penguins and auks do, it is a different matter. Their plumage must be completely waterproof, and the use of preen oil may be a help in achieving this. However, the cormorants, which feed by swimming and diving even in the colder parts of the world, have plumage that is imperfectly waterproof; they must come ashore periodically to dry their feathers. It is a common sight to see them perched on a rock, in a tree, or on pilings, with their wings spread out to dry.

Some special types of down feathers break off at the tips to form a fine powder, and have a special function in dressing the bird's feathers. In some birds, such as the hawks, these powder-down feathers may be scattered over the body among the other feathers. In other birds, such as the herons, they are massed in paired patches on the sides of the breast, flanks, and rump. Preening by the bird distributes this fine powder from the down feathers over the contour feathers and gives the blue-grey bloom that is seen on the back of the goshawk and the night heron.[4] It is another aid to dressing feathers, comparable to the oil from the preen glands so commonly used by birds, and perhaps also helps in waterproofing the plumage.

As has been mentioned earlier, the preen gland, also called oil gland or uropygial gland, is the only gland that birds have with an external opening.[5] The bird nibbles at the gland to get the oil on its bill and distributes it over the feathers. Presumably this oil helps in keeping the feathers in good condition, but this view has been questioned, and there are birds without oil glands.

The evolution of bird feathers from reptile scales is often regarded as having taken place in one of two ways. According to one view, primitive feathers were down feathers, much like those that clothe newly hatched ducks and chickens. These evolved into feathers with loose webs, such as those that form the body plumage of young owls when they leave the nest. In the next stage came feathers with firm webs, the adult feathers of present-day birds. This view stresses the insulating function of feathers, their contribution to the development of the warm-blooded condition. The other point of view is that feathers evolved first on birds' wings, as an aid to locomotion, in a hot climate. The specialized down feathers came later, as birds invaded colder climates. Probably flight and warm-bloodedness developed together and feathers evolved for various purposes early in the history of the bird. Unfortunately the fossil record throws no light on this.

We have concentrated on the various types of feathers which serve as body covering and as aids to flight, and have not mentioned what are often the most conspicuous of the modified feathers, those used for display – the flank plumes of birds of paradise, the trains of peacocks, the capes of pheasants, and the like. These are adaptations for social communication, their

Figure 38. *Feather tracts of a song-bird. On only a few primitive birds do feathers grow uniformly over the body.*

function grafted on to the basic uses of feathers, as it were, and will be considered in the discussion of display in a later chapter.

The contour feathers on a bird have actually been counted for a number of species.[6] They have been found to run from 940 on a humming-bird to 25,216 on a whistling swan.[7] It is probable that the counts for penguins would go much higher. They have numerous minute feathers on their flipper-like wings, perhaps as many as 3,800 on the upper surface of the 'forearm' alone in the emperor penguin.[8] In birds of roughly similar shape and feathering there is, as one might expect, an inverse relationship between weight and number of feathers.[9] Larger birds have fewer feathers per unit of weight than do smaller ones. This difference reflects the relationship between the volume and the surface of a body. As the size of the bird changes, the skin area, which is two dimensional, increases as the square, while the volume of the body, and consequently the weight, increase as the cube. A large bird has a proportionally smaller surface to cover. There is also a seasonal difference; a bird has more feathers in winter than in summer.[10] It is probable that arctic birds have more feathers than birds of similar size in the tropics, because their environment is colder and their need for insulation greater.

There are some birds, such as the kiwi and penguin, whose feathers are more or less uniformly distributed over the body. But in most birds the feathers are arranged on the skin in well-defined patterns, called feather tracts, or pterylae.[11] The vanes of the feathers spread out to overlap each other and conceal the bare areas of skin, the apteria, in an imbricated pattern, and cover the bird smoothly.

The overlapping long wing quills, the remiges, are arranged in rows, one row on each 'hand' and each 'forearm', and for each species there is a definite number of remiges in each row. The number of primaries (the remiges on the 'hand') varies from nine in the tanagers and related New World song-birds and ten in most other song-birds (even if the outermost is rudimentary) to twelve in the grebes and storks. The number of secondaries (flight feathers on the 'forearm') varies from nine in most song-birds to thirty-two in certain albatross. Smaller feathers, the coverts, overlap each other and the bases of the remiges to fill in the spaces at the bases of the quills and between them and the body. Of course, in some flightless birds the remiges are much reduced in structure and number.

Most of the area of the tail consists of a row of overlapping quills, the rectrices, attached to the fleshy stump of a tail, the pygostyle. Six pairs of rectrices are common, but some birds have as few as four, and some, such as the pheasants, as many as sixteen.

There are birds of the tropics, such as the marabou storks, vultures, and certain fruit-eating parrots and cassowaries, whose heads are mostly bare. But in the Arctic, where protection from the cold is important, the ptarmigan are completely muffled in feathers. Some types even protect their nostrils from snow and others their legs and their toes.

The growing feather emerges from the skin as a dark, blood-rich pin-feather with a greyish, scaly sheath. New material is added at the base, and the tip is pushed out. As the feather grows, it bursts the sheath which flakes off as the vane expands. A grown, dry feather is in effect a dead structure; material cannot be added or withdrawn by the physiological processes of the bird. Damage by wear or breakage is not repaired.

Although a feather cannot be repaired, the bird's plumage, its whole complement of feathers, can be repaired by the replacement of damaged feathers. A broken feather is not immediately replaced, but, if it is pulled out, the growth of a replacement is stimulated.

Feathers become worn with use and age, and ordinarily the complete plumage is replaced once a year through moult.[12] The old feather falls out, or is pushed out as the replacement begins to grow.

Moult is an adaptive affair and varies with the biological cycles of different birds – their breeding and migration customs – and their habitats and habits. In most species the moult proceeds gradually, a few feathers at a time, so that the bird is always clothed in feathers and always has usable wings, even if a quill is missing here and there. The bird can continue its normal activities while this is going on.

The simplest sequence of moults and plumage growth is shown by many song-birds of the tropical rain forest. First, a scant natal down is lost in a post-natal moult and is replaced by the nestling plumage. This is moulted in the post-nestling moult, soon after the bird leaves the nest, and the first-year plumage develops. In this plumage, which is very similar to the adult's, the bird may breed. Subsequently there is one complete moult a year, after the breeding season.

A more complex situation is found in many arid-country birds, and in some from the Temperate and Arctic Zones. These have a second seasonal moult each year, which may involve some of the head and neck feathers only, or all the body feathers, or the contour feathers and tail quills, or all the feathers, including the wing quills. A pre-nuptial moult, usually incomplete, produces a breeding plumage, and a post-nuptial moult, usually complete, produces an off-season, non-breeding, or eclipse plumage, as it is variously called. Both plumages may be very similar, as in the leaf warblers (*Phylloscopus*), or they may be quite different, as in the male scarlet tanager, whose breeding plumage is red while the non-breeding plumage is green.

In small birds the process of becoming adult may be a rapid one, but even in these the first winter plumage, though in some species similar to the adult's, as in sparrows, may be quite different from the adult breeding male's, as in many wood warblers.

In larger birds the adult plumage may be acquired quickly, as in the mallard drake, which changes from a first plumage similar to that of the female directly to the adult breeding plumage. However, in the gannet and some eagles, there is a succession of immature plumages over some years before the adult plumage is achieved.

In the adult American bald eagle the head and tail are white, while in the young these parts are blackish brown, like the rest of the plumage. When a very young bird was brought to the Bronx Zoo in New York, Dr Lee S. Crandall, curator of birds there, had the opportunity to follow the changes in colour with each succeeding annual moult.[13] When the bird was three years old its head and neck were blotched with white and its tail feathers with grey. When the bird was five, the head and neck were all white, as in the adult, but the tail, though largely white, was still heavily blotched with blackish brown. Not until the eagle was ten years old were the new tail feathers all white, so that the bird was in completely adult dress.

In their early stages precocial young, active from hatching, are thickly covered with natal down; a few, such as divers, have two successive coats of down. In gallinaceous birds the flight quills develop early in life while the body is still downy and there is a quick replacement of quills at the post-juvenal moult. In gulls, among others, the first wing quills are worn during the first winter.

Noteworthy is the fact that in ducks, some rails, cranes, and divers the flight feathers are shed all at one time and grow in all at once, an arrangement only possible for water- and marsh-birds that can get along for a time without flying.

Penguins are perhaps the only birds which are immobilized by their moult.[14] In Antarctica the emperor penguin fasts during the three weeks or more that it takes to renew its feathers. During this time it stands on the ice and the new growing feathers push out the old ones, which finally come away in big patches.

While feathers are retained by most birds for a year at the longest, there is some evidence that the golden eagle may moult only part of its body plumage each year, thus keeping some of its feathers for two years.[15] An Oriental hornbill (*Rhinoplax vigil*), with a pair of extremely long central tail feathers, moults them alternately, one every other year.[16]

The development of ways to replace feathers once a year or oftener with the least risk of inconvenience to the species has provided ample scope for the operation of natural selection. The more obvious critical times for the bird are the breeding and nesting season, the migratory periods in spring and autumn, and the cold winter. Thus timing of the moults may be influenced, directly or indirectly, by all the factors that influence breeding or migration. In part, feather growth and colour are fixed and inherited; in part they are under the influence of hormones and physiological processes controlled by many external factors. To add to the complexity, there are such contingencies as severe climatic conditions of drought or cold and the abrasive action of the vegetation in the habitat; these also are factors in selection. Small wonder that, looked at the world over, the moult patterns which have evolved present a wealth of diversity.

CHAPTER 19

Flight, Walking, and Swimming

FLIGHT is one of the most distinctive attributes of birds and has been a major factor in shaping the course of their evolution. It has made it possible for them to exploit freely habitats little used by other vertebrates, such as the open air and the tips of branches. It has enabled them to colonize widely, even on far-distant islands, and to develop migration on an unprecedented scale, so that seasonally favourable habitats can be occupied on a part-time basis. Flight, facilitating quick movement away from an enemy, has allowed birds to substitute distance for concealment, and to become bright-coloured, noisy, and conspicuous.

However, birds as a group would have been much less successful if they had not also retained the efficient use of their legs. There are birds that have over-specialized for flight and have legs of use for little beyond perching, like swifts and frigate birds, and there are birds that have lost their power of flight, like some rails and the ostrich-like birds. But the common birds which occupy most of the available habitats utilize their wings and their legs alternately for locomotion. Thus they share in two worlds: the world of air and the world of land or of water. Accordingly, the wing must be limited in its development to a size that can fold up neatly.

Birds fly by flapping their wings, which are powered by the great breast muscles. The downward beat of the spread wing is the power stroke, giving both upward lift and forward thrust; however, some forward thrust may be added by the flick of the outer wing quills during the upstroke, or recovery stroke, made with partly flexed wing. The muscles which power the wings compose about twenty per cent of the weight of many birds, and in most species the muscles that power the down-stroke are about ten times as large as those that power the up-stroke, perhaps an indication of the relative role, in general, of each in propulsion.[1]

The flying bird, with its streamlined shape and its wings, invites comparison with the aeroplane, but there is a big differ-ence. In the aeroplane the wings supply the lift only, and the propellor or jet provides the thrust.[2]

The aerodynamics of flight is very complicated, but as Oskar and Katharina Heinroth of the Berlin Zoo point out in their charming little book, *The Birds*,[3] one can see how lift operates by putting a hand out of the window of a moving car. The flat hand, tilted upward in front to meet the current of passing air, is pushed upward. The faster the forward movement, the stronger the lift. A paper kite on a string keeps aloft in much the same way on a windy day; the wind substitutes for forward movement as the source of a moving stream of air. A gliding bird acts much like a glider. In still air it loses altitude in order to maintain enough speed to achieve the lift necessary for staying in the air. By taking advantage of thermal up-draughts rising from heated ground, and of up-currents of air caused by winds deflected by waves and hills, birds such as vultures and albatrosses can glide for hours.

In flapping flight the basal part of the wing, which moves relatively little, provides most of the lift, and the wing tip, which moves most, provides the thrust. Thus the bird's wing has the functions of both the wing and the propellor of an aeroplane. There are many delicate adjustments in the structure of the bird's wing that the aircraft designer recognizes: the curved rather than flat wing surface to promote air flow and give added lift; the jagged tips of the wings – caused by the spread of the tips of the primaries and augmented in some birds by emarginated quill tips – which reduce turbulence; and the alula, consisting of the feathers on the 'thumb', that can be moved to open or close a gap, comparable to the slot in an aeroplane wing, and as useful in controlling flight.

Some experimental aircraft have been designed with wings capable of major adjustments, but the adjustments possible in the standard aircraft's wings are small indeed compared with those possible in a bird's wing. There is the major adjustment accomplished by flexing the whole wing on the joints in the skeleton, so that an eagle can soar on fully extended wings and then, with wings partly closed, can plunge earthward. There are also minor adjustments, made by the movements of the individual flight feathers. Watching a bird gliding on nearly motionless wings, such as a gull or an albatross riding the up-draught over the stern of a ship, one can see the continued adjustment of the quills and wings to varying air currents, adjustment quite impossible with the rigid wing and body of an aircraft. The function of the tail, presumably, is to steer. Many of the most aerial of birds, such as the swifts and the albatrosses, have short tails, but tails are so variable in other birds that one is forced to conclude that their size and shape are not rigidly controlled by the needs of flight.

The shape of the wing correlates with the type of flight, though it must be repeated that in most birds flying is an alternative way of getting about. Even flying may be used for different purposes – hurrying, cruising, landing, taking off, and manoeuvring. Some birds make display flights. Even the fastest and most aerial of birds, the swifts, falcons, and doves, have more than one type of flight. The following generalizations simply indicate some of the extremes in shape in a bird's wings.

A long, broad wing may be correlated with soaring, as in vultures, eagles, and storks, and may also be associated with slow, measured flight, as in pelicans, herons, and hornbills. Very long, narrow wings are correlated with sailing, as in the albatross and the gulls. Long, pointed wings are correlated with a great deal of rapid flying, as in swallows, falcons, and some waders. Moderately short, pointed wings may be correlated with direct, rapid movement from one place to another, as in ducks. Short, rounded wings are usually an indication of short, slow flights from place to place, as in many song-birds and in partridge, in which flapping often alternates with gliding.

The role of the tail in flight is less clearly evident, as we have mentioned, and birds seem to get along with a variety of types. Certain forest-hunting hawks have a long tail that would seem of value as a rudder for manoeuvring in confined woodland spaces; certain birds that have long, pointed wings and do much manoeuvring on the wing in the open seem to be

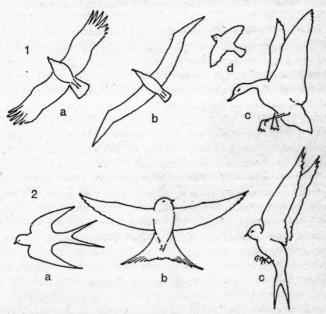

Figure 39. (1) *Types of bird wings:* (a) *long and broad (vulture),* (b) *long and narrow (albatross),* (c) *short and pointed (duck),* (d) *short and broad (song-bird).*

(2) *Different poses of same bird in flight: a swallow* (a) *gliding on partly closed wings,* (b) *with wings fully extended and tail spread,* (c) *coming in to a landing.*

served to advantage by a deeply forked tail that provides a long steering organ with a comparatively small surface. Among these birds are swallows, red kites, and frigate birds. However, certain birds that spend much of their time on the ground or in the shrubbery, among them coucals and some of the pheasants, have very long tails, while others, such as pittas and quail, have very short ones. The scissor-tailed fly-catcher, with elongated outer tail feathers, feeds much as does its relative the king-bird, with its square tail. Hence one may conclude that the exact size and shape of the tail are less correlated with locomotion than are the size and shape of wings and feet.

As birds become larger, if all their parts grow proportionately, the addition in wing length is linear, while the wing area increases as the square and body weight increases as the cube. If growth continued, sooner or later the limbs would be unable to support the weight; this fact may be the controlling factor in limiting the increase in size of birds.[4]

Among existing birds, the behaviour of the individual species, and the type and function of its flight, have had a profound effect in evolving wing–weight relationships. Birds that feed by walking or swimming have much shorter wings in relation to their weight than do those that feed on the wing, in the air, as the figures (from various sources) show (Table VIII).

The same type of relationship is apparent when one compares the wing load of a duck, which flies with small, fast-beating wings, with that of a gull, which floats along easily with long, slow-moving wings. The duck's wing has a load of 2·6 pounds per square foot, while the gull has a wing load of 0·8 pounds per square foot.

TABLE VIII

Wing Size and Feeding Methods

Bird	Method of Feeding	Wing Length (millimetres)	Weight (grammes)
Pied-billed grebe	feeds by swimming	130	343
Grackle	feeds on foot, but flies freely	142	122
Martin	feeds on the wing	144	43
Leach's petrel	feeds on the wing	157	26

TABLE IX

Wing Length and Wing Beat

Bird	Wing Length (millimetres) (wrist to tip)	Wing Beat (times per second)
Small humming-birds	33–54	38–78
Large humming-birds	65–88	18–28
Chickadees	65–82	22–24
Thrushes	125	6
Crows	325	3·6

The frequency of wing beats during flapping flight has a basic correlation with wing length.[5] It is highest in small birds, lowest in large ones (Table IX).

Variation in the shape of wing and relative body weight, however, prevents any close correlation between wing length and wing beat. For instance, the coot with broad wings and relatively heavy body beats its wings at an average of 5·8 beats per second, while a plover with a similar wing length but with a much lighter body and narrower, more pointed wings beats them at an average of 2·3 beats per second. These figures are for flapping flight, which small humming-birds use all the time; many small birds flap a few times and then glide, and soaring birds may sail without perceptible wing strokes for long periods.

The speed at which birds fly varies from that of the humming-bird hovering in one place and then slowly moving forward into a flower to that of a racing pigeon flying at 94·3 miles an hour.[6] There has been much written about even greater speeds: Indian spine-tailed swifts flying 200 miles an hour in level flight; frigate birds flying 261 miles an hour in level flight; the peregrine reaching 360 miles an hour in a dive; and a golden eagle getting up to 570 miles an hour in its dive, but none of these records is acceptable by modern standards.

Ground speed of birds is not the same thing as air speed, the rate at which the bird is actually going through the air. A herring gull flying with a strong wind may have a ground speed of 60 miles an hour, double its air speed, while if it were flying against this same wind, its progress might be near zero. Col. Meinertzhagen, who made a recent survey of bird speeds, watched an eider duck trying to fly away from him into a heavy gale.[7] The eider has a maximum air speed of about 55 miles an hour, but in this gale it drifted downwind, approaching Meinertzhagen as it tried to fly away.

Birds that swoop on flying prey, like the peregrine, can undoubtedly increase their speed above that of their cruising rate, though it is very doubtful that a golden eagle, which ordinarily does not reach 60 miles an hour, can actually speed up to 570 miles an hour in a mile-long dive.[8] However, whether a bird in level flight is actually doing its best also makes a difference. A crow in India that cruised at 25 miles an hour in the shelter of trees speeded up to 35 miles an hour when it was crossing open fields and attack was likely. King-birds are recorded as making only 11 to 15 miles an hour, but I have seen one overtake and strike a fleeing American crow that was certainly doing more than the 26 miles an hour usually credited to it.

Birds in level flight seem to have a 'normal' cruising speed and an accelerated migration speed, the latter also being used when the birds are going to roost. Starlings have been recorded as cruising at 28 miles an hour and flying to roost at 47 miles an hour, while the corresponding figures for ravens are 22 and 37 miles an hour.

The following are some general estimates of the speed of birds in calm air in level flight:

10–20 miles an hour – many small perching birds (e.g., sparrows, wrens, cat-birds, fly-catchers)

20–30 miles an hour – many medium-sized birds (e.g., American robins, grackles, meadowlarks) and some larger, broad-winged birds (e.g., herons, pelicans, gulls)

30–40 miles an hour – many small and medium-sized birds (e.g., starlings, chimney swifts, flickers, mourning doves)

40–60 miles an hour – the faster-flying birds (e.g., falcons, ducks, geese, rock doves)

There are birds which probably spend month after month in a few acres of land, where their daily rounds require very few miles of flying; certain birds, such as rails and grebes, may not fly at all on some days. On the other hand, such birds as swallows and kites, which feed in the air or search the ground while in flight, may spend much of their day on the wing. The aerial-feeding swifts in particular certainly cover many miles in a matter of minutes. That superb flyer, the bateleur eagle of Africa, is said to survey a territory of 250 square miles daily.[9] The great blue herons and white pelicans nesting on islands in the Great Salt Lake, which because of its salinity is fishless, must fly daily to fishing waters some forty miles away.[10]

A particularly interesting instance of long flights to feeding grounds was discovered by the British naturalist R. M. Lockley, who has a special interest in North Atlantic sea birds.[11] When studying the Manx shearwaters that nest on the island of Skokholm, off the coast of Wales, he marked breeding birds with numbered rings. He found that some of these were being killed during the breeding season by Spaniards in the southern part of the Bay of Biscay. Apparently the individuals of a pair take turns at the nest, remaining there from three to five days at a time. While one bird stays at the nest, fasting, the other is away at sea, feeding, and may go as far as six hundred miles from its nest.

When migration time comes to the northern latitudes, many small birds may fly from Canada to South America or from northern Europe to South Africa. We have already mentioned the distance some migrating birds have been known to fly, including the common crossing by small birds of five hundred miles of water in a single flight.[12]

The plasticity of avian characters is well shown by the loss of flight in eight major groups of modern birds, i.e., rails, cormorants, pigeons, grebes, ducks, penguins, auks, and also the ostrich-like birds. Flight, one of the most characteristic avian attributes, has thus been lost independently at least eight times. Presumably this loss is adaptive, and as in so many adaptations no one pattern fits all the instances. The most common pattern is exemplified by the rails. These are running, skulking birds, especially good at colonizing oceanic islands, and especially prone to becoming flightless in the isolation of these oceanic islands, where there are no mammal predators and where wandering flights are likely to end in disaster.

The single flightless cormorant of the Galápagos and the giant pigeons – the dodo and the solitaire of the eastern Mascarene islands – are, or were, all island birds. Two grebes – one (*Centropelma micropterum*) restricted to Lake Titicaca, Bolivia, in South America; the other (*Podilymbus gigas*), to Lake Atitlán, Guatemala, in Central America – may be considered as inhabiting 'water islands' on continents. But the flightless steamer duck lives on the South American coast alongside a close flying relative, and the great auk of the North Atlantic was apparently much like the other North American auks in its general habits and its range.

In none of the flightless birds just mentioned have body structures been greatly modified from what they are in the birds' flying relatives, except for the smaller size of wings and related flight muscles. Only two of them, the great auk and the dodo, were notably larger than their relatives, so only in these may size have been a factor in their becoming flightless.

The penguins, all flightless pelagic birds of the southern oceans that swim with their paddle-like wings, have no close relatives; their life is much like that of the great auk, which they superficially resemble. The ostrich, rhea, emu, and cassowary are all very large running birds of the continents, and the ostrich lives where mammal predators like the lion and the leopard are common. They have no close relatives, and their structural modifications include not only the reduction in wing size, but also the disappearance of their breast muscles and the heavy bony braces for muscle attachment. One wonders if perhaps their flightlessness evolved because they grew too big to fly and were able to survive because they were large, watchful, and fleet of foot. Certainly in different places similar results arose from different causes.

Just as there are birds with very small wings, useless in locomotion, so there are birds with superb powers of flight which have small feet ineffective for locomotion and useful for little but perching. These include the humming-birds, the swifts, and the frigate birds. But most flying birds have retained considerable powers of bipedal locomotion, and some, such as the mallard duck, are equally at home flying in the air, walking on the

land, and swimming in the water. Just as some of the best
flying birds can use their feet very little, so some of the most
expert swimmers, the grebes and divers, can barely shuffle along
on the land. One would not expect land birds to swim, but it is
surprising what unlikely ones can occasionally do so; even
cassowaries swim across wide rivers in their swampy habitat.
The flightless cassowary has an extra handicap in swimming,
for unlike most birds, whose specific gravity is lighter than
water, the cassowary's is not; when it stops paddling, it sinks.

The lightness of a bird's body must be overcome when it
dives. This is no problem for birds, such as terns and kingfishers, that barely go below the surface for their food, for the
momentum of their plunge carries them far enough. But the
gannets and boobies that go deeper may start their dives a
hundred or two hundred feet in the air and send up a striking
splash of water as they disappear. So great is the force with
which gannets dive, that – it is said – they used to be captured
by attaching a fish to a water-logged floating plank. When the
bird dived at it, it broke its neck.

Underwater swimming probably is accompanied by a voluntary increase of the bird's specific gravity. One can see this
reduction of buoyancy by watching a pied-billed grebe on a
pond. At rest, the grebe's body is a plump oval, floating lightly.
But when the bird is alarmed, the oval decreases in width as the
feathers are pressed close against the body, expelling the air
from the plumage and perhaps from the air sacs too, and the
bird gradually sinks until only the head is above the water.
Then this is pulled down and the bird is gone. More often,
swimming and diving birds simply duck their heads into the
water and with thrusts of their feet force themselves down at an
angle. However, some, such as mergansers, may at times leap
clear of the water in diving.

Many dabbling ducks that are quite able to dive – as indeed
they demonstrate when crippled by a gunner – rarely do so, but
feed underwater by reaching down with their long necks. They
may extend their reach by 'tipping up' so that only the tail, the
rear part of the body, and occasionally the kicking feet, are
above the surface as the birds grub on the bottom of a shallow

pond. Other ducks, like the scoters, dive to the bottom for shell-fish; while cormorants, divers, auks, and penguins pursue their prey through the water. Our records of the extreme depths to which birds dive are rather unsatisfactory, for they are obtained by noting the depths at which birds are caught in nets or on fish-lines.[13] Such records indicate that divers may dive to two hundred feet, while ducks, cormorants, gannets and grebes have been found at depths exceeding seventy-five feet. But the dives of most birds probably take them only a few yards below the surface and do not last more than a minute. It is probable that additional oxygen in the blood (more than in non-diving birds' blood) and possibly a circulation of air back and forth through the lungs and air sacs may be adaptations for underwater swimming, when breathing is not possible.

Swimming speed has been measured for some birds. Certain penguins swim at twenty miles an hour, and the five-foot vertical leaps they make from the water on to the edge of floating ice are visual demonstrations of the speed they can attain.[14] Penguins swim with their wings, as do the auks, but more commonly swimming is done with the feet, these being webbed or lobed. However, gallinules, which swim regularly, have neither webs nor lobes, and dippers, which are song-birds of streams and ponds, feed under water although their feet are as unspecialized as a robin's.

Some birds swim by striking out with both feet at once, while others use them alternately. This alternation is easily seen when a canvas-back duck takes a running start off the water to become airborne, while the cormorant does the same thing with both feet striking at once. These are the aquatic equivalents of the running and hopping of land birds.

Hopping seems adapted to a life among swaying, uncertain branches and twigs, while walking or running seems better suited to a terrestrial existence, where the footing is more solid. But parrots – predominantly tree birds – walk, and some song-birds that feed commonly on the ground hop, while others walk. The American robin on a lawn does both.

Penguins, birds of the southern oceans, have two odd ways of locomotion.[15] Birds of this Antarctic group crossing snow fields on the way to their nesting grounds may abandon their upright walking pose and toboggan along on their breasts, using both wings and legs to get up a speed of as much as ten miles an hour. Later, when the breeding season is over and the ice is breaking loose, some of the penguins move up to the edge of the water, and when the floes break loose and drift north, the penguins ride on them in the start of their northward migration.

CHAPTER 20

Voice and Display

BIRDS, like humans, communicate by vocal and visual signals. Man has developed a language in which complicated abstract ideas can be expressed, but even civilized man of the cities still uses simple signals, such as the policeman's upheld hand that stops traffic at street intersections, and the short 'hi' or 'hello' with which old friends greet each other. Birds, at a pre-lingual stage, have evolved auditory and visual signals that are standardized and current through a species. These were developed from more primitive sounds such as squawks of alarm and from movements such as those made just before fleeing or going to feed.

In some ways the methods of bird communications can be compared to the sign language and the sounds indicating pleasure and alarm used by travellers in communicating with people whose language they do not know. By gauging the emotional content of the voice and by seeing what actions follow certain signs and sounds, one can build up a basic vocabulary. But the situation must be played by ear and the signs interpreted by context. A snap of the fingers by the side of the head, indicating the release of a bowstring, may signify that the speaker shot the bird lying in front of the traveller, or may have reference to a planned attack on a neighbouring village, in which aid is being sought.

Birds too may use similar sounds and signs in different circumstances. In my garden one morning a cat-bird gave a cry of distress because a cat was prowling the shrubbery for the short-tailed young hidden there. Later in the day it gave a similar call when it could not find the apple from which it had been taking pieces to feed its young. (The apple had fallen to the ground in the bird's absence.) In each case the bird was disturbed and indicated its disturbance in much the same way, but the reasons for its distress were different in each instance.

A display too may be used in a variety of situations. A common type of display among birds is the fluttering of partly open wings. This is used by the young bird in begging, by the adult in ritualized courtship feeding, and by the female in soliciting mating and in feigning injury.[1]

Some years ago a discussion arose in ornithological circles when it became known that the glossy cuckoos of Africa (genus *Chrysococcyx*) sometimes fed their young when they were out of the nest.[2] These cuckoos are parasitic, laying their eggs in other birds' nests, and the young are raised by foster parents. At first this feeding of the young by a social parasite was thought to be atavistic behaviour, a left-over piece of the cycle of normal care of egg and young that was otherwise lost in the species. But more likely, as was soon pointed out, these cuckoos, which practise courtship feeding, mistook the well-grown begging young for potential complaisant mates. In interpreting the signal system of birds, one must be continually aware that the same signal may be used for different things, and different signals for the same thing.

Vocal and visual signals are alternative methods of communication, and most birds use both to some extent. A bird that sights a stalking cat may raise its head, chirp, and flit its wings, before it actually flies. Both the call and the intention movements help to tell its neighbours that danger is near.

A gaudy displaying bird of paradise announces its presence with loud, ringing calls that carry through the forest far beyond the distance from which the display can be seen. In general, where display is highly developed, the sounds that call attention to it are simple even if loud. On the other hand, in species with elaborate songs, the displays are simple. By and large, loud noises and songs are more characteristic of birds of the denser

vegetation, where visibility is limited. Birds of the open country
with good song may sing in flight, however, and this flying may
be considered a form of display since it makes the bird conspicuous.

Both song and display reach their most complex development
in relation to pair formation and nesting. They have developed
differently in each species to prevent mismating. The male is
ordinarily the songster or the displaying partner. But among
some song-birds the female sometimes sings with her mate,[3] and
among some other species, such as grebes, both sexes may join
in mutual displays.[4]

In the family life of parents and young some special signals
are required for communication between them with respect to
feeding and danger from enemies. It is because these tend to be
less specific than the signals connected with mating that social
parasites are able to leave their young to the care of foster
parents.

As most birds are social, to some degree, for at least part of
the year, there must be continual social communication. At
its simplest this may be achieved through the call notes that
locae birds in the shrubbery or the movements seen in more
open country, or through the squawk of alarm or the rattling
of quills as a bird flies to escape a predator. These signals are
often understood not only within a species but by other species.
This mutual understanding is indicated by the cohesion of the
big, mixed flocks so characteristic of tropical forests, mentioned earlier, and by the way in which the wintering flocks of
icterid blackbirds – which often consist of grackles, red-wings,
and cow-birds, and perhaps also starlings, which are not blackbirds, but are somewhat similar in appearance and habits –
keep and move together. It is also evident in the way that a
scolding tattler or spur-winged plover, seeing a hunter approach,
may rouse all the game birds in a marsh with its calls.[5]

That bird voices may be interpreted correctly by animals
other than the birds themselves is often demonstrated. For example, on the plains of Alberta I saw a coyote that was successfully hunting a scattered brood of young sharp-tailed grouse by
heeding their location calls.

No two people classify bird sounds and signals alike. In attempting refinements, one soon encounters bewildering complexities. Dr A. A. Saunders of Canaan, Connecticut, who has a remarkably keen ear and has spent a lifetime studying bird song in the United States, writes that no two individual birds sing exactly alike and each individual bird sings differently from time to time.[6] In his opinion, the song sparrow (*Melospiza melodia*) shows these two types of variation more obviously than any other bird. This sparrow's song consists of strongly rhythmic introductory notes, a central trill, and a final series of rather irregular and indefinite notes. A single song sparrow may sing from six to twenty-four different songs.

In classifying 884 recorded song-sparrow songs, no two of which are alike, Saunders groups them into five types, two of which are further subdivided into eight sub-types each. In addition there are eight 'irregular' songs that do not fit into the classifications. The songs vary in length, rhythm, pitch, intensity, quality, nature of consonant sounds, and number of component parts. Yet rarely is one in doubt about what species is singing.

Bird voices may vary not only individually, but also geographically. In the same study Dr Saunders found that a few song sparrows living along the Allegheny River within a half mile of Quaker Bridge, New York, all sang with characteristic downward slurs, rare in the song sparrow. However, an African study made by C. W. Benson, officer of the Department of Game and Fisheries of Northern Rhodesia, reports a more comprehensive comparison of the songs of birds in eastern Africa, from Ethiopia to South Africa.[7] He found 176 species without voice variation and only 33 instances of variation, most of them slight. Perhaps the smallness of geographical variation, rather than its existence, is the important point. Voice would seem to be no more variable than plumage.

While bird song serves only a few main functions – to announce the presence of the bird, its sex, its emotional state or physiological condition, and perhaps its individuality – call notes serve a much wider range of uses.[8] Dr W. H. Thorpe, reader in Animal Behaviour at Cambridge University, the foremost English student of bird song, divides functional call notes into ten groups: pleasure calls, distress calls, territorial-defence calls, flight calls, feeding calls, nest calls, flock calls, aggression calls, general alarm calls, and specialized alarm calls, such as those for terrestrial and those for aerial enemies.[9]

In commenting on various sounds and displays of birds I am using the following classifications. Not infrequently the behaviour under discussion has been referred to in other sections of this volume, where it is discussed in context, while here it is presented as an aspect of display or song.

   I. Visual signals
     A. Intention movements
     B. Displays
       1. Miscellaneous
       2. Ritualized fighting
       3. Courtship and mating
  II. Mechanical sounds
     A. Miscellaneous
     B. Courtship and mating
 III. Voice
     A. Expressions of well-being
     B. Expressions of alarm and distress
     C. Location and directional calls
     D. Song

Intention movements are the many small movements that a bird may make as a preliminary to action, such as the stretching up of the head or the flick of a wing preparatory to flight. Gregarious birds, which are continually being influenced by what their flock mates are doing, are quick to use such movements as signals. The speed with which they can respond to visual cues is nowhere more apparent than in flocks of sandpipers that wheel and swirl in unison, the birds in the rear apparently taking their cues from the birds in front.

Special display poses are used to convey special information in a variety of situations. Often they involve some motions, as in the feigning of injury, or in the begging-to-be-fed posture of young birds, and in the spreading of wings and erecting of feathers to indicate readiness to fight, which can be called an intimidation display.

Ritualized fighting often replaces actual combat as a means of repelling rival males at breeding time, and along with singing, it may be used to defend territory limits. Of course, actual fighting may occur too; the spurs on screamers' wings and on the legs of pheasants have been developed for real combat.

Display in birds reaches its height during courtship and varies greatly from group to group. In a grackle it consists of a simple fluffing out of the feathers as the bird forces out its rusty squeals. Specialized plumes of various kinds are seen in herons and grebes; these are present in both sexes and are used in mutual displays. But the greatest development of ornamental plumes is seen in such birds as pheasants and birds of paradise, which are polygamous and characterized by a strong sexual dimorphism. Among the pheasants ornamentation includes the elongated upper tail coverts which constitute the eyed train opening into the fan of the peacock; the elongated, eyed, inner secondaries of the argus pheasant; and the colourful capes, hackles, and wattles of a number of others. Among the birds of paradise are many elongated plumes, some wire-like, with iridescent 'flags', and some brightly coloured and forming capes, breast shields, flank tufts, breast tufts, and strangely shaped tails.

The birds have developed unusual postures to display these plumes to best advantage, the strangest being the upside-down, hanging pose of the blue bird of paradise, which allows the long, lacy, blue flank plumes to fall away at each side to frame a red and black area on the body. Many of the extravagant displays come to a climax in a frozen pose as the splendour is presented to the female. But in other species the climax of the display is a dance, performed singly or in parties depending on the species.[10] Special display areas are used, and some of the birds, such as the magnificent bird of paradise, clear them of vegetation for this purpose.

But dances and displays are not restricted to species with prominent plumes or sexual dimorphism. Some of the polygamous grouse that have only slight sexual dimorphism perform elaborate dances, motion largely replacing plumage decoration as the focus of the display, and the polygamous bower-birds, with little or no sexual dimorphism, have substituted a decorated display area, where they dance, for decorated plumage. Mutual display by monogamous birds finds its parallel in the mutual dance of monogamous, plain-coloured species, such as the bouncing dance of the cranes.

Though birds in general are the most vocal of animals, some groups, such as storks, pelicans, and vultures, are nearly or entirely voiceless. The storks compensate in part by making loud, clattering noises with their bills; owls, which do have good voices, also snap their bills and hiss when they are giving their intimidation displays. Also, the swishing and clattering noises of birds' wings in flight constitute mechanical sounds that can convey information. But the most elaborate and conspicuous mechanical sounds have been developed in connection with courtship. The rolling tattoo of the woodpecker has almost completely replaced its song, although the bird has quite a good voice. It produces this drumming by pounding rapidly on a resonant piece of wood with the bill. Though an unlikely way of making a 'song', the drumming is a logical outcome of the bird's way of feeding and the sound is quite as conspicuous as a vocal song, and serves the same purpose.

The male ruffed grouse has a different way of drumming. He stands upright on a log and beats the air with his wings. At the start the individual thumps are distinctly audible, but they soon quicken and merge into a continuous drumming sound. This practice fits into a courtship pattern quite different from that of the woodpecker, for it is used to announce the mating station to which the female grouse will come.

Other mechanical sounds used in courtship are the rustling and whistling of wings, the rattling of quills by the peacock when he has spread his train, the snap of the manakin's wing quills, the boom from the neck pouches and the stamping of feet of the prairie chicken, and the bleating noise made by the

Figure 40. *Some types of display:* (a) *red-winged blackbird,* (b) *frigate bird,* (c) *blue bird of paradise,* (d) *king-bird of paradise,* (e) *turkey,* (f) *bower-bird.*

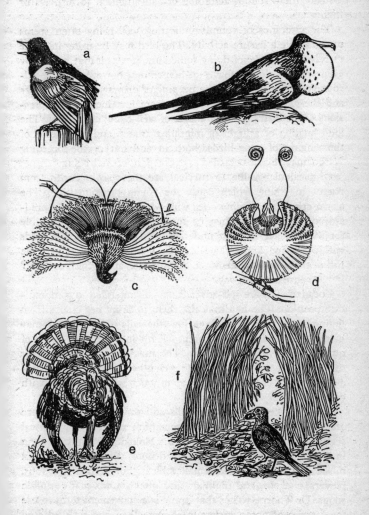

air going through the tail feathers of a snipe in courtship flight. Usually these sounds reinforce or call attention to displays or flights.

The utterance of sounds indicating well-being often seems to constitute a leisure activity. The bird may be using its voice merely for the sake of doing something, just as it may hop or fly even when it doesn't have to. Sometimes, however, contented-sounding noises, such as the peeping of drowsy, well-fed chicks and the gabbling of feeding ducks, are just incidental expressions of the bird's sense of a state of well-being or comfort. The loud bugling of a flight of migrating cranes, and even some of the singing of song-birds, both in and out of the breeding season, may also be regarded as expressions of well-being.

Of particular value to survival are the warning cries from parent to young which cause the young birds to hide. The alarm cries and scolding cries with which a wren greets a predator, or the jay an owl, may be important in making it impossible for the attacker to hunt undetected in the area. All the birds within hearing know that there is a predator about, and the racket they make as many of them gather and 'scold' or 'mob' it may cause it to go away.

Location calls are self-advertising calls intended to communicate position. The hen may use them to bring her chicks from hiding and gather them about her; the calls of a lost chick may help to reunite it with its parents. Birds in a scattered covey of quail often give rallying cries. The members of a mated pair may call back and forth to locate each other, and the members of a winter flock of forest birds keep in touch with each other with occasional calls.

Drawing the line between calls and song is difficult. There are melodious calls, and their repetition results in a musical series of sounds which may serve the biological function of song in courtship. In general, 'song' denotes the more complex musical utterances of the smaller birds, but certain tinamous, plovers, cuckoos, and nightjars also utter sounds that resemble songs. Dr Thorpe writes that 'song' is a convenient term to use for a series of notes, generally of more than one type, uttered in succession and forming a discernible pattern.[11] This is perhaps the most nearly objective definition one can employ. We have discussed song's biological function in courtship, and here we will pay particular attention to its relation to music, as explored by Dr Charles Hartshorne, former professor of philosophy at the University of Chicago.[12]

If the 'melodious, musical and beautiful' bird songs, some of which are found on every continent, are thought of as primitive music, an objective comparison is possible. Dr Hartshorne points out that the sounds constituting music consist predominantly of pure 'tones' each consisting of a single frequency or a frequency and its natural harmonics rather than a miscellaneous blend of frequencies. Birds utter both tones and noises but tones are more conspicuous in the better songs. Bird songs commonly include flute-like sounds, and there are also guitar-like, bell- or chime-like, and even organ-like tones.

Birds' notes are usually short, and in simple, less melodious songs are arranged into patterns, or phrases, which are repeated at intervals and with little variation hundreds or even thousands of times a day. More complicated and more musical songs involve variations in phrase and in their sequence, and the bird may sing a medley, sometimes including imitations of other birds' songs in a variable sequence of different songs. Singing of this sort is the most showy and attracts the most attention, as witness the reputation of the mocking-bird. This bird gives a wonderful performance, incorporating into its own song, among others, phrases borrowed from wood thrush, wren, and cardinal. But its brilliant performance is relatively loose, and has not the musically unified variation on a single pattern that characterizes the wonderful performance of the wood thrush itself.

Randomness or unpredictability in the arrangement of the phrases is also a factor in producing a highly rated song – the aesthetic principle of surprise and novelty. Hartshorne's example is the wood thrush, which has perhaps ten songs which can follow one another in ninety different combinations. The bird can produce scores of different contrasts in the course of a few minutes' singing.

Any really simple element of musical form can probably be illustrated in the singing of birds. Though simultaneous harmony or polyphony in bird music is meagre, some birds do sound two or more harmonious notes at once in a song.

We also have elementary rhythmic effects – *accelerando* in the field sparrow, *ritardando* in the yellow-billed cuckoo, *crescendo* in certain robin chats of Africa – as well as interval inversions, simple harmonic relations, changes of key, and themes with variations.

In one respect, Hartshorne finds the best bird music radically inferior to human music, and that is in the brief time span of each musical unit. Three seconds is perhaps average, six seconds long, and ten seconds extreme. Of course, some bird songs consist of a phrase that lasts for a minute or so, but these, like some insect songs, are patternless prolongations of a single sound, such as a trill, buzz, or whistle.

Bird song, according to Hartshorne, is usually intelligible as simple music. The birds that we consider the best songsters are those that put the most variety and complexity into the use of elementary musical devices. And the birds that we rate the best songsters are those that sing the most.

We must now examine this bird music against the biological background. How does it arise, and for what is it used?

Despite geographical and individual variation, the song of a species remains fairly constant over the breadth of a continent year after year. This is strong presumptive evidence that the song, like other species characters, is inherited.[13] Experimental work with young birds raised in sound-proof rooms indicates that in general the basic song, at least, is inherited. But the refinements of the song in some species seem to be acquired later, as the bird hears others of the species sing and works out the fine details in competitive singing with them.[14] Some species, brought up in isolation, may learn the songs of a strange species when opportunity offers. The European bullfinch is well known for this ability to learn different songs, and, more than most birds, can be taught various fancy songs, played on a special pipe, the bird flageolet.[15]

In the wild certain species may imitate strange songs and incorporate them into their repertoire. Notable for this are the mocking-bird of America and the lyre-bird of Australia. Yet, in hearing one of these singing, one is never deceived for long. The imitators are adding a variety and a distinctiveness to their own songs which make the singer unmistakably a mocking-bird or lyre-bird. Also, each singer tends to be individualistic; each song is surely that of one individual mocking-bird or lyre-bird. Both of these qualities are an advantage, the first in the life of the species, the second in the successful reproduction of the pair.

The imitation of human speech by 'talking' parrots and mynah birds in captivity seems to be in a different category.[16] There appears to be no use for such imitation in the life of the wild bird. The capacity is latent. In captivity it seems to be brought out by a relationship between a particular human and a bird. The suggestion has even been put forward that this relationship resembles that between the human mother and the child learning to talk.

While bird song developed in connection with courtship, where it has its main use, birds do sing outside the breeding season. It is possible that some of this singing is for social communication, but it is probable that much of it is leisure activity, carried on for its own sake. The bird is, in effect, playing with sounds. It is also practising, and here we may recall that the best songsters also sing most. Practice makes perfect. The similarity in musical content of the best bird song over the world suggests that a unifying principle exists. The most logical conclusion is that there is a measure of congruity between the bird's feeling for sound pattern and ours.

CHAPTER 21

Behaviour,
Instinctive
and Learnt

WHEN a young lapwing is following its parent and an enemy
approaches, the parent gives a warning cry and the young one
crouches motionless on the ground, beautifully camouflaged by
its colour and pattern. By repeated warnings the female may
keep the young one quiet for several hours. There is no learning
involved, nor any appreciation of the situation by the young
bird. Upon receiving a certain stimulus – the warning cry – the
chick uses an instinctive pattern of behaviour, as much inherited
as the pattern of the downy feathers, and together they give the
chick concealment.

Instinctive behaviour and the use of special equipment start
in the egg. As has already been pointed out, the twisting, turn-
ing young bird breaks the shell as it emerges, using a special
structure, the egg tooth, to cut the shell and a special muscle,
the hatching muscle, to force the tooth against the shell.[1] The
egg tooth is soon shed and the hatching muscle dwindles and
disappears. Here, at a critical time at the very start of the bird's
life, are a structure and a behaviour pattern that are transient,
used but once. They are essential for survival and are employed
before there is any possibility of learning. The behaviour is
timed by maturation alone and is independent of any external
stimuli.

Throughout the bird's life we find such inherited behaviour patterns operating; for some examples see Figure 41. Some of these in the early days of the bird depend in part on maturation of bone and muscle, in part on maturation of the nervous system. Some become evident when external stimuli trigger a related readiness to respond in the bird itself, as in its reaction to an enemy, in its daily feeding, and in its seasonal breeding (brought about on a longer rhythm by endocrine effects).

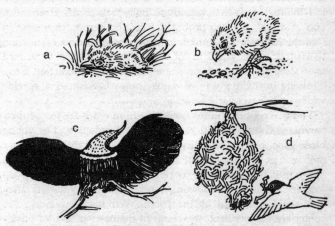

Figure 41. *Some instinctive behaviour patterns:* (a) *chick crouching motionless, freezing at the danger call of the parent;* (b) *young chick pecking at an object;* (c) *rifle-bird giving its stereotyped mating display;* (d) *weaver-bird building the complicated nest of its species.*

Since many, perhaps most, small birds live only a year or so and breed but once or twice, much of the bird's behaviour, especially that dealing with reproduction, must be instinctive. Without training and without experience, the Baltimore oriole of the United States, still less than a year old, makes a round-trip migration to Central America and then mates, builds a nest that is characteristic of the species, and raises a family.[2]

But despite all this unlearnt behaviour, the bird is no automaton. Its basic patterns may be set, but they can be varied and their use adapted to a wide variety of conditions. How else could the species survive in its diversified world?

The Baltimore oriole chooses a maple tree for its nest in Quebec, an elm in Maine, and a birch in Minnesota, and when poplars appeared on the plains of Alberta, following the settlements, the bird moved into them. For nest materials, it uses a variety of available fibres. Near human dwellings, string, bits of cloth, and horsehair are used, and in the south Spanish moss. The oriole eats a wide variety of food, from hairy caterpillars, leaf-mining insects, and snails to hollyhock seeds, green peas, and cherries, and also probes flowers for nectar. In winter in Central America this bird is common both in arid cactus and thorn-tree country and in lofty rain forests. At night the bird may sleep in tall grass or among the foliage of orange trees. Thus its instinctive way of doing things is adapted to a wide variety of materials and situations.

Young song-birds in the nest and just out of it are fed by their parents and a reciprocal recognition is instinctive. The young birds gape, open their bill wide, give a special call, and flutter their wings, and the parent bird thrusts food into the bill. As the young birds develop coordination they begin to pick up food for themselves, and soon, unless they are very hungry, they may avoid being fed by the parent. Within a few weeks the young are independent, the result of maturation both of physical equipment and of mental behaviour patterns.

But this change in behaviour can be indefinitely delayed even when the physical equipment develops normally, as I showed when working at the Archbold Biological Station in Florida.[3] I took four young loggerhead shrikes (Lanius ludovicianus) from the nest and raised them together, by hand, until they were twenty-one days old. At about this time they normally begin to change to self-feeding. Then I divided them into two lots, housed separately. The subsequent care of each lot was quite different. The first two birds had food before them constantly and hand feeding was discontinued as soon as possible. The second two birds were allowed no free food, and I fed them by placing pellets of food in their mouths.

There was a pronounced difference in the duration of infantile begging. The first two birds fed themselves well at the age of twenty-eight days, though they still begged when hungry. After the age of forty-five days they were never seen to beg. The second two birds, with no chance to feed themselves, did not try to pick up food from my fingers until they were thirty-nine days old.

One individual of each lot survived, and these two birds were kept under observation for about six months longer. When the experiment was terminated, the bird from the first lot had not begged for six months. The bird from the second lot, which had received excessive care, still begged for food, though it was able to feed itself. This was shown when it picked up some food that had been dropped accidentally on the floor of its cage. Abnormal excessive care had caused the delay in its attempts at self-feeding and had prevented the normal sequence of patterns.

This also happens occasionally in the wild. On an islet off Mexico where frigate birds nest, an adult of the species was found in good condition except for a withered wing. The frigate bird is a sea bird that flies out over the ocean to get its food of fish. But this bird evidently had never flown, and all of its life had retained its infantile method of begging for food, depending successfully on the bounty of its fellows.[4]

In interpreting changes in the growing bird, the effects of maturation must be separated from the acquisition of skill through practice and learning. Some young birds, when the time approaches for leaving the nest, spend some time fanning the air with their wings. This activity could be interpreted as a way of practising coordination of the wings, in preparation for flying. However, when the birds actually make their first flight, they use their wings so differently that this explanation seems improbable. So, experimentally, some young pigeons were fitted with a harness that prevented their wing exercise in the nest.[5] The harness was removed at the time when the birds normally start to fly, and they flew as well as their fellows who had been allowed to exercise their wings.

That skill can be acquired with practice is shown in bird song. Some species, such as the chaffinch, inherit their basic type of song and with practice and imitation work out the adult pattern.[6]

Feeding and the avoidance of enemies are fundamental for survival and the activities involved are fairly standard. Indeed, there are only a few basic ways in which the bird can handle food (with its bill, sometimes aided by its feet) or escape its enemies (by flight and by concealment). But there is a wide range of objects to which it can respond, and here experience can play an important part.[7]

There may be an inherent tendency to feed on certain types of things, such as lizards, hairy caterpillars, or berries, or, more generally, moving things in the water. But when birds are hungry their preferences relax and they try all sorts of food until they find something that is suitable, even if they have to eat it in an unaccustomed way. Swallows prefer to eat flying insects which they catch on the wing, but in times of scarcity, tree swallows will feed on berries; American robins unsuccessfully hunting earthworms in the cold weather of early spring will eat bread crumbs or pieces of apple put out for them.

The role of learning in the development of birds' feeding

Figure 42. *A bird learns to eat palatable food in one dish and ignore ill-tasting food in the other.*

habits is most clearly shown in their use of the trial-and-error method to find out what things to eat and what things to avoid. I once raised a barred owl (*Strix varia*). One day when it was hungry I gave it a toad. The owl seized it in its feet, then took it into its mouth. A moment later the owl shook the toad out and then moved its head violently with evidence of distaste. There was no question of the nauseous quality of the toad's skin secretions. After that, the owl refused not only toads but good-tasting frogs which had similar appearance.

The kea parrot of New Zealand is an omnivorous bird, and earlier we pointed out that its hooked bill may be considered a pre-adaptation for preying on sheep (pp. 50–51). Here is an excellent example of trial-and-error learning leading to a new source of food. The kea parrot grubbed out roots and insects from clumps of moss, among other things. When sheep were introduced into New Zealand and skin, offal, and hides from slaughtered animals became available, some keas, probably through trial and error, tasted them and acquired a liking for the flesh and fat of dead sheep.[8] Eventually, these parrots learnt to perch on the backs of live sheep and tear through the skin to get at the flesh and fat, killing the sheep on which they fed. Apparently not all the keas did this; only some individuals learnt to secure this new food. In doing this they used the old way of feeding that had been successful in getting grubs from the ground.

In recent decades, as has been mentioned (p. 52), tits in Britain have learnt to open both cardboard-stoppered and metal-capped milk bottles left on the doorsteps and to drink the cream.[9] Once some birds learnt this habit, others in the same area did too, so that the habit spread quickly. These birds were able not only to learn to recognize the bottle and to open it, but also, it appears, to learn from one another.

A tit, nuthatch, or jay quickly learns to solve the problem of getting food that is suspended on a string below its perch by pulling up part of the string in its bill, holding this under one foot, and pulling up another length and holding it, until the food is within reach.[10] This manoeuvre is so well known that it is included in the repertoire of caged birds in

Figure 43. *A tit learns to pull up a container of food suspended by a string from its perch.*

the Orient. In the wild there seems to be no parallel to this method except for the bird's habit of holding food under its foot. Here, then, is a new way of getting food. Students of bird behaviour have even suggested that 'insight learning' is involved, for the bird seems to solve the problem without the laborious trial-and-error process. This same procedure almost qualifies as an example of tool-using as well.

The unequivocal use of a tool must be credited to the Galápagos woodpecker finch.[11] This bird feeds on insects that it finds in crevices in trees. Sometimes when the crevice is too narrow and too deep for the bird, it picks up a thorn, holds it in its bill, and employs it as a probe to get the insect out of the hole. (See Figure 13, Chapter 7.) The ontogeny of his tool-using has not yet been studied, and an investigation should yield results of great interest.

Detour problems set for birds by experimental biologists have resulted in very poor performances.[12] The domestic hen has demonstrated a lack of ability in this area, making repeated pecks at a piece of glass separating it from food instead of attempting to go round the glass. The significance of this inability in the life of the bird is doubtful.

The manner in which a bird learns its own territory so that

it can fly quickly with food to its nest when feeding its mate
or its young, even if the nest is not within sight, certainly
demonstrates an integration and reorganization of previous experience – learning of a sort. Apparently the results of this type
of learning can be retained for some time. Birds seem to have a
remarkably persistent memory of their precise wintering
grounds and breeding grounds and will return to the same spot,
garden, or clearing in the forest year after year. The bird's
knowledge of its home area, acquired by earlier learning, must
be of considerable value to it in finding food and in escaping
predators.

Birds have been considered lamentably lacking in the understanding of numbers. It is commonplace for a bird photographer
entering a hide to take a companion with him. When the
companion departs noisily the bird's suspicions seem to be
allayed. It is as though the birds are unable to count, and, seeing
one person leave, assume that both are gone.

Strangely, in view of this, birds score rather highly in tests
involving concepts of numbers. When a man counts objects –
one, two, three – he obviously needs names for the numbers.
But he can recognize the number of objects present, such as
marks on a cardboard, without counting by a sort of pre-
linguistic number sense. Many people can distinguish groups of
up to five units without counting; exceptional people can distinguish groups of up to eight. Birds can do about as well. In a
test a raven was presented with a card on which were a certain
number of spots and several boxes, each with a different number
of spots. The problem was to choose the box containing food –
the box which had the same number of spots as the card.[13] The
raven's score indicate a non-lingual number sense about equal
to that of many people. Perhaps there is great variation from
species to species in this ability.

Moreover, I have known duck shooters using decoys who
asserted that ducks could distinguish between more than
twenty-five or thirty and less than that number. They claimed
that a flock of more than thirty decoys was much more effective in attracting ducks than a flock of less than twenty-five.

The role of learning in the recognition of enemies by birds

Figure 44. *Koehler's experiment in which a raven learnt to select from a number of small food boxes the one marked with the same number of spots as appeared on a large card. This experiment demonstrates not only learning but also a pre-linguistic number sense.*

has also been investigated. In experimental work in Arizona, on the curve-billed thrasher, I found that a wide variety of objects larger than the thrasher, potential predators and otherwise, were ignored unless they were moved towards the bird.[14] Then it fled, showing alarm. Only snakes seemed to be objects of special interest, as if they were instinctively recognized as enemies.

Probably the general picture of enemy recognition is somewhat as follows: there is instinctive response to large or strange objects only if they move, except for a few cases in which owls or snakes are instinctively recognized as enemies. In general, birds have to learn not what to fear, but what not to fear – a form of habituation.

This habituation is well seen in the birds that come to a bird-table outside a window. In the early winter the chickadees, cardinals, and sparrows are shy. When a face appears at the window or a curtain is twitched, the birds fly up and away. But as the winter progresses the birds get used to being watched and learn to ignore the watchers. A similar habituation towards people is seen in the waterfowl that visit a city park in winter and learn to eat the bread thrown to them even though, some miles away, where they are shot at, they are very shy.

The learning by young birds of appropriate responses to both dangerous and safe situations can be facilitated by the behaviour of adult birds. Young American crows sitting in a tree or wrens in a bush are not alarmed by the approach of a man. But the parent bird that sees the man and sets up a cawing or a chattering and flies back and forth will soon influence the young birds to regard the intruder as an enemy and to flee from him, following the parent.

Old experienced ducks and geese that return year after year to the same sanctuaries along their migration routes and spend the winter in certain preserves bring young birds with them and thus teach them to stop in the safe places. So fixed are some of these routes that students have spoken of the 'traditions' of wildfowl [15] that govern some of their routes and stopping places.

The ability to profit by the experience of others was shown by the great flocks of crows that were destroying almond crops in the Pacific area.[16] The problem became so bad that poisoning was resorted to. Only a few birds were actually poisoned; the rest recognized that the area was dangerous to them when they saw the fate of some of their fellows, profited from the experience of the poisoned birds, and fled.

Quite evidently, the bird is in part little more than a reflex machine, responding blindly to stimuli. But birds can and do modify some of their behaviour in the light of their own experience, and they may even profit by the experience of others. That is to say, they have both instinctive and learnt behaviour.

The study of behaviour leads into the fields of psychology, physiology, and philosophy, and to special schools of each.[17] Discussions within these disciplines concern what goes on inside the bird and its brain, as well as how the external stimuli can set the responses in motion, and they deal with such central themes in biology as purposiveness and directiveness – meanings in their widest sense.

But in considering much of bird behaviour certain subjective interpretations seem to fit. The exploring jay seems to have 'curiosity'; 'fear' would seem to be the motivation in enemy avoidance, and 'anger' or 'pugnacity' would seem best to describe the vicious attacks of one woodpecker on another. Sometimes the drives spoken of by the psychologist seem synonymous with the 'moods' and even the 'emotions' of more general terminology. Often such terms, used as figures of speech, provide the best way to convey a description of what appears to be happening.

CHAPTER 22

Bird
Geography

As I remember it, the geography of my school days was filled with statements like 'Europe is bounded on the west by the Atlantic Ocean', 'The capital of Germany is Berlin', and 'The principal products of Barbados are sugar, rum, and molasses. The climate is mild and salubrious.' It seems a far cry from these to the zoo-geography, the animal geography, which I have studied in later years.

'Geography' is defined in Webster's *Third New International Dictionary* as 'a science that deals with the earth and its life; *esp:* the description of land, sea, air, and the distribution of plant and animal life including man and his industries with reference to the mutual relations of these diverse elements.'

The scope of geography is thus enormous, and for convenience the study has been broken down into subdivisions – for example, physical geography, political geography, military geography, plant geography (or phytogeography), and zoo-geography. Bird geography, a further subdivision of zoo-geography, is our present concern.

Even with the subject so restricted, the discussion must be severely limited to fit a single chapter. In brief, it deals with the major patterns revealed by a survey of the ranges of many species of birds, and the main evolutionary, environmental, and dispersal factors involved.

The major world patterns of land-bird distribution are correlated with the patterns of the continents.[1] Each continent has had enough isolation to allow the evolution in it of many species of birds, numerous endemic genera, and from one to thirty-one endemic families. This isolation has been provided mostly by the seas that separate the continents, but other physical, climatic, and related vegetational barriers have played a part. The Sahara Desert helps separate the African fauna from that of extreme northern Africa and Europe, and the Himalayas and the Tibetan highlands separate the tropical fauna of southern Asia from the more temperate fauna of the rest of Asia. Despite the barriers between them, each continent is near enough and accessible enough to another continent for some birds to have crossed to it, and, indeed, only in this way did the outlying continents receive any birds at all.

A speeded-up view of the rise and spread of the birds that gave us our present-day avifaunas might be somewhat as follows. Birds arose in the humid African–Indian tropics, which were at one time larger and more continuous than they are today. Wave after wave of newly evolved faunas spread out from this centre of origin. Some of them went to South Africa, which proved to

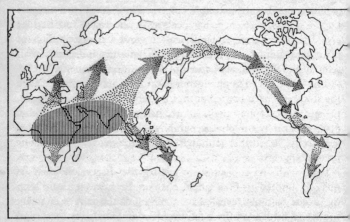

Figure 45. *The main routes of colonization taken by birds radiating from their presumed area of origin in the Old World tropics.*

be a dead end. Some went south and east across what is now the East Indian archipelago, helped at times by the fact that the islands now on the continental shelf as far as Java and Bali and including them were part of the continent of Asia. Beyond these, passage was more difficult, for it involved island-hopping across the Lesser Sundas and the Moluccas until the birds reached New Guinea and Australia. Here they evolved into the present-day faunas and even sent a few birds back along the route as far as southern Asia to recolonize. New Zealand, a thousand miles or so to the east of Australia, was so far away that only a smattering of birds at long irregular intervals arrived; there they evolved into a limited but very distinct fauna. The fauna also spilt over into the far-flung islands of the south-west Pacific.

Another route from the presumed tropical centre of distribution was northwards over Europe and Asia, for a time more or less cut up by the Tethys Sea, of which the Mediterranean is a remnant. There temperate and arctic conditions acted as a barrier to many of the diversified forms which had developed in the ancestral tropical forest. The birds that were able to survive and adjust formed a new centre of radiation, and their offspring carried on across the Bering Strait, aided occasionally by temporary land bridges. North America was so like Europe and northern Asia that little adaptation was necessary.

Then the route turned south to a new tropical area in Central and South America. The early arrivals found a land bridge all the way, and a new, mostly tropical continent open to them. Somewhat later the Central American area became an archipelago. This change gave South America and the islands of Central America the isolation necessary for the evolution of new types of birds. A rich avifauna developed, including many descendants of the primitive perching birds that were the early colonists. When the islands of the Central American archipelago merged into an isthmus again, forming a continuous land connection between the Americas, this tropical fauna sent colonists in numbers back north to flavour strongly the North American avifauna, and a very few groups sent colonists back along the invasion route into Eurasia.

We cannot prove that all this happened in quite this way, but this account agrees best with what we know about the geology of the world during the time birds were evolving. Basically it assumes that continents have retained much the same location, size, and shape over this period, except that the Tethys Sea at one time extended the Mediterranean, and there have been minor changes in Central America, the Bering Strait, and the east Indian archipelago. These changes increased the ease of dispersal at times and made it more difficult at others, but never created absolute barriers.

The effect of past barriers and colonization corridors on the fauna of an area is well shown by the comparison of an oceanic island with a continental island. The island of Madagascar is an oceanic island in the sense that it has had no land connection with a continent, since birds began to evolve, and all its birds arrived from overseas. The result is that the avifauna of Madagascar, which has an area of almost 230,000 square miles, is composed of less than two hundred species, a comparatively small number for a territory of this size. Most of these birds are derived from African forms, and a few come from Asiatic forms, but now many are very distinct. Other notable oceanic islands are New Zealand, the islands of Polynesia and Micronesia, the Galápagos Islands, and Tristan da Cunha.

On the other hand, the Greater Sunda Islands, which stand on the Sunda shelf, are continental islands. They were part of the Asiatic mainland as late as the Pleistocene, when the sea level was lower. One of these islands is Borneo, with an area of close to 290,000 square miles. The avifauna of Borneo, which includes more than four hundred species, is much richer than that of Madagascar but has comparatively few endemic genera and no endemic families. The land connection that allowed so many birds to colonize this island destroyed the isolation needed for endemics to arise, and Borneo has an Asian continental fauna. Some other well-known continental islands are New Guinea, the Japanese islands, the British Isles, Newfoundland, and Trinidad.

The fossil record of birds is insignificant compared with that of mammals and provides relatively little information for tracing phylogenies and dispersal routes.[2] But the summary just given accords fairly well with the picture of mammal spread and distribution based on a much better fossil record, and there is some avian palaeontological data to support this view of the movements and changes of the faunas. However, much of our reconstruction of the past must be deduced from the distribution patterns of present-day bird forms and the antiquity of the patterns as indicated by the distinctiveness of species, genera, and families comprising the faunas.

Because fossil birds are scarce, the fact that they do not occur in the geological deposits of an area cannot be taken to indicate that birds were non-existent there during the period in question. However, when fossil records are found they may give striking and unexpected evidence of the former occurrence of species or groups where they no longer occur. For example, the discovery of fossils has demonstrated the former presence of the California condor in eastern North America [3] and of the Old World vultures (a different group) in North America.[4] Even

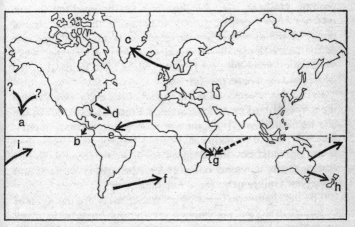

Figure 46. *Some minor routes of colonization over water to* (a) *the Hawaiian Islands,* (b) *the Galápagos Islands,* (c) *Greenland,* (d) *Bermuda,* (e) *South America,* (f) *Tristan da Cunha,* (g) *Madagascar,* (h) *New Zealand,* (i) *Pacific Islands.*

more striking is the recent finding of three species of fossil
flamingos in Australia,[5] since at present no species of flamingo
is found closer to Australia than India. Along with the spread
and dominance of one group, we may have the withdrawal and
disappearance of another. It is assumed that primitive non-
singing passerine groups were exterminated in the Old World,
except for a few relic groups, by the more recently evolved
dominant song-birds. Only in the isolation of South America
were the primitive passerine birds which had evolved earlier,
such as tyrant fly-catchers, oven-birds, and wood-hewers, able
to flourish and radiate, and now some of them have successfully invaded North America in competition with the more
advanced song-birds, as we have mentioned.

The capacity of birds to expand or contract their ranges is
evident even in records covering the short period since naturalists in eastern North America began keeping records of birds
seen. The early naturalists found the dickcissel, a sparrow of
the grasslands, common along the Atlantic coast from New
England to the Carolinas and west on to the prairies, but the
evening grosbeak, a seed-eating finch of the northern forests,
was not known east of the Great Lakes. With the passage of
the years the dickcissel has retreated westwards, until now east
of the Mississippi valley it is known only as a straggler, while
the evening grosbeak now regularly visits New England in the
winter and even nests that far east.

Even more spectacular is the spread of the cattle egret, which
used to be a bird of Africa, southern Europe, and Asia.[6] In the
late 1920s and early 1930s the species began to expand, colonizing west to South America and east to New Guinea. Since then
it has spread from the Guianas north to the central United
States – two thousand miles in less than thirty years – and
from New Guinea to northern Australia as well.

The distribution patterns which we see today are the result of
continual evolution not only in one centre, but also in many
secondary centres. There has been colonization and re-coloniza-
tion, the extinction of some faunas and their replacement by
others. Viewed in the perspective of geological time, the picture is fluid. But it is useful to have a classification of these

data based on present conditions. The most workable is a system of zoo-geographical regions based on a classification proposed by the British ornithologist P. L. Sclater in 1859.[7]

Sclater wrote the paper embodying his proposals before Darwin published his *Origin of Species*, which also appeared in 1859, and the thinking was pre-evolutionary. Sclater was attempting to find the primary areas of distinct creation. With this in mind he wrote, the '. . . awkward necessity of supposing . . . [the] colonizing [of] Polynesia by stray pairs of Malays floating over the water like coconuts, and all similar hypotheses, would be avoided'.

But whatever his philosophy, his approach and his methods were scientific and his results sound. He set about 'ascertaining the most natural primary divisions of the earth's surface, taking the amount of similarity or dissimilarity of organized life solely as our guide'. Working only with birds he outlined the six major faunal 'regions'. Though Sclater was the first to recognize these six regions, it was the British naturalist-explorer Alfred Russel Wallace, the co-discoverer with Darwin of the theory of evolution, who correlated zoo-geography with evolution in two books that have become the classics in the field. These books, *The Geographical Distribution of Animals* and *Island Life*, earned him the title of 'Father of Zoo-geography'.

Sclater's six regions are the Ethiopian, the Oriental, the Australian, the Palearctic, the Nearctic, and the Neo-tropical. An outline of each region and a brief treatment of bird distribution follows.

Ethiopian Region. This includes Africa south of the Sahara, and southern Arabia.[8] It is mostly tropical, and the major habitats are associated with varying amounts of rainfall. The rainforest area of the Congo basin and West Africa constitutes one habitat, and enclosing it in a half circle to the north, east, and south are the drier habitats – deciduous forests, savannas, grasslands, and areas of desert. The high mountains of Africa are small and scattered, some with humid forests. They have a small endemic avifauna, derived from the lowlands.

Africa is the mammal continent, especially rich in big game, but it also has a rich and varied avifauna. There are seven endemic families with from one to eighteen species in each. These are the ostriches, whale-headed storks, secretary birds, guinea fowls, turacos, colies (mouse-birds), and wood hoopoes. Another family, the hammerhead storks, is shared only with Madagascar.

Certain more widely distributed families have notable elements in the Ethiopian Region, such as certain bee eaters, honey guides, hornbills, larks, shrikes, weaver-birds, sun-birds, the aberrant starlings called tick-birds that feed on the ticks on big game, and the aberrant hawks called vultures that feed on the animals that fall from the herds.

The oceanic island of Madagascar is usually included as a sub-region of the Ethiopian Region because of its physical location and because most of its birds whose ancestry can be deduced show African affinities. However, as has been mentioned, the distinctiveness of its fauna is shown by the evolution there of six families of birds which are not found elsewhere, including vangas, mesites, philepittas, and two roller families. In addition the extinct *Aepyornis*, or elephant bird, is known only from Madagascar.

Oriental Region. This includes tropical southern Asia from the Himalayas and Burma southward and the Malay archipelago as far as Java, Bali, and Borneo.[9] The eastern boundary is traditionally 'Wallace's line', drawn between Bali and Lombok, but there is a wide band of intergradation, so the exact position of the line itself is not of great importance. The eastern part of the region is mostly rain forest, while India is drier, with deciduous forests, brush, and even deserts.

The rich and diversified avifauna is basically like the Ethiopian, with which it shares many Old World tropical families. But this region does have one endemic family, that of the leafbirds and fairy blue-birds. It is notable also for the number and diversity of the pheasants, babbling thrushes, and broadbills which can claim it as their headquarters.

This region shares with the Australian Region tree swifts, frogmouths, megapodes, wood swallows, and flower-peckers, which find their north-western limits here.

Australian Region. This region of marsupials and gum trees is partly tropical and partly temperate.[10] New Guinea, with a range of high mountains down its length, is largely a humid, forested tropical island, with an important bird fauna in both its lowland rain forest and its humid mountain forest; in the south it has an area of dry grassland. Australia is largely a warm, arid country of open, dry forest, brush, grassland, and in the centre some desert. In northern Queensland there is a small area of rain forest very like the New Guinea tropical forests, and there are some moist forests in the south.

The fauna of this region, whose ancestors arrived overseas by island-hopping, is not nearly so rich in species as that of the Oriental Region, but its endemism is relatively high. It has three endemic, non-passerine bird families: emus, cassowaries, and owlet frogmouths. It is also notable for seven endemic families of perching birds: scrub-birds, lyre-birds, bell magpies, magpie larks, bower-birds, birds of paradise, and honey eaters. There are also some peculiar groups of birds resembling respectively warblers, fly-catchers, creepers, nuthatches, and orioles, birds that are doubtfully related to the corresponding ecological

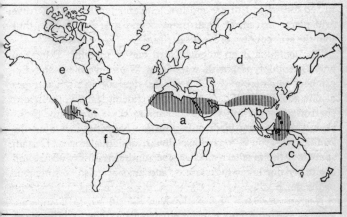

Figure 47. *The six main continental zoo-geographical regions:* (a) *Ethiopian;* (b) *Oriental;* (c) *Australian;* (d) *Palearctic;* (e) *Nearctic;* (f) *Neotropical.*

groups in the Indian Region. There are, too, a number of peculiar genera of babbling thrushes. The abundance and diversity of parrots and lories, pigeons, cuckoo shrikes, kingfishers, and flower-peckers is unequalled elsewhere.

New Zealand, a group of oceanic islands, is usually included here because of its proximity and its small present-day avifauna, which indicates Australian origins – when they can be deduced. However, there are three modern families – kiwis, New Zealand wrens, and wattle-birds – which are restricted to New Zealand, as were the extinct moas. The avifauna of the Pacific islands originated mostly in the area of Australia and New Guinea, with a striking endemic species in New Caledonia, the kagu, the sole member of a family related to the cranes. Hawaii, however, is considered part of the Nearctic Region.

Palearctic Region. This Old World North Temperate and Arctic Zones region includes Europe, northernmost Africa, and Asia north of the Himalayas.[11] Its northern edge is covered by tundra; next comes a band of coniferous forest, or taiga. Both of these have their counterparts in the Nearctic Region of the New World. In the middle latitudes there are deciduous and mixed forests in Europe and in China and Japan, and extensive arid plains in central Asia; these extend into Arabia and thus join the arid country of North Africa.

The avifauna is an impoverished one of modified Ethiopian and Oriental types, with many Old World warblers and flycatchers common, and with a general decrease in tropical types as one goes north. There is only one endemic family, the hedge sparrows. In the taiga and the tundra there are many forms shared as breeding birds only with the Nearctic, including the families of grouse, waxwings, divers, and phalaropes. Certain sparrows, the northern finches, the tundra-nesting waders, and the many northern ducks, gulls, and auks are also conspicuous in the north.

Nearctic Region. This is the New World North Temperate and Arctic Zones region, extending south to meet the tropics in southern Mexico.[12] Tundra covers the Arctic islands and the northern edge of the continent, followed by a band of taiga, as in the Palearctic. In the middle latitudes the eastern part of

the region is characterized by deciduous or mixed forests; the
central part is more arid, with extensive grasslands. In the west
are the great north–south mountain ranges – the Rocky Mountains and the coastal ranges; their higher altitudes bring Alpine
grass and coniferous forests far south and they have complex
valleys, often arid in the south, with desert, cactus, and mixed
forests. Humid forests occur on the west coast in the middle
latitudes, deserts in the south.

The bird fauna is mixed, more so than the Oriental. That the
region received much of its fauna from the Palearctic is especially evident in the tundra and forests of the north, which even
share with the Palearctic some of the same genera or species of
divers, ducks, waders, chickadees, nuthatches, creepers, northern
finches, and the like; the secondary invasion of Neo-tropical elements, represented by the humming-birds, icterid blackbirds,
tanagers, and tyrant fly-catchers, becomes more and more noticeable as one goes south.

The only truly endemic families are the wren-tits and the
turkeys, but the abundance of species and genera suggests that
several more widespread groups of less than family rank have
their headquarters here. These include the grouse, the American
wood warblers, the American quail, and the streaked sparrows.

The oceanic Hawaiian Islands are regarded as part of the
Nearctic Region, from which came most of their fauna, including the ancestors of the endemic family of Hawaiian honey
creepers, but a few Polynesian groups, such as a honey eater
and a warbler, have also colonized there.

Neo-tropical Region. This is primarily a tropical region, with
a small area in the South Temperate Zone.[13] It is dominated by
the great north–south range of the Andes and the great rain
forests of the Amazon basin, the Guianas, and Central America.
Outside the rain forests, the country becomes covered with drier
forests, scrub, and grasslands, and in the south and along the
southern west coast are deserts.

While Africa is the mammal continent, South America is the
bird continent. It has an unrivalled bird fauna, which remains
today the least known of any. It has had a history of isolation
during much of the period birds have been in existence, and

evidently had an influx of birds early in their history – a colonization that has resulted in the evolution of more than two dozen
endemic families in addition to those that have spread northwards to colonize North America. The presence of the Andes,
extending north and south for several thousand miles, has
resulted in a unique development of bird faunas correlated with
altitude.

Among the notable endemics of South America are the rheas,
tinamous, hoatzins, trumpeters, sun bitterns, cariamas, seed
snipe, potoos, and oil-birds, most of them unknown even by
name to all but ornithologists. There are also six families of
non-singing perching birds and seven families of song-birds
found nowhere else.

Certain absences should be noted, such as those of the tits
and nuthatches, and although parrots and pigeons are represented by many species, they lack the variety which is theirs
in the Australian Region.

The oceanic Galápagos Islands and the Tristan da Cunha
groups were colonized from this region. Trinidad is a continental Neo-tropical island. The West Indies, as far as birds are
concerned, seem to be oceanic islands close enough to the mainland to have received considerable numbers of birds, most from
the Neo-tropics but some from North America. The avifauna is
not rich but there are a number of endemic genera and one endemic family, the todies, related to the Neo-tropical motmots.

Though the regions which have been outlined are useful in
discussing zoo-geography, they fall far short of fitting all the
data. At the species level many local forms do not occupy more
than a fraction of a continent. In the great continent of Africa
there are about ninety species with ranges of less than a hundred miles. On the basis of the distribution of groups of bird
species, it is possible to subdivide each region into sub-regions
and provinces. These usually are correlated with ecological
factors, such as the type of vegetation in a particular part of a
region. At the other extreme, there are species that range over
several continents, such as the barn owl, the peregrine falcon,
and the osprey.

At the family level, a distribution approaching the cosmopolitan is shown by such groups as the rails, swallows, and hawks, while other families, such as the sun-grebes and the barbets, are pan-tropical but do not reach Australia. Still others, such as the pigeons and the parrots, have general headquarters in the tropics but spread into temperate zones.

The seas cover much more of the earth than the land does, and they are in more intimate contact with each other than are the continents. As a result, land barriers have not had the effects on sea birds that sea barriers have had on land birds.[14] Rather, sea birds have been affected by ecological factors in the sea, such as those that marine biologists have used in mapping marine faunas. Sea birds can be considered as broadly falling into three groups – southern, tropical, and northern. The birds do require the presence of islands or land for annual breeding sites, and some groups, such as frigate birds and cormorants, come ashore daily to sleep.

The southern group of sea birds is dominated by albatrosses, penguins, and some petrels and cormorants; the pan-tropical group by terns, boobies, frigate birds, and tropic birds, and in some areas by petrels; while the northern group (found in Palearctic and Nearctic waters) is notable especially for its auks and gulls.

A somewhat similar latitudinal zonation can be seen on the land, but quite unrelated species may be ecological counterparts on different continents, and an analysis of this zonation calls for a synthesis of zoo-geography and ecology.[15]

CHAPTER 23

The Nature
of Species

MUCH of what we know about the mechanics of evolution has come from studies of present-day species. Behind these living species is a long history illuminated by a study of the fossil record. Though the record is imperfect, we can read in it the story of the interrelationships of all living things.

This theme has been suggested in the preceding chapters, and here, before we go on to examine the nature of species, it may be well to mention the great landmarks in the process of this evolution as it has affected birds and their ancestors.[1]

Evolution was well under way 500,000,000 years ago, when there was a rich invertebrate fauna in the seas. This fauna left its record in the fossil remains entombed in the rocks of the Cambrian period. The record of the first vertebrate animal goes back nearly as far. Primitive, marine, armour-plated fish, called Ostracodermi, existed during the Ordovician, some 450,000,000 years ago. The amphibians, first vertebrates to occupy the land, came 100,000,000 years later, in the Devonian. Some 50,000,000 years after that, in the Carboniferous, reptiles appeared. Another 150,000,000 years elapsed, and then the first known bird, *Archaeopteryx*, climbed and glided about the cycads fringeing the Jurassic coral lagoons of western Europe. This gives birds, the class Aves, an age of more than 150,000,000 years. During this period of time the birds we know today have evolved.

The process of evolution has been long, and it has also been

– and continues to be – slow. In the course of geological time one species has changed to another or has evolved several daughter species. Of course, not all species have been successful; some species, and even groups, have become extinct without leaving replacements. The moas of New Zealand, for example, became extinct within the Christian era.

Different groups have not all evolved at the same rate. For example, oysters of the Mollusca have changed little in the whole period during which birds and mammals evolved from their reptile ancestors to their present forms.

Even within a particular class, species have not evolved at a continually uniform rate. Evolution went on faster where there were great changes in the land; thus when great mountain ranges such as the Andes of South America were thrust up, the mountain avifauna evolved to occupy the new altitudes.[2] Evolution also received an impetus when new foods became available. Grass seed became available when the grasses were developed in the Miocene, and then the seed-eating finches, sparrows, and weaver-birds evolved. On the other hand, when the environment remained more quiet and stable, evolution proceeded more slowly. It is still going on today.

Palaeontologist Pierce Brodkorb has provided an example of the different rates at which birds in an area may evolve.[3] The mourning dove (*Zendaidura macroura*) of the United States has existed unchanged since the Pliocene, as its fossil remains show. But during the same period the fossil quail (*Colinus hibbardi*) of the Pliocene was replaced by the quail (*C. suilium*) of the Pleistocene, which in turn was replaced by *C. virginianus*, the bobwhite quail of the present-day eastern United States.

Taking into account such complexities in determining the life-span of fossil-bird faunas, Dr Brodkorb concludes that the average longevity of a bird species may be half a million years.

Ascertaining the point at which one fossil species evolves into another species, which replaces it, is a matter of subjective judgement based on the degree of difference of the forms concerned. But when two species co-exist in time and space their status can be objectively determined. Most important is the absence of hybridization, for it is only because they do not interbreed that they can co-exist and not lose their identity. The attainment of species status, a process called speciation, is a critical part of evolution.

Species are the units of the many evolutionary series built up from protozoans to fish to reptiles to birds. To understand how these series came into being, one must understand species formation. Let us first, therefore, examine the nature of the species itself.

The local naturalist is rarely in doubt about the reality of the species he encounters. He knows that robins differ from wood thrushes and barn swallows are not cliff swallows. He also recognizes that, since the red male scarlet tanager and the green female mate, they are members of the same species. Even if the red-headed woodpeckers have grey-headed young, they all belong to one species. A pair of dark-coloured purple martins with a brood containing an abnormal white (albinistic) young bird still forms only one species.

Our bird student recognizes each species by its particular combination of size, shape, and colour – the 'species characters' used for practical identification. But he knows that each is a species because the individuals are part of an interbreeding population that does not interbreed with any other species.

When our local naturalist leaves his own area and studies the birds of other places, perhaps on other continents or archipelagos, he may find some of the species he knew at home, but he will also notice that the characters vary slightly from place to place. The birds may be larger or darker in a colder or more humid area, smaller or paler in a warmer or more arid place; they may differ in song, in eggs, in nest, and in colour characters for no obvious reason except that they come from widely separated areas. In his travelling the naturalist finds that many of the different-looking populations intergrade or hybridize in geographically intermediate areas, and some meet and live together just as did the species that he knew at home. No longer can his concept of a species be a simple, static one. Observations such as these, especially in regard to the Galápagos finches, were what led Darwin to formulate his theory of evolution and the origin of species.

Before Darwin's time, the prevailing species concept was a static one. Species had been created one by one and were fixed, unchanging entities. Each was definable in morphological terms, and the individual was the unit of study. Then, in the middle of the nineteenth century, Charles Darwin made his trip round the world as a naturalist on the *Beagle*, and made biological history. From his new experiences with living animals and fossils came his idea that species do not always stay the same. Instead, they change from place to place and they also change with geological time. One species may turn into another and one species may give rise to two species through evolution.

Darwin's theory of evolution postulates that in animals and in plants individual variations of all degrees occur, and that a great many more young individuals come into the world each year that can survive to adulthood.[4] There is therefore a struggle for existence, and natural selection results in the survival of the fittest. Accordingly, there is descent with modification – the individual variations most useful for survival are most likely to be retained. The concept of static species received a blow from which it has never recovered.

In the second quarter of the twentieth century, the concept of evolution expanded and evolution became the 'modern synthesis', integrating all aspects of biology into a central comprehensive scheme.[5] Genetics, physiology, behaviour, ecology, zoo-geography, palaeontology, and other special branches all bring evidence to bear on evolution.

From one of these disciplines – genetics – came the particulate theory of inheritance, in which the idea of information coded in separate particles, the genes, replaces the earlier idea of blending inheritance. According to this theory, now generally accepted, variation depends on mutations and recombinations of genes. With the adoption of this view came the realization that the population rather than the individual should be the unit of study.

But even more important than the understanding of how variation occurs is the understanding of how natural selection deals with it. Students of bird evolution are not blessed with such wonderful series of fossils as are students of mammals. These

allow mammalogists to trace with assurance such histories as
that of the horse, for instance. By comparison, and with a few
exceptions, bird fossils in the older strata of the rocks are few,
scattered, and fragmentary.[6] The process of reconstruction must
follow a different path. Evolution is a continuing process and we
can see examples of evolution and speciation in progress in
present-day fauna all over the world. By piecing together these
examples we can illustrate how bird species arise just as if we
had a fine series of bird fossils from every geologic age and
could reconstruct the process from the record of the past.

These modern changes are most easily seen in the comparable developments of breeds of domestic animals, such as dogs,
domestic fowl, and pigeons. The breeds of domestic pigeons
include such extremes as the knip, weighing thirty-six ounces,
and the parlour tumbler weighing seven ounces; the jacobin,
with elongated neck feathers that can be raised to hide the
head, and the swallow spot, with elongated feathers on its feet;
the owl, with short bill and bent upper mandible; the carrier,
with fleshy wattles about the eyes and bill; and some tumblers,
with up to forty quills instead of twelve.[7] All these types and
many more have been developed from the ancestral rock doves
of Europe by man's artificial selection of desired inheritable
variations. When this artificial selection is relaxed and the breeds
are allowed to mingle, the birds revert to something like the
ancestral type seen in the flocks of pigeons in city parks.

Among wild birds, we find a similar type of individual
variation producing a range of variants; natural selection directs
the development of the more favourable types, replacing man's
artificial selection; and natural barriers, first extrinsic geographical ones and later intrinsic biological isolating mechanisms, replace man's cages in preventing interbreeding.

The process of species formation can be illustrated by pos-
tulating a hypothetical group of three oceanic islands far out in
the sea. A flock of small birds blown off its course finally colonizes the three. Since each island is slightly different from the
others, natural selection results in the development on each
island of a population with different characters, adapted to the
local conditions. At first a rare stray from one island reach-

ing the next across the water barrier is absorbed into its resident population. But with the accumulation of small differences generation after generation, intrinsic biological isolating mechanisms develop within the birds themselves. Then fertile interbreeding with their relatives cannot take place. Each of the three populations has now reached species level on its own island. They are allopatric species; that is, their ranges do not overlap. Without competition on its island, each species occupies all the habitats there, feeding on the ground, in the shrubbery, and in the trees. Now, when birds stray from one island to another they are not absorbed into the resident population but establish a colony of their own. Each island is finally occupied by three sympatric species, species that live in the same area. In the course of colonization that brought these three species together, there was competition among them, and it was lessened by one species living in the trees, one in the shrubbery, and one on the ground. They divided the habitat among them, and in the course of time each became specialized for its particular part of the habitat. The stage is set for further differences due to the interspecific competition, and for additional recolonization and additional speciation. This is in effect a simplification of the situation which Darwin found among the finches on the Galápagos Islands and which helped him to formulate his theory of evolution.[8]

Let us now look at examples in some present-day birds of the various aspects of species formation. First we have individual variation. This may be hard to see in a flock of starlings feeding on a lawn, but each member of a flock of hens may be known by name to the farmer's children. They may be recognized not only by differences in plumage, but also by variations in posture and behaviour: one is greedy, one is aggressive, another is tame, and so on. Starlings look alike on a lawn, but when I examined museum specimens of starlings, I could find no two that were exactly alike. Some of the differences were due to age and to wear, it is true, and in one case a bird had some abnormal white feathers, but the fact remains that each individual bird did show some minor difference from every other starling. The presence of individual variation is further demonstrated by the

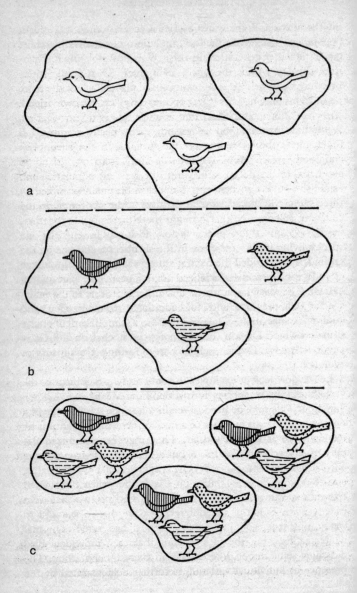

a

b

c

ability of individuals in a flock of hens or a covey of quail that have been together for a long time to recognize each other by sight.

Also essential to species formation is the fact that many more individuals are born than can survive. The enormous reproductive potential of birds is easily shown by a consideration of the American robins that nest in my own garden at home. Every year there are two pairs, each of which raises two broods in succession, laying four eggs each time. Thus the two pairs have the capacity to produce sixteen young in one season. If this went on year after year, in eight years the four original birds would have about a quarter of a million descendants. But from my observations over eight years I know that the population in my garden has remained the same – two pairs breed there each year.

Obviously, a variety of factors have eliminated most of the increase.[9] We know some of them: predation, parasites, climate, food supply, weather, accidents; all may take their toll. Population structure of a species may limit the number of its breeding individuals in the area, as is shown in territorial birds like the robin. There may be an unmated surplus, birds that are not able to find an unoccupied territory and lack the vigour to usurp part of an occupied one. Also, competition by other species may reduce the amount of food and the number of nesting sites available.

No two areas that support a population of birds are just alike, and the young that survive in one area are those whose individual characteristics best fit them to do so in that particular area. Here we have an explanation for geographical variation: the existence of differences between the populations of species from different areas.

Presumably, when techniques are refined sufficiently we can show that every population is at least slightly different from

Figure 48. *Three stages of species formation on a group of three hypothetical islands: (a) all three islands are colonized by one species from the mainland; (b) in isolation, the birds on each island develop into a different species; (c) each new island species colonizes the other two islands.*

every other one. When we look at the avifauna of a continent, we find many cases in which the populations of different areas look different and behave differently from one another. When these populations or groups of populations become distinct enough to be recognized easily, the taxonomist calls them geographical races, or sub-species.

In North America the best-known example of a species with many sub-species is the song sparrow.[10] This species is very widely distributed and very variable. The varying populations have been grouped into thirty-one named sub-species. The extremes are a small, pale red-brown, desert song sparrow from Arizona, and a large, dark, soot-coloured bird from the Pacific north-west. In areas covering a good part of the United States from the Atlantic coast to the Pacific, and extending into central Canada, there are intermediate populations with varying combinations of size, width of streaking and redness, buffness, and blackness in various parts of the pattern. Wherever these populations (sub-species) come into contact, they interbreed. Even the isolated sub-species on Amak Island, near the western end of the Alaska peninsula, is so similar to the others that one assumes the birds would interbreed if the physical barrier of island isolation were removed.

In the absence of actual contact and intergradation the assumption that isolated populations belong to the same species has only a subjective basis. The conclusions of students of geographical variation do not always coincide. The Savannah sparrow is an American species, related to the song sparrow, with sixteen recognized sub-species. On the tiny islet of Sable Island, in the Atlantic off Nova Scotia, lives the Ipswich sparrow – obviously a larger, paler, geographical representative of the Savannah sparrow. No one doubts the relationship, but in the absence of objective criteria such as interbreeding or intergrading, opinion is divided as to whether it should be considered a sub-species of the mainland bird or a separate species.

Such isolated breeding populations are common. In some, no sub-species have developed. The Caspian tern, for instance, has eighteen or more colonies scattered over the North American continent, and others in Asia, Africa, Madagascar, Australia, and New Zealand.[11] But, despite the isolation, the populations throughout this wide range show no morphological differences that we can use to define sub-species.

In archipelagos, such as the Philippine Islands, isolated populations of many species of land birds which have developed into quite distinctive sub-species are common.[12] In the Philippines some of them occupy an island less than a dozen miles across, and some live on islands which are separated from their neighbours by only a few miles of water.

While isolation does not always result in the evolution of quite different populations, the evidence is that where new species do evolve, they always do so in isolation. A population is regarded as forming a new species when it has developed not only distinctive physical characters, but also, with the accumulation of small differences, the inability to interbreed with the parent species. An intrinsic biological isolating mechanism thus replaces the extrinsic geographical one. This intrinsic barrier may be a variation in courtship behaviour, so that mixed pairs do not form; or it may be incompatibility in the reproductive cells, so that cross matings are sterile; or if the cross mating is fertile the hybrids may be sterile, as is the mule, offspring of horse and donkey.

The next step in speciation is the range extension by which newly evolved species come to share an area occupied by related species; it is interesting to note, however, that rarely do the ranges of two species coincide completely throughout. It is by means of this sequence – first speciation in geographical isolation and then range extension – that avifaunas are built up; in this way the two to three hundred species recorded in a square mile of rich tropical forest came into being. But this process is easier to see where the species are fewer, notably in archipelagos.

An example is the little yellowish leaf warbler of the genus *Phylloscopus*, rather widely distributed through the Philippine Islands.[13] Some populations are more yellow, some more grey and green. Four forms have been described. These have all been called sub-species of one species, and still would be if it were not that on one island, Negros, two forms occur, making it apparent that they no longer interbreed. This is a case of double invasion, and, as in the hypothetical island example outlined earlier, the two colonists reached species status between the time of the first invasion (in which the warbler came to the Philippines) and the second invasion (which resulted in two new species occupying the same island). Evolution may still operate on the two species in one area, to make the isolating mechanisms more effective in preventing cross mating, and to make their ways of life more unlike, so that the competition between them is reduced.

The kinds of difference that may develop are illustrated in Table X, comparing two species of tyrant fly-catchers in eastern North America, closely related and very much alike in appearance.[14]

The scarcity on continents of cases of incipient speciation and the fact that many of our modern bird species are known from as far back as the Pliocene, at least, have led some students to believe that evolution proceeds rapidly only in times of tectonic change, as has been pointed out. Most modern bird types may have evolved by the Lower Cenozoic, their development correlated with the Laramide revolution that built the great mountain chains of the present-day world and affected climates and environments.

Certain it is that most cases of incipient speciation seen today in North America are easily correlated with the great changes that accompanied the glaciation of the Pleistocene.[15] The ice that covered the northern part of the continent pushed the northern biota into a few restricted ice-free locations: one or more within the largely glaciated territory in the Yukon–Bering Sea area; one or more south-east of the ice, in what are now the Middle Atlantic states; and two or more south-west of the ice in the Rocky Mountain area.

There were thus three main refugia, areas with semi-boreal forest conditions in which the plants and animals could survive. When the glaciers melted and retreated, the plants and animals spread out to reoccupy the northern part of the continent.

But the isolation in these refugia had given the fragmented population time to evolve independently. When the descendants

TABLE X

Two Related Fly-catchers

	Acadian Fly-catcher (Empidonax virescens)	Least Fly-catcher (Empidonax minimus)
1 Length	5¾ inches	5½ inches
2 Colour	Back – greener olive Lower mandible – yellower	Back – greyer olive Lower mandible – more dusky
3 Breeding range	Southern – Florida to New York and Nebraska	Northern – North Carolina to Wyoming, north to Quebec and the Yukon
4 Winter range	Southern – chiefly northern South America	Northern – Mexico to Panama
5 Arrival date in Maryland	Early May	Late April
6 Habitat	Dense shade of mature woods	Open woodlots and scattered trees
7 Voice	An abrupt ka-reep, the second syllable having a rough quality, accompanied by a twitching of the tail	An emphatic chebec accompanied by a toss of the head and a flick of the tail
8 Nesting period in Maryland	Peak reached in early June	Peak reached in late May
9 Nest	A basket suspended by its edges in a slender horizontal fork near end of branch	A cup wedged in a substantial crotch
10 Eggs	White, spotted with brown	White, unspotted

of these several populations met, they did so with less inter-breeding and less intergradation than one would expect if they were all of the same species. Still, a certain amount of hybridization and intergrading did occur. It seems that here we had a natural experiment that lasted just long enough to cause speciation to proceed half way.

By a sequence involving individual variation, geographical variation, geographical isolation allowing the populations concerned to proceed to the species level, and the overcoming of geographical isolation so that the new species live together, separated by intrinsic biological barriers and ecological preferences, faunas have been built up in the past – and the process continues today.

CHAPTER 24

Birds and Man

BIRDS have played a part in man's life since Neanderthal man ate great auks at Gibraltar and left the bones in his refuse heaps. Palaeolithic man drew pictures of them on the walls of his caves in Spain, Chinese and Egyptian scribes incorporated bird forms into their written characters, and soothsayers in Borneo and Greece used birds to foretell the future. Today people write letters to the newspapers about many aspects of bird life – for instance, the effect of pesticides, on the place of birds in the balance of nature, the open season on mourning doves in Illinois, or the results of the latest Christmas bird census. Man has always been aware of birds, and they still supply material and inspiration for recreational, intellectual, and scientific pursuits, as well as fresh eggs for breakfast.

The flesh and the eggs of most birds are palatable, but they have supplied only seasonal or incidental food in most parts of the world. Birds are too small and too scarce, and their populations too susceptible to depletion and over-use, for wild birds to supply a staple food where the human population is large. This vulnerability is well illustrated by the almost disastrous effects of market hunting on game birds in the United States during the last half of the nineteenth century. Only small, isolated human populations can harvest a bird population on a continuing-yield basis.

Until recently the Seychelles Islanders got an important

part of the protein in their diet from the eggs of certain tropical terns and gannets which nested on the islands.[1] In colder latitudes where there is a seasonal abundance of nesting birds it has been possible to catch and store the birds for food. In the Tristan da Cunha group – abandoned late in 1961 because of volcanic activity, and since resettled – the settlers used to make annual visits to an outlying greater-shearwater colony in November, when the young were well grown, to harvest the birds for their fat.[2] The fat extracted provided a supply of cooking oil for the whole year. The polar Eskimos of Greenland harvested great numbers of little auks in summer and stored them for winter use, a practice that prevented starvation when other game was scarce.[3]

Civilized man's main use of birds for food has been confined to a few domesticated species, especially the domestic fowl, a descendant of the jungle fowl (*Gallus gallus*) of India or Siam;[4] the turkey, whose ancestor was the wild turkey of North America;[5] the ducks, most of which are descended from the European wild mallard, though in recent years the large Muscovy duck, whose original home was in the American tropics, has increased in popularity; and the geese, some descended from the greylag of northern Eurasia, and others (among which the male has a knob on his forehead) from a Chinese goose.[6]

Wild birds contribute in another way to man's food supply: they provide guano, which is used as fertilizer for crops. The best-known deposits are on the coastal islands of Peru, where the arid climate allowed the droppings of the swarming cormorants, gannets, and pelicans to accumulate over the centuries into veritable mountains of fertilizer.[7] In the last century this was mined and loaded into ships until the supply was threatened so that now only a certain amount may be harvested annually. Though the Peruvian deposits are the best known and the most important, others exist in South America, and on the coasts of South Africa and southern Australia.[8]

Bird skin is too tender, feathers are too fragile, the quantities produced by each bird are too small, for competition with mammal skin and hair as the material for much of man's clothing.[9] But feathers do have good insulating properties, and some

Eskimos make inner garments that will last a season from the
skins of ducks and auks. The feather cloaks of Hawaiians,
Maoris, and Brazilian Indians belong in a different category.
Like many of the feather head-dresses and feather bands so
widely worn by savages and by ladies of fashion, these cloaks,
notable for the beauty of the feathers, have a social rather than a
utilitarian importance.

Trade in feathers has taken various forms. Papuans traded
bird-of-paradise plumes westwards through native trade routes,
so they reached Europe before New Guinea was discovered by
western travellers. For hundreds of years China imported the
feathers of kingfishers from the Malay countries for use in
jewellery, pictures, and panels. In Europe and America fashions
in feathered millinery, and the trade to obtain the feathers from
newly opened lands, reached a peak in the 1880s. But such
large-scale commercial exploitation of wild birds has almost
ceased.

There still exists trade in some luxury items provided by
birds, supporting industries which are important to a few local
groups and which are on an annual-harvest basis. There is the
eider-down industry of Iceland, utilizing down from the ducks'
nests;[10] the bird's-nest-soup industry, processing the nests of
certain swiftlets of the Malaysian area;[11] and the industry of the
Tasmanian area which produces canned 'squab in aspic', the
'squab' being the young of the slender-billed shearwater, or
Tasmanian mutton-bird.[12]

Bird products have also been put to a host of minor uses. In
prehistoric times birds' bones provided awls, needles, and
whistles. The eggs of ostriches still provide the desert-living
Kalahari bushmen with containers for water. The islanders of
St Kilda, who depended on nesting sea birds for food, also
formerly burnt oil from young fulmars for light, and in place
of the traditional stone lamp sometimes used the sternum of a
gannet;[13] in New Britain it is said that the oil of the cassowary
is a specific for rheumatism, while the long, sharp inner toenail
is used to tip hunting arrows.

Hunting was a serious business to primitive man, and his
ways of catching birds showed great diversity.[14] He used throw-

ing sticks, spears, arrows, blow-pipe darts, and bolos, as well as snares, nets, and birdlime; all these are still being used in parts of the world today. In more civilized communities the leisured class practised bird hunting as a sport. Netting waterfowl in the marshes was a sport of the Pharaohs, as depicted on the walls of chambers in the pyramids. Falconry was known in England in the Bronze Age and was the sport of kings in medieval Europe.[15] During the Middle Ages ladies also might accompany their gallants on a day's sport of netting partridge. In the Orient cormorants have long been trained to catch fish. This used to be to secure food. Today these birds are one of the tourist attractions in Japan. In Japan, also, an intriguing sport was the taking of ducks in a decoy. Wild ducks were enticed up narrow canals, or 'pipes', with high banks, and fowlers armed with long-handled nets arose from behind the banks and scooped up the ducks from the water.

With the introduction of gunpowder in the western world, a new type of sport, 'gunning' for birds, arose. A man of the modern Western world seeking to kill birds is likely to be a gunner and a sportsman, and to round out his sport by eating his game. He may wait in the ambush of a duck hide or a goose pit for waterfowl, or he may go out on foot with his shotgun hunting upland game birds, perhaps with the aid of a dog.

But today in many of the more civilized parts of the world, the blood sports are being replaced by bird photography, bird watching, and bird listing. Practised as hobbies, these activities may yield data for the ornithologist as well as provide recreation for the hobbyist.

Many primitive people raise birds in captivity. Sometimes they do so simply to add flesh to young birds before they are eaten, and the domestication of birds may have originated in just such a practice. But sometimes native peoples keep parrots apparently just because they like to have them about. The practice of keeping birds in cages seems most common in the Orient and least so in North America, where only a few birds are regularly kept. These include the canary, valued for its singing, the Java sparrow, for its appearance, mynah birds, and parrots; three of the parrots – the African grey, one of the green

and yellow Amazons, and the Australian budgerigar – are the
most popular pet birds. Aviaries, of course, often have a wide
range of species, including many tropical and insect-eating birds.
Certain species, tame but not domesticated, such as pheasants,
peafowl, ducks, and geese, and in warmer latitudes macaws
and flamingos, are used to ornament estate grounds. The
activities of amateur bird raisers, which may overlap those of
zoo keepers, have contributed substantially to our knowledge of
birds.

To consider man–bird relationships on another plane, we can
turn to the role played by birds in the magico-religious thought
world of primitive peoples. The Iban Dyaks of Borneo are a
polytheistic people, and birds are woven into the whole texture
of their thought and belief.[16] When their principal deity appears
he usually takes the form of a kite, but more often he makes
known his will by sending lesser deities in the form of other
birds. Their calls and actions convey his message, according to
Dr J. D. Freeman of the National University, Canberra, who
has studied this people.

For instance, if a trading party just starting out hears the cry
of a trogon with the notes running together, future happy
laughter over good trading is assured and the party can proceed
with confidence. On the other hand, if men starting to clear the
forest for a rice field hear the alarm call of the rufous piculet
(*Sasia abnormis*), they know that if they persist in their work
one of them will cut himself with his axe. The only wise course
is to abandon work for the day and go home. Sometimes when a
canoe trip has been decided upon, the Dyaks avoid the chance
of hearing an unfavourable omen by having someone in the
canoe beat a gong continually, or the men may plug up their
ears with leaves.

To interpret the actions or the calls of these augural birds is
not easy. The meaning varies not only with the type of call or
the direction in which the bird flies, but even without these
differences. When a certain trogon enters a long house, as it
sometimes does, its laughing cry and bright plumage may indicate future happiness, or its bright-red breast may symbolize
the flames which will soon devour the long house. These

auguries for the whole community may be interpreted by one man skilled in such interpretation, and he has great ritual and social importance among his people.

That beliefs like these were widespread among ancient peoples may be concluded from the similar nature of augury in early Greece and Rome. Dr Freeman, in this connection, quotes from the *Odyssey* the episode in which unwelcome suitors were pressing for the hand of Penelope during the long absence of her husband, Ulysses. Her son prayed to Jove for guidance, and he answered by sending two warring eagles directly over the roof. Halitherses, the best-qualified reader of omens, saw correctly in this the return of Ulysses and the bloody doom of every suitor.

The founding of the city of Alexandria also involved augury. According to Plutarch, Alexander the Great selected the site and ordered the plan of the city to be laid out on the black soil. For want of chalk the lines were drawn with flour. This was barely finished when a great number of birds arose like a black cloud from the near-by Nile River and ate all the flour. At this omen even Alexander himself was troubled, fearing pestilence and famine for his city, but the augurs told him it was a sign that the city he planned would feed the whole world, and so the building of the city went ahead.

Birds had a part in the founding of Rome too.[17] Not only did a she-wolf suckle Romulus and Remus, but the birds also brought them food. Later, when the twins had grown and were founding Rome, a dispute arose over the exact site for the city: was it to be on what is now Roma Quadrata or on the Aventine Mount? Following the custom of the time, they settled the matter by divination from a flight of birds. Remus saw six vultures which was a very good sign, but Romulus saw twelve, and as this was much better his choice was accepted.

While divination from flight of birds largely disappeared in the Western world with the advent of Christianity, it is worth remembering that flights of birds may have a real meaning even if not a supernatural one. Even today the arrival and the departure of the migrant yellow wagtails in Borneo each year help the Dyaks to time their agricultural activities.[18] In the Kelabit highlands the rice is harvested by January, else the crop may be devoured by the weaver finches which arrive in hordes in February. The people watch for the last yellow wagtail to depart in March; then they know they have two free moons, until June, before they must start to prepare the fields for the next crop.

When the first wagtails arrive in September, they know that the fields should be ready to plant, and when the birds come back in really great numbers, a month or so later, the farmers know that they can no longer delay but must work in the fields in earnest if the rice is to be ready for harvest before the weaver finches come in February. This mixture of astronomical and ornithological timing is an ideal one, enabling the people to adjust to the variable seasons there and to find the best times for doing such things as travelling to trade salt, building a house, or marrying off the chief's daughter, as well as planting and reaping their rice crops.

The southward migration of birds in the autumn of 1492 played a part in the discovery of America. When Columbus left Spain and passed the Canary Islands in the summer of that year, he put the known world behind him. In late September and early October he was passing north of the West Indies and was headed towards the coast of Florida, but out of sight of both. His sailors were discontented and mutinous, thinking that they would perish on the boundless area. But on 7 October the birds that had been passing on their autumn migration became so plentiful, all flying to the south-west, that Columbus changed his course to follow them.[19] Because of the birds, Columbus landed in the Bahama Islands instead of on the coast of Florida.

More recently, the great auks that were once seen so commonly on the Grand Banks of Newfoundland also played a part in navigation, for they were used to help fix the position of the sailing ships.[20] Thus some 1743 sailing directions for the North Atlantic include this statement: 'None [birds] are to be minded so much as the Penguins [an old name for the great auk] for these never go without the Bank as others do: for they are always on it . . .'

Birds have also figured prominently in the arts through the years. Dancing is probably the oldest form of art, and some primitive dances seem to have been borrowed from the courtship dances of birds. Among the dances of the New Guinea natives is a bird-of-paradise dance in which the Papuans hop through imitations of the displaying birds. The resemblance is strengthened by the fact that the dancers are decorated with plumes of the birds. In North America the artist-naturalist E. T. Seton has pointed out the resemblance of a Cree Indian dance in Manitoba to that of the sharp-tailed grouse (*Pedioecetes phasianellus*).[21] The dancing and the stamping *hi, hi*'s of the Crees correspond to the wing drumming, tail rattling, stamping, and crowing of the birds.

In ballet, which as we know it began about the sixteenth century, we have, among many others, *Swan Lake* and *The Dying Swan*. In the former the ballerina uses the story to show her dancing ability; in the latter, with simpler steps, a mood is created around the death of an ephemeral being. Creating still another mood, in another medium, Leoncavallo in his opera *I Pagliacci* makes Nedda sing the 'Bird Song', a happy, carefree aria in which she likens the freedom of flight to the way her heart and dreams soar and wander.

In early literature birds commonly appear in their symbolic, magical role, functioning as omens. But they may also appear as characters, even if rather improbable ones, as in Aristophanes' satire *The Birds*, with its amazing list of birds in the *dramatis personae*. Some of these do impossible things like carrying building bricks from Africa, while the pelican hews timbers with its big bill. It is from this play that we get the saying 'carrying owls to Athens', dating from long before the British equivalent, 'carrying coals to Newcastle'. Birds also appeared in Aesop's fables and in such familiar sayings as 'Don't kill the goose that lays the golden eggs', 'A bird in the hand is worth two in the bush', and 'One swallow does not make a summer'.

That there was a considerable body of scientific knowledge during the classical period is evident from the works of Aristotle and Pliny.[22] During the next thousand years science, including natural history, practically disappeared. Perhaps the best-known works during the Middle Ages were the Bible and the bestiary.[23] The Bible has many zoological references, such as the statement that the Lord marks the fall of each sparrow, but its allegories are in the form of parables, generally not involving animals; those of the bestiaries are in the form of fables with animal actors.

The bestiary, enormously popular in the Middle Ages, was a descendant of the *physiologi*, combining natural history and religious instruction, which came into being during the first centuries of the Christian era.[24] The historian T. H. White writes that the bestiary should be considered serious natural history, but a reading of the material he translated gives the impression that its natural history is puerile and that it is a direct descendant of Aesop's fables. To the readers of the bestiary it did not matter whether or not the animals actually existed or did what they were said to do. If the birds and the stories about them helped men to lead virtuous lives, the stories were considered to have served a good purpose. For instance, in the account of the pelican, who is supposed to bring her dead young back to life by opening her breast and pouring her blood over them, a similarity to Christ is pointed out. The pelican therefore became a favourite in heraldry as a symbol of Christ, piety, charity, and hospitality.

One cannot help wondering whether such beliefs did not exist chiefly among 'educated' people and whether, among the unlettered people who lived close to the soil and the wood, there were not men who knew enough about the habits of birds to catch them.

With the beginning of the Renaissance came a more modern attitude towards nature: people looked at birds and wrote down what they saw. Among the great naturalists of the 1500s, of special interest to us is William Turner, an English clergyman who published his *Avium praecipuarum* (History of Birds) in Cologne in 1544.[25] In this work he took up where Aristotle and Pliny left off and added new knowledge of his own.

The appearance of this modern book on birds marked the start of our present era in bird study, an era in which there has been an increasing number of papers and books on birds written and published, until today several thousand papers and many books, both serious and popular, appear each year.[26]

In the literature written in the period following the publica-

tion of Turner's book, prose and verse are often embellished
by references to real birds, as they actually are. The extent of
these allusions is suggested by the existence among the current
works of literary historians of volumes on the birds in the writings of such authors as Spenser (1552–99), Drayton (1563–
1631), Shakespeare (1564–1616), and Milton (1608–74). We
find poems like Shelley's 'To a Skylark', and others with birds
as conspicuous as the albatross in Coleridge's 'Rime of the
Ancient Mariner'.[27]

Today we have mystery stories with the scene laid in a
natural-history museum and detective stories with the main
characters portrayed as bird watchers. Sean O'Casey wrote at
least two short stories with birds as important characters, giving
their everyday lives the dignity of human ones.

But nothing gives a better idea of people's interest in birds
today than the contents of the daily newspapers. Over a two-
year period I gathered 250 clippings about birds from four
Chicago daily papers.[28] A survey of them gives gratifying evidence that people are bird-conscious. In addition to references
in the nature columns, the Sunday supplements, and the
sporting pages, an amazing amount of bird material appeared
during these two years in the news columns alone. The items
range in length from a few lines to a half column or more, and
many are illustrated. They cover a wide variety of bird news,
and 130 kinds of birds are mentioned. Since the combined daily
circulation of the four papers totals more than 2,500,000, the
public reached by these stories is substantial. Such an audience
makes the several thousand readers of the scientific bird journals seem few indeed.

The general impression one gets is that city people are interested in birds, for these clippings represent real happenings.
The standard of accuracy in all of these accounts is high. The
reporters knew what they were writing about or consulted those
who did. Developments relating to the educational, conserva-
tional, and economic importance of birds, or to scientific findings
concerning them, are of interest in this medium only as they are
news. The stories are not aimed at the hobbyist or the bird
lover, for whom there are special columns, but the birds are

treated as interesting beings, with births, lives, and deaths. Silly as well as tragic things happen to them. They get mixed up with the police, are lauded or joked about. Their private lives, their comings and goings, their effect on the community in which they live are all reported. While we cannot say that birds are on their way to becoming citizens, we can see that citizens are certainly becoming aware of birds. As far as birds are concerned, the newspaper-reading public has a chance to be biologically literate.

Ornithology would seem to have achieved a signal success in making birds and their ways familiar to the man in the street, in making its findings the material of everyday reading and conversations, in making the general public aware of birds as part of the environment, and in putting bird lore in the public domain. This spread of knowledge is one of the ultimate goals of any science. What better method of measuring this success than to examine what the daily press presents to its urban readers?

We have come a long way from the time when man's chief interest in birds was to eat them. We have passed the time when they figured only in magic and appeared in stories chiefly to help teach a moral lesson, and have come to the time when a knowledge of birds has become a part of our culture in science, literature, and recreation. Ornithology has played a significant role in opening our eyes to the living world around us – its meaning and our place in it.

APPENDIX I

Classification

A SEARCH for ancestors is a hobby with many people. By searching old records, church registers and tax rolls, and the like, they hope to establish an unknown line of relatives from the present back to the Pilgrim Fathers who travelled on the *Mayflower*, or to those who fought at Hastings at the time of the Norman invasion. This study of family pedigrees is called genealogy, and is variously described as a science or an art.

However, 'genealogy' also has a wider meaning; it denotes an account of the regular descent of a group of organisms from an older form. The tracing of the ancestry of modern species of birds is the goal of the people who study bird classification. The grouping together of related genera into families of birds (whose names always end in 'idae') and of the families into orders of birds (with names ending in 'iformes') indicates degrees of relationship (see also Chapter 5). This relationship is deduced from external characters, from internal anatomy, and from the fossil record. In zoology the term 'genealogy' is seldom used. 'Phylogeny', the commonly used word, may be defined as the race history or evolutionary history of a group of organisms (members of a species, family, order, or the like). Though the study is practised as science, the subjective evaluations required make it at times partake of the nature of an art.

A family tree is often used to indicate the relationships among a group of birds. For birds as a whole a shrubby tree would represent the class Aves. The main branches would be the orders, the small branches the families, the twigs the genera, and the leaves the species. When these groups are reduced to lineal lists, an attempt is made to start with the most primitive and to place nearest relatives next to each other.

The resulting simplicity of arrangement provides a clarity and definiteness that is inherent in the system, but also obscures the many uncertainties and gaps in our knowledge. The idealized family tree well illustrates how birds must have arisen. If we had samples of all the species that have ever existed, the family tree, or phylogeny, could be accurately reconstructed.

But the data we have to work with are the present-day species, some ten thousand of them, plus some 834 known fossil species. This last, the known fossil species, are but a minute fraction, about 0.05 per cent, of those that probably existed. Consider the problem one would have in reconstructing the shape of a banyan tree if one had only a narrow section through the top of the tree – many leaves and twigs, and a few bits of branches – representing present-day birds, and a few slices of larger limbs and trunk, representing the fossil birds. Small wonder that our knowledge of the phylogeny within the class Aves is so uncertain.

The characters which are evaluated as indicators of relationships include a wide range of structures and behavioural traits. Among them are the external characters, such as the shape of the bill and feet, the colour patterns of the feathers and occasionally of the soft parts, and many aspects of breeding behaviour. These are useful for determining relationships even up to the family level. However, at the level of the order, the next higher category, distinctions are based on such characters as the structure of the skull, the arrangement of the muscles and tendons in the legs, the convolutions of the intestines, and the condition of the young at the time of hatching. The classification at this level must be done from a broad point of view, and has been the province of a few bird specialists, not all of whom agree. The following system (Table XI) is that of Dr Alexander Wetmore, former secretary of the Smithsonian Institution and an outstanding authority on fossil birds as well as modern ones. His system recognizes twenty-seven orders and starts with the older, more primitive birds. While it might be argued that the

TABLE XI

The Orders of Living Birds

1	Sphenisciformes	Penguins – flightless swimming birds
2	Struthioniformes	Ostriches (Africa and Arabia)
3	Rheiformes	Rheas (South America)
4	Casuariformes	Cassowaries and emus (Australia and New Guinea)
5	Apterygiformes	Kiwis (New Zealand)
6	Tinamiformes	Tinamous (Central and South America)
7	Gaviformes	Divers – water birds with three toes webbed
8	Podicipediformes	Grebes – water birds with lobed toes
9	Procellariiformes	Albatrosses, shearwaters, and petrels – sea birds
10	Pelecaniformes	Pelicans, tropic-birds, boobies and gannets, anhingas, cormorants, and frigate birds – water birds with four toes webbed
11	Ciconiiformes	Storks, herons, ibis, spoonbills, and flamingos – large water birds specialized for wading
12	Anseriformes	Ducks, geese, swans, and screamers
13	Falconiformes	Hawks, vultures, falcons, etc. – diurnal birds of prey
14	Galliformes	Domestic fowl, megapodes, pheasants, quail, grouse, etc. – gallinaceous, or fowl-like, birds
15	Gruiformes	Cranes, rails, etc.
16	Charadriiformes	Waders, gulls, and auks
17	Columbiformes	Pigeons and sandgrouse
18	Psittaciformes	Parrots, macaws, cockatoos, etc.
19	Cuculiformes	Turacos, cuckoos, and roadrunners
20	Strigiformes	Owls – nocturnal birds of prey
21	Caprimulgiformes	Nightjars, frogmouths, etc.
22	Apodiformes	Swifts and humming-birds
23	Coliiformes	Colies (Africa)
24	Trogoniformes	Trogons (tropics)
25	Coraciiformes	Kingfishers, rollers, etc.
26	Piciformes	Woodpeckers, etc.
27	Passeriformes	Perching birds, more than half of all living species

Sub-orders	a. Eurylaimi	Broadbills
	b. Tyranni	Tyrant fly-catchers, manakins, etc.
	c. Menurae	Lyre-birds, etc.
	d. Passeres	Larks, warblers, thrushes, jays, swallows, etc. – Oscines, or song-birds

penguins and the ratites, which together form the first five orders, are extremely specialized in certain respects, they do have in common their retention of a greater number of primitive anatomical characters. Thus they can be considered low side branches of a family tree whose crown is occupied by birds that are generalized in form but specialized in detail, like the songbirds.

Known birds are classified as ancestral birds and true birds. Alone in the first group is *Archaeopteryx*, the fossil, lizard-tailed, toothed bird of the Jurassic.

All the other known birds, fossil and living, belong in the group of true birds. The most primitive of these are the fossil birds *Hesperornis*, the large flightless swimming birds with teeth (and related *Enaliornis* and *Baptornis*), and *Ichthyornis*, the tern-like bird (and the related *Apatornis*). Whether or not the latter possessed teeth is not known; the toothed jaws earlier thought to belong to this species have proved to be reptile jaws. The vertebrae are biconcave, a primitive character. Both groups are known only from the Cretaceous, mostly of North America.

The brief analysis presented next, with the accompanying figures (Figures 49, 50, and 51), gives an idea of the general characters of each order.

The penguins are pelagic, flightless, swimming, and diving birds of the Southern Hemisphere. They are duck- to swan-sized, and have short necks. Although their feet are webbed, they swim with their wings, which are paddle-like and covered with small, scale-like feathers. The young are down-covered and semi-altricial.

Then come three orders of giant, flightless, running birds which are grouped together along with the kiwis as ratite birds, or ratites, because the breast bone in each lacks a keel. The ostriches, which may stand up to eight feet tall, are found in Africa and Arabia; the emus and cassowaries live in Australia and New Guinea; and the rheas live in South America. The interrelationships of these groups are still under discussion, which is centred especially on the interpretation of the anatomy of the skull. The ostriches, the largest, are the only birds with just two toes; the cassowaries, emus, and rheas are noted for the length of the after-shaft of the feather, which is as long as the main feather part. The young of all are precocial.

The extinct moas of New Zealand, some of which were larger than ostriches, and the extinct elephant bird of Madagascar were similar in general form to the living ratites and are presumably related to them.

The kiwis of New Zealand are flightless, walking birds with wings very much reduced, a silky plumage, and a long slender bill. Thy have semi-precocial young; presumably they are related to the moas.

The tinamous of South America are walking, flying birds, somewhat grouse- or quail-like in appearance, size, and habits. However, the bill is weak, and details of the anatomy relate them to the ratites. Like them, their young are precocial.

Placed next are two orders of specialized swimming and diving birds, the divers and grebes, with fair powers of flight but with little walking ability (a few species are flightless). Their young are precocial. Most of these birds live on fresh water and come out on to land only to nest. Northern species may winter on salt water. The divers, found in the Northern Hemisphere, have the three front toes webbed; the grebes, of world-wide distribution, have the toes lobed. Both have straight, pointed bills.

The albatrosses and their allies are pelagic water birds. They range from thrush- to swan-sized and have the three front toes webbed and the bill hooked at the tip. They are unique in having as nostrils external openings modified into tubes. Their young are altricial. The albatrosses, shearwaters, and petrels have specialized long narrow wings and glide and sail over the waves in seach of their food. However, the thrush-sized storm petrels flutter over the water, sometimes dabbling their feet in it, and the diving petrels dive from the air.

Yet another group of specialized aquatic birds follows, consisting of the pelicans and their allies, which range from the size

Figure 49. *Bottom third of the family tree of birds, by orders:* (a) *penguins;* (b) *ostriches;* (c) *cassowaries, etc.;* (d) *kiwis;* (e) *rheas;* (f) *tinamous;* (g) *divers;* (h) *grebes;* (i) *petrels, albatrosses, etc.;* (j) *frigate birds, boobies, pelicans, cormorants, etc.*

of small ducks to the size of swans. They are the only birds with all four toes connected by webs. Their young are altricial. The pelicans are the most unusual in appearance, having long, broad bills, capacious gular pouches, and long, broad wings. They dive from the air and swim on the surface, fishing. The other species have straight, pointed bills or long bills hooked at the tip. Some dive from the air for their food (tropic-birds and gannets); others swim and dive (anhingas and cormorants). The frigate birds have superb powers of flight and parasitic feeding habits, robbing other birds without alighting on the water.

With the stork, heron, ibis, and spoonbill assemblage, we switch from aquatic birds to an order of birds which are specialized for wading but still feed chiefly on animal life. These birds range from pigeon- to goose-sized, and have long bills (with a few exceptions), long necks, long legs, and (again with a few exceptions) long toes. The young are mostly altricial. A small, highly aberrant sub-group consists of the flamingos which have very long necks and legs, but short, webbed toes. Their short, bent bill has a sieving device of lamellae, similar to that found in ducks, and their young are semi-precocial. The flamingos seem to form somewhat of a link between their own order and the next.

The ducks and their near relatives, the geese and swans, are included with the screamers in one order. As the storks and their close relatives are wading birds whose habitat overlaps that of some walking birds, so the ducks and their relatives are swimming birds whose habitat – primarily marshy areas – overlaps that of some wading and walking birds.

Vegetable food is important to them, and their young are precocial. Some ducks are mostly swimming, diving, and fish-eating birds, while the geese walk on the land and graze on vegetation. The three front toes are webbed in ducks and their relatives, and they have flattened bills with lamellae along the edge for sieving their food from the mud and water. The related screamers, with their big feet webbed only at the base of the toes, and with spurs on the bend of the wing, are rather fowl-like marsh birds of South America.

Now we come to a group of land birds – the hawks and

their allies. Few of them walk, but they fly well, and they perch freely on trees and rocks. They seize their animal prey in their grasping feet, which are armed with sharp, curved claws, and tear it with their short, hooked beak. The young are altricial. Goshawks, kites, buzzards, falcons, eagles, and vultures are all included in this order. The vultures have weaker feet than the hawks and have bills adapted for feeding on carrion. A single aberrant species, the secretary bird of Africa, is a long-legged broad-winged running bird of the plains, with the bill and feet of a hawk.

The gallinaceous, or fowl-like, birds in the next order are typified by our domestic fowl. They are adapted for walking, and have a short bill and short, rounded wings. Their diet is generalized, with vegetable food preferred. A muscular gizzard aids in breaking up this food. They range from the sparrow-sized quail to the giant turkey and peacock. They have precocial young. This well-known group includes partridge, pheasants, peafowl, francolins, grouse, ptarmigan, and guinea fowl. The American curassows, guans, chachalacas, and a few others form a rather distinct sub-group of birds with longer tails than most and a more arboreal habitat. The single aberrant species, the tree-dwelling hoatzin of South America, has a long tail and a crest. Its young have distinct claws on the tips of certain 'fingers'.

The cranes, rails, and their relatives, like the gallinaceous birds, are chiefly terrestrial and eat both animal and vegetable food. Their powers of flight vary from good to poor; some are flightless. The young of most species are precocial or semi-precocial; in a very few they are altricial. The rails – sparrow- to fowl-sized – are the most numerous type; they have short rounded wings, moderately long legs, and long toes for living in the marshes. The cranes are much larger, and have long legs, long necks, and long, broad wings. They too are wading birds, but favour open grass country as well. In the Old World the bustards, running birds of the plains, are well-known repre-sentatives of this order; as are the little, quail-like bustard quail. Especially noteworthy is the cariama of South America, a crane-like bird that is somewhat predatory in habits but is not as

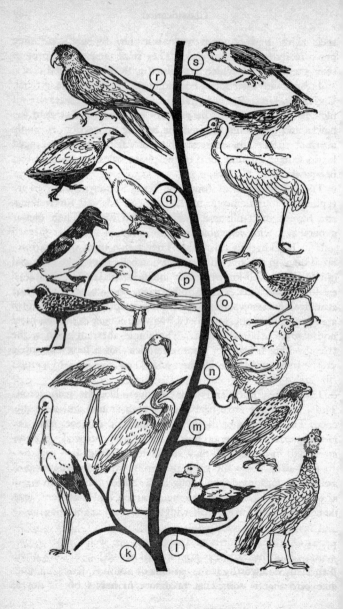

specialized for predation as is the secretary bird, of a previous order. There are a number of other small groups of walking, swimming, or wading species within this order.

The wader, gull, and auk assemblage has four main groups. The waders, sparrow- to fowl-sized, include sandpipers and plovers, and are chiefly walking and running birds with good powers of flight; their home is the edge of the water. The gulls, terns, and skuas are aerial water-feeders with webbed feet and long, narrow wings. The auks, which are swimmers and divers, have webbed feet and rather short, narrow wings, which they use in swift, direct flight and in swimming under water. The jacanas resemble rails and live in the marshes. There are a few other small groups in this order, such as the sheathbills and the seed snipe. The young are precocial or semi-precocial.

The pigeons, seed and fruit eaters, are well typified by the domestic pigeons of our city parks. They range from the size of thrushes to the size of small turkeys. Some are mostly arboreal and have very short legs, but some have longer legs and spend much time walking on the ground. Included in this order are the sandgrouse, which, as their name implies, somewhat resemble grouse. They live in dry, open country and have small feet and pointed wings. The extinct flightless dodo of Mauritius was related to the pigeons. The young of this group are altricial.

Usually placed next to the pigeons are the seed- and fruit-eating parrots, macaws, cockatoos, lories, and their close relatives. The stout, hooked bill and grasping feet, well known from caged species, characterize all members of the compact, species-rich group. Most of them are tree birds, and they range from sparrow- to raven-sized. Their young are altricial.

Some of the cuckoos are tree birds with short legs; others are walking birds with longer legs. Both have two toes in front and two behind. They range from sparrow- to fowl-sized, and their young are altricial. Some specialize in animal food, but

---

Figure 50. *Middle third of the family tree, by orders:* (k) *storks, herons, flamingos, etc.;* (l) *screamers, ducks, etc.;* (m) *hawks, etc.;* (n) *domestic fowl, etc.;* (o) *rails, cranes, etc.;* (p) *plover, gulls, auks, etc.;* (q) *pigeons and sandgrouse;* (r) *parrots;* (s) *roadrunners, cuckoos, etc.*

others are fruit eaters. The roadrunners and the plantain-eaters, or turacos, of Africa are also placed in this order.

The owls are the nocturnal birds of prey, the ecological equivalent of the hawks, the diurnal birds of prey. Owls' hooked bills and sharp claws are quite hawk-like, but the disc-like feathering around their eyes and their soft, fluffy feathers give them a distinctive appearance. The young are altricial.

In the next order, the nightjars and their relatives, we find nocturnal birds, which resemble owls in that they are mottled and barred in soft browns, greys, and black, and have large eyes. The frogmouths and the owlet frogmouths of the Indo-Australian area, and the potoos of the American tropics, are perching tree birds. They have very small feet and a short bill more or less hooked and with a very wide gape, and are somewhat owl-like in appearance if not in habits. The nightjars, while similar, have weaker bills and longer wings and feed on the wing, catching insects. The related oil-bird has a much more hooked bill and feeds on fruit. The young are altricial or semi-precocial.

The most aerial of all birds are the swifts, and included with them in the same order are the humming-birds. The swifts' bill is reduced to little more than a narrow rim around a wide gape, and they have tiny feet and long, narrow wings. Swifts are aerial feeders *par excellence*, gleaners of insects from the air, and an ecological equivalent of the nightjars and the swallows. The humming-birds, all from the New World, have long, needle-like bills for probing flowers and tiny feet. In flight they make a buzzing sound. The young of this order are altricial; those of all the following orders are also altricial.

The colies, or mouse-birds, form a separate order of small, fruit-eating African birds with very long pointed tails, short legs, and the ability to turn all their toes forwards. The trogons, of pan-tropical distribution, form a distinct order of medium-sized tropical birds with beautiful colours, rather long

---

Figure 51. *Top third of the family tree, by orders:* (t) *owls,* (u) *nightjars and frogmouths;* (v) *swifts, humming-birds, etc.;* (w) *colies;* (x) *trogons;* (y) *hornbills, kingfishers, rollers, hoopoes, etc.;* (z) *woodpeckers, toucans, jacamars, etc.;* (aa) *perching birds, such as swallows, crows, robins, etc.*

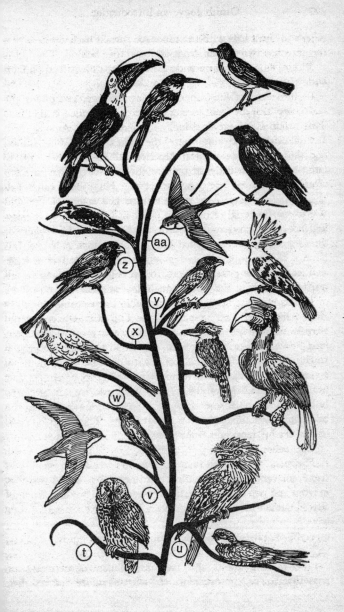

tails, and short legs with the inner toe turned backwards so that the bird has two toes in front and two toes behind. The bill is short and stout but has a wide gape, and the birds feed on fruit and insects.

In birds of the kingfisher–roller assemblage, except for the cuckoo-rollers, the front toes are more or less united at the base. This group is a large one, including ten families. Among them are the widespread kingfishers, the todies of the West Indies, and the motmots of tropical America. All of these have rather large bills, and usually sit up straight and dart down to earth after their animal prey. A few of the kingfishers catch fish rather than insects. Also included are bee eaters of the Old World, partly aerial feeders that often sit up watching for passing insects which they dart out to seize in flight. The rollers of the Old World are somewhat like the bee eaters in habits, but have a short, stout bill and a broad gape instead of a long, slender bill. The ground rollers, found only in Madagascar, are terrestrial birds of the forest and brush, and the cuckoo-rollers of Madagascar are strange birds, notable in this group for their cuckoo-like feet. The hoopoes of the Old World have a long, slightly curved bill and a strange flattened crest. They often feed by walking on the ground. The wood hoopoes comprise a small group of African birds, often with metallic black plumage, a long curved bill, and a habit of climbing about trunks and branches of trees. Hornbills, of the Old World tropics, are large birds with big bills, sometimes with an elaborate casque on the bill; they have small feet and broad wings. They feed on fruit or insects in trees, and some species of hornbills catch insects on the ground.

The woodpeckers and their relatives are tree birds, ranging in size from very small to medium, and normally having two toes in front and two toes behind, like the cuckoos. They are structurally so similar to the perching birds of the next order that they have been united with them in one order. This order includes a diversity of birds, among them toucans, honey guides, barbets, and jacamars.

Finally we come to the great assemblage of perching, or passerine, birds, an order which contains more species than all the rest put together. They range in size from a honey eater three inches long to the raven more than two feet long, and the lyre-bird which with its magnificent tail reaches over three feet in length. Most of the species in this order are rather generalized in bill, wings, tail, and feet. The feet are designed for perching, with three toes in front and one, well developed, behind. However the various birds are very diversified in behaviour.

The song-birds, called Oscines by some authors, comprise the greater part of this order; their syrinx is more complex than that of other birds. The common garden birds, such as thrushes, sparrows, warblers, and swallows, are song-birds.

Nomenclature

To designate each bird by one name, and one name only, sounds much easier than it is. A European bird which an American would think of as some kind of a chickadee is called the 'great tit' in England, the *Kohlmeise* in Germany, the *Talgmees* in Sweden, the *mésange charbonnière* in France, and the *cinciallégra* in Italy. No wonder the scientists of various countries use an international system of nomenclature in which the bird is known to all students, regardless of their nationality, as *Parus major*.

Even people who speak the same language do not always use the same name for a bird. The great northern diver, the moorhen, the sand martin, and the goldcrest of England become the common loon, the Florida gallinule, the bank swallow, and the kinglet of North America.

Within the United States itself the same bird passes under different names among country people in different places, despite the standardization that official lists and bird books are bringing. The ruffed grouse may pass as a birch partridge in New England and as a pheasant in the Carolina mountains; the coot of New England may be a scoter, which is a duck; while the proper coot of the bird books, which is a rail, may be known as a mudhen.

While country folk in different parts of the United States continue to use various names for the same bird, book-conscious people attempting to keep to standard names by following the 'official' American Ornithologists' Union checklist may find they have to adjust to some changes in terminology with each new edition of the list. The duck hawk of the 1931 edition disappears in the peregrine falcon of the 1957 edition, the willow thrush of 1931 in the veery of 1957, and so on, while the Bartramian sandpiper and the prairie hen of the 1895 edition subsequently become the upland plover and a prairie chicken.

When the world was being explored and novelties were being brought in from its four corners, people had to find names for the many unfamiliar birds which were encountered. 'English' names were adopted from a variety of sources: 'emu' and 'albatross' from Portuguese, 'cassowary' from Malay, 'mynah' from Hindi, 'kiwi' from Maori, and 'tinamou' from Gelibi (spoken in French Guiana). For some, names were coined: 'rhea' from mythology, 'tropic-bird' from its habitat, 'roadrunner' from its habit, and 'bobwhite' from its call.

That all is not yet plain sailing where English names are concerned can easily be demonstrated by asking an ornithologist the difference between a pigeon and a dove, or between a parrot, a parakeet, a paroquet, and a parrotlet.

William Turner, the Englishman whose *Avium praecipuarum* (1544) is the Western world's first printed bird book, is sometimes called the Father of Ornithology. He tried to use one name for one bird, but though he dealt only with the birds mentioned in Aristotle and Pliny, with some additions of his own, he had trouble doing so.

Writing of the woodpeckers (Latin *Picus*) he says, '... the first kind the English call the Specht and Wodspecht, which the Germans name elsterspecht. The second kind Englishmen term Hewhole, that is, hewer of holes, the Germans grunspecht.' Thus for the bird now known as *Dendrocopos major* (great spotted woodpecker) he has three names, two in English and one in German, and for the bird now known as *Picus viridis* (green woodpecker), two names. (Evans, A. H., 1903, translated as 'Turner on Birds'.)

While Turner wrote in Latin, the Englishman Mark Catesby, author of the first natural-history book on North America, the two-volume *Natural History of Carolina, Florida, and the Bahama Islands* (1731, 1743), wrote in English. But he did coin

Latin names for his birds. This was the custom of that day, foreshadowing our present-day employment of Latin scientific names. But with five new woodpeckers to name, he used what were really whole descriptive phrases, as is evident in both his Latin and his English versions:

Latin Names	*English Names*
Picus medius quasi villosus	the hairy Wood-pecker
Picus varius minimus	the smallest Spotted Wood-pecker
Picus varius minor, ventre luteo	the yellow-belly'd Wood-pecker
Picus niger maximus capite rubro	the larger, red-crested Wood-pecker
Picus major alis aureis	the Golden-winged Wood-pecker

The system of descriptive Latin names was becoming too cumbersome to be practical. This problem was solved by the great Swedish naturalist and cataloguer Carolus Linnaeus (later ennobled as Carl von Linné). In the tenth edition of his *Systema naturae*, published in 1758, he listed all the birds he knew with binomial, or two-word names. The *Picus niger maximus capite rubro* of Catesby became *Picus pileatus*, for instance.

Linnaeus's great work was the starting point for modern nomenclature. Birds not named in Linnaeus were given binomial names by later authors. The first part of the binomial name is the generic name, indicating the group, or genus, to which the bird belongs; the second part, the specific name, indicates the species. For the relations of these to classification, see Chapter 5, pp. 42, 43.

Scientists generally are agreed on this procedure, and an international commission has drawn up a set of rules governing the naming of animals.

Linnaeus's system of binomial names has been modified by the addition of a third name, or trinomial, to indicate geographical races or sub-species. For example, some sub-species of the house, or English, sparrow (*Passer domesticus*) are *Passer domesticus domesticus* (often written *P. d domesticus*), the house sparrow of northern Europe; *P. d. biblicus*, the paler sub-species of Palestine; and *P. d. niloticus*, the small, pale sub-species of Egypt.

Names may be changed for a variety of reasons related to

changed ideas of biological relationships. Linnaeus named the kestrel *Falco tinnunculus*, the European sparrow hawk *Falco nisus*, and the European goshawk *Falco gentilis*. Later authors, thinking that the relationships of these birds were not close enough to justify keeping them in the same genus, proposed additional genera, including *Accipiter* in 1760 and *Astur* in 1799. The names of these three birds then stood as *Falco tinnunculus*, *Accipiter nisus*, and *Astur gentilis*. More recently most ornithologists have agreed that the birds in the genera *Accipiter* and *Astur* are not different enough to be kept separate, so the goshawk and the sparrow hawk have been put in the same genus, *Accipiter*, the older of the two, and the European goshawk's name has become *Accipiter gentilis*.

The North American goshawk was named *Falco atricapillus* in 1812; this name was later changed to *Astur atricapillus* and then to *Accipiter atricapillus*. Then the view was accepted that the American and the European goshawk are geographical representatives or sub-species of one species, for which the oldest name is *gentilis*, and now the two sub-species are known as *Accipiter gentilis gentilis* and *Accipiter gentilis atricapillus*. Thus scientific nomenclature reflects changing biological concepts.

APPENDIX III

Field-Study Techniques

THIS aspect of ornithology is outside the scope of the present volume. However, many readers may want to become familiar with birds at first hand, for any number of reasons. Some may wish simply to watch them as a hobby, while others may become interested in birds to the point of making serious studies. Probably no aspect of biology is more attractive and fruitful for the amateur student.

The many techniques for watching and studying living birds include attracting and feeding wild birds, putting up nest boxes, and establishing sanctuaries and providing protection; the observer may conceal himself in a hide, use binoculars, camera, or tape recorder, and consult bird guides, or identification manuals; his activities may include bird banding or ringing, colour marking, and studies in zoos or aviaries.

Field studies may result in the writing of life histories, studies of single species, or faunal or ecological reports concerning the species of an area. Studies in museums where specimens are housed may be combined with field studies; they are likely to deal with classification, moult, or anatomy. Some laboratory and experimental studies, employing specialized techniques, deal with physiology, orientation, or behaviour.

For those interested, the following selected bibliography is added:

Barton, R., *How to Watch Birds*, New York, Toronto, and London, 1955.

Hickey, J. J., *A Guide to Bird Watching*, London and New York, 1943.

Hutson, H. P. W., *The Ornithologists' Guide. Especially for Overseas*, London, 1956. Aimed at the amateur who may want to do independent research.

Pettingill, O. S., *A Laboratory and Field Manual of Ornithology*, Minneapolis, Minnesota, 1956. Planned for use in college teaching.

APPENDIX IV

Notes and Suggested Reading

Chapter 1. Introducing Birds

A text on characteristics of birds compared with other animals:

1. Storer, T. I., and Usinger, R. L., *General Zoology*, New York, Toronto, and London, 1957.

A text on bird-fossil history:

2. Romer, A., *The Vertebrate Story*, Chicago, 1959.

General, comprehensive reference works on ornithology:

3. Grassé, P.-P., ed., *Traité de zoologie*, Vol. XV (*Oiseaux*), Paris, 1950.
4. Stresemann, E., 'Aves', in *Handbuch der Zoologie*, edited by Kükenthal, W., and Krumbach, T., Vol. VII, Part 2, Berlin and Leipzig, 1927–34.
5. Thomson, Sir A. Landsborough, ed., *A New Dictionary of Birds*, New York and London, 1964.

General textbooks:

6. Wallace, G. J., *An Introduction to Ornithology*, New York, 1964.
7. Welty, J. C., *The Life of Birds*, Philadelphia, 1962.

Important surveys of the present status of many aspects of ornithology:

8. Marshall, A. J., ed., *Biology and Comparative Physiology of Birds*, 2 vols., New York and London, 1960, 1961.
9. Wolfson, A., ed., *Recent Studies in Avian Biology*, Urbana, Illinois, 1955.

Literature and history of ornithology:
  10. Newton, A., *A Dictionary of Birds*, London, 1893.
  11. Wood, C. A., *An Introduction to the Literature of Vertebrate Zoology*, London, 1931.

  1. For origin of birds, Swinton, W. E., 'The Origin of Birds', in reference 8, Vol. I, pp. 1–14.
  2. For fossil record, Wetmore, A., 'Paleontology', in reference 9, pp. 44–56.

Chapter 2. Size and Shape of Birds

  1. For essay on the size of animals, Huxley, J., *Man in the Modern World*, New York, 1952, pp. 75–90. For problems of size in birds, Storer, R. W., 'Adaptive Radiation in Birds', in reference 8 (Ch. 1), Vol. I, pp. 17–19.
  2. For largest-known bird, Amadon, D., *Condor*, Vol. XLIX (Berkeley, California, 1947), pp. 159–69.
  3. For discussion of bird shape and adaptation to habitats, Storer, R. W., 'Adaptive Radiation in Birds', in reference 8 (Ch. 1), Vol. I, pp. 15–55.

Chapter 3. The Bird Body

For general references see those of Chapter 1, numbered 1–8. For anatomy of birds, reference 1, pp. 544–54.
  1. For skeleton, Bellairs, A. d'A., and Jenkins, C. R., 'The Skeleton of Birds', in reference 8 (Ch. 1), Vol. 1. pp. 241–300.
  2. For musculature, Berger, A. J., 'The Musculature', in reference 8 (Ch. 1), Vol. I, pp. 301–44.
  3. For digestive system, Farner, D. S., 'Digestion and the Digestive System', in reference 8 (Ch. 1), Vol. I, pp. 411–67.
  4. For excretion, Sperber, I., 'Excretion', in reference 8 (Ch. 1), Vol. I., pp. 469–92.
  5. For reproductive system, Witschi, E., 'Sex and Secondary Sexual Characters', pp. 115–68, and Marshall, A. J., 'Reproduction', pp. 169–213, in reference 8 (Ch. 1), Vol. II.
  6. For egg structure, Romanoff, A. L., and Romanoff, A. J., *The Avian Egg*, New York and London, 1949.
  7. For circulatory system, Simons, J. R., 'The Blood-Vascular System', in reference 8 (Ch. 1), Vol. I, pp. 345–62.
  8. For respiratory system, Salt, G. W., and Zeuthen, E., 'The Respiratory System', in reference 8 (Ch. 1), Vol. I, pp. 363–409.

9. For structure of syrinx, Thorpe, W. H., *Bird-Song*, London, 1961, p. 106.
10. For central nervous system, Portmann, A., and Stingelin, W., 'The Central Nervous System', in reference 8 (Ch. 1), Vol. II, pp. 1–36.
11. For endocrine glands, Höhn, E. O., 'Endocrine Glands, Thymus, and Pineal Body', in reference 8 (Ch. 1), Vol. II, pp. 87–114. Also Sturkie, P. D., *Avian Physiology*, Ithaca, New York, 1954, pp. 301–408.

Chapter 4. The Senses of Birds

The following is a selected bibliography:
1. Marshall, A. J., ed., *Biology and Comparative Physiology of Birds*, Vol. II, New York and London, 1961.
2. Pumphrey, R. J., 'The Sense Organs of Birds', *Ibis*, Vol. XC (London, 1948), pp. 171–99.
3. Sturgis, P. D., *Avian Physiology*, Ithaca, New York, 1954.

1. For eye and sight, reference 3, pp. 229–38, and Pumphrey, R. J., 'Sensory Organs: Vision and Audition', in reference 1, pp. 55–68.
2. For ear and hearing, reference 3, pp. 239–42, and Pumphrey, R. J., 'Sensory Organs: Vision and Audition', in reference 1, pp. 69–85.
3. For olfactory, taste, and tactile senses, reference 3, pp. 243, 244, and Portmann, A., 'Sensory Organs: Skin, Taste, and Olfaction', in reference 1, pp. 37–48.
4. Stager, K. E., 'The Role of Olfaction in Food Location by the Turkey Vulture (*Cathartes aura*)', *Contributions in Science*, No. 81 (Los Angeles County Museum, 1964), pp. 1–63.

Chapter 5. Patterns of Diversity

The following is a selected bibliography:
1. Lack, D., *Darwin's Finches*, London, 1947.
2. Storer, R. W., 'Adaptive Radiation in Birds', and 'The Classification of Birds', Chapters II and III in *Biology and Comparative Physiology of Birds*, edited by Marshall, A. J., Vol. I, New York and London, 1960, pp. 15–93.

1. For classification, 'The Classification of Birds', reference 2, pp. 57–93.

2. For adaptation, 'Adaptive Radiation in Birds', reference 2, pp. 15–55.

3. Friedmann, H., *Scientific Monthly*, Vol. LXIII (1946), pp. 395–8.

4. Fisher, J., *The Fulmar*, London, 1952, pp. 433–53.

Chapter 6. Social Feeding

The following is a selected bibliography:

1. Allee, W. C., *The Social Life of Animals*, New York, 1938.
2. Rand, A. L., 'Social Feeding Behavior of Birds', *Fieldiana: Zoology*, Vol. XXXVIII (Chicago, 1954), pp. 1–71.

1. For vultures leading others to carcasses, reference 2, pp. 8, 9.

2. Jackson, F. J. J., *The Birds of Kenya*, Vol. 1, London, 1938, pp. 128–35.

3. Bates, H. W., *Naturalist on the River Amazon*, revised ed., London, 1864, p. 403.

4. Reference 2, pp. 46–58.

5. Reference 2, p. 21.

6. Reference 2, p. 21.

7. Rand, A. L., *Auk*, Vol. LXX (1953), pp. 26–30.

8. Reference 2, p. 25.

9. Reference 2, p. 25.

10. Reference 2, p. 26.

11. Reference 2, p. 30.

12. Friedmann, H., *U.S. National Museum Bulletin 208* (Washington, D.C.), pp. 25–71.

13. Reference 2, pp. 13–15.

14. Reference 2, p. 12.

15. Reference 2, p. 32.

16. Reference 2, pp. 35–7.

17. Reference 2, p. 15.

18. Reference 2, pp. 15, 16.

Chapter 7. Food and Water

1. For physiology of birds, Sturkie, P. D., *Avian Physiology*, Ithaca, New York, 1954. For food habits of birds, Henderson, J., *The Practical Value of Birds*, New York, 1934; and Hartley, P. H. T., 'The Assessment of the Food of Birds', *Ibis*, Vol. XC (1948), pp. 361–81.

2. Schmidt-Neilson, K., and others, 'Extra Renal Salt Excretion in Birds', *American Journal of Physiology*, Vol. CXCIII (1958), pp. 101–7. Also *Auk*, Vol. LXXXI (1964), pp. 160–72.

3. For energy metabolism, King, J. R., and Farner, D. S., 'Energy Metabolism, Thermoregulation, and Body Temperature', *Biology and Comparative Physiology of Birds*, edited by Marshall, A. J., Vol. II, New York and London, 1961, pp. 215–88.

4. For time required for food to pass through digestive system, Sturkie, P. D., op. cit., pp. 155–7.

5. Lincoln, F. C., *Migration of Birds*, Garden City, New York, 1952, p. 53.

6. Kendeigh, S. C., 'Resistance to Hunger in Birds', *Journal of Wildlife Management*, Vol. IX (1945), pp. 217–26.

7. Sims, R. W., 'The Morphology of the Head of the Hawfinch', *Bull. Brit. Mus. (Nat. Hist.), Zoology*, Vol. II (London, 1955), pp. 369–96.

8. Wetmore, A., *Auk*, Vol. XXXVI (1919), pp. 190–97.

9. North, M. E. W., *Ibis*, Vol. XC (1948), pp. 138–41.

10. Morris, D., *British Birds*, Vol. XLVII (London, 1954), p. 33.

11. Ritter, W. E., *The California Woodpecker and I*, Berkeley, California, 1938.

12. Richards, T. J., *British Birds*, Vol. LI (1958), pp. 497–508.

13. Swanberg, P. O., 'Food Storage, Territory and Song in the Thick-billed Nutcracker', *Proceedings 10th International Ornithological Congress* (Uppsala, 1951), pp. 545–54.

14. Chapin, J. P., *Bulletin of the American Museum of Natural History*, Vol. LXXV (New York, 1939), p. 473.

15. Gorsuch, D. M., *University of Arizona Biological Science Bulletin, No. 2* (Tucson, Arizona, 1934), pp. 39–40.

16. Tordoff, H. B., *Miscellaneous Publications of the Museum of Zoology, University of Michigan, No. 81* (Ann Arbor, Michigan, 1954), p. 17.

17. Frings, H. F., and Frings, M., *Condor*, Vol. LXI (1959), p. 305.

18. Amadon, D., and Rothwell, R., *Auk*, Vol. LXXXI (1964), p. 82.

19. Bowen, W. W., *American Museum Novitates*, No. 273 (New York, 1927), pp. 1–5.

20. Emlen, J. T., and Glading, B., *University of California Agricultural Experiment Station Bulletin 695* (Berkeley, California, 1945), p. 34.

21. Bartholomew, G. A., and Dawson, W. R., *Ecology*, Vol. XXXV (1954), pp. 181–7.

Chapter 8. Activity and Rest

1. Pearson, O. P., *Condor*, Vol. LVI (1954), pp. 317–22.
2. Koford, C. B., *National Audubon Society Research Report No. 4*, New York, 1953, p. 25.
3. For sun-bathing, Lanyon, W., *Wilson Bulletin*, Vol. LXX (1958), p. 280. Also Whitaker, L. M., *Wilson Bulletin*, Vol. LXXII (1960), p. 403.
4. For birds and fire, Conway, W. G., *Wilson Bulletin*, Vol. LXXI (1959), p. 189. Also Goodman, J. M., *Wilson Bulletin*, Vol. LXXII (1960), pp. 400–401. Also Burton, M., *Phoenix Re-born*, London, 1959.
5. Whitaker, L. M., *Wilson Bulletin*, Vol. LXIX (1957), pp. 195–262.
6. For song-sparrow awakening, Nice, M. M., *Transactions of the Linnaean Society of New York*, Vol. VI (1943), pp. 99–114.
7. For activity in continued daylight, Armstrong, E. A., *Ibis*, Vol. XXIX (1912), pp. 307–27. Also *Auk*, Vol. XXX (1913), pp. 512–37.
8. Fisler, G. F., *Condor*, Vol. LXIV (1962), pp. 184–98.
9. For swifts sleeping on the wing, Lack, D., *Swifts in a Tower*, London, 1956, pp. 125–36.
10. For activity in continued daylight, Armstrong, E. A., *Ibis*, Vol. XCVI (1954), pp. 1–30.

Chapter 9. Start of the Breeding Cycle

A selected bibliography on breeding behaviour and the breeding cycle follows:

1. Davis, D. E., 'Breeding Biology of Birds', in *Recent Studies in Avian Biology*, edited by Wolfson, A., Urbana, Illinois, 1955, pp. 264–308.
2. Hochbaum, A., *The Canvasback on a Prairie Marsh*, Washington, D.C., 1944.
3. Howard, H. E., *Territory in Bird Life*, London, 1920.
4. Kendeigh, S. C., *Parental Care and its Evolution in Birds*, Urbana, Illinois, 1952.
5. Lack, D., *The Life of the Robin*, London, 1943, pp. 1–200.
6. Nice, M. M., 'Studies in the Life History of the Song Sparrow, I', *Transactions of the Linnaean Society of New York*, Vol IV (1937), p. 1–247.
7. Nice, M. M., 'Studies in the Life History of the Song Sparrow,

II', *Transactions of the Linnaean Society of New York*, Vol. VI (1943).
8. Stoddard, H. L., *The Bobwhite Quail*, New York, 1931.

1. Wetmore, A., *United States National Museum Bulletin 133* (1926), pp. 154–7.
2. For summary of thought on factors controlling breeding seasons and migration, Marshall, A. J., 'Breeding Seasons and Migration', in *Biology and Comparative Physiology of Birds*, edited by Marshall, A. J., Vol. II, New York and London, 1961, pp. 307–39.
3. Rowan, W., *The Riddle of Migration*, Baltimore, Maryland, 1931.
4. For displays, Armstrong, E. A., *Bird Display*, London, 1942.
5. Gilliard, E. T., *Scientific American* (August 1963), pp. 38–46.
6. For courtship feeding, Armstrong, E. A., *Bird Display*, London, 1942, pp. 1–381.
7. For a review of territory, Nice, M. M., 'The Role of Territory in Bird Life', *American Midland Naturalist*, Vol. XXVI (South Bend, Indiana, 1941), pp. 441–87.

Chapter 10. Nests and Eggs

For a selected bibliography see references of Chapter 9, numbered 1–8.
1. For types of nests and eggs of various families and species, Austin, O. L., *Birds of the World*, New York, 1961.
2. For nest construction, reference 1 (Ch. 9), pp. 268–70.
3. Allen, R. P., *National Audubon Society Research Report No. 2*, New York, 1942, pp. 60–65.
4. For share of sexes, various species, in building, reference 4 (Ch. 9), pp. 173–302.
5. For eggshell characters, Romanoff, A. L., and Romanoff, A. J., *The Avian Egg*, New York, 1949, pp. 61–171.
6. For egg laying, reference 1 (Ch. 9), pp. 270–73.
7. For clutch size, reference 1 (Ch. 9), pp. 273–82.
8. For factors affecting clutch size, reference 1 (Ch. 9), pp. 282–4.
9. For factors affecting laying of domestic hen, Romanoff, A. L., and Romanoff, A. J., *The Avian Egg*, New York, 1949, pp. 5–59.
10. ibid., pp. 7–9.
11. Phillips, C. L., *Auk*, Vol. IV (1887), p. 346.
12. For re-nesting, reference 1 (Ch. 9), p. 272.

13. For incubation, reference 1 (Ch. 9), pp. 284–8.
14. For incubation, share of sexes, and attentive periods, various species, reference 4 (Ch. 9), pp. 173–302.

Chapter 11. Parents and Young

For a selected bibliography see references of Chapter 9, numbered 1–8. Also the following:

9. Nice, M. M., 'Development of Behavior in Precocial Birds', *Transactions of the Linnaean Society of New York*, Vol. VIII (1962).
10. Romanoff, A. L., *The Avian Embryo*, New York, 1960.

1. For hatching, reference 1 (Ch. 9), p. 288.
2. Reference 9, pp. 14–27.
3. For share of sexes in care of young, various species, reference 4 (Ch. 9).
4. Skutch, A., *Auk.*, Vol. LII (1935), pp. 257–73.
5. Reference 9, pp. 128–9.
6. For development of a young song-bird, reference 6 (Ch. 9), pp. 12–34.
7. Moreau, R. E., *Proceedings of the Zoological Society of London* (1936), pp. 336, 337.
8. For parental care, many species, reference 4 (Ch. 9), pp. 173–287.
9. Lack, D., *Swifts in a Tower*, London, 1956, p. 90.
10. Reference 4 (Ch. 9), pp. 173–302.
11. For development of young bobwhite quail, reference 8 (Ch. 9), pp. 37–47.
12. For young megapode development, reference 9, pp. 35–40.
13. For young duck development, ibid., pp. 42–55.
14. Heinroth, O., and Heinroth, K., *The Birds*, Ann Arbor, Michigan, 1958, pp. 36–7.
15. For parental care of young grebes, reference 9, pp. 92–100.

Chapter 12. Social Nesting

1. For nest of sociable weaver-bird, Friedmann, H., *Natural History*, Vol. XXX (New York, 1930), pp. 205–12.
2. For pygmy falcon in sociable weaver-bird's nest, ibid.
3. For bird, wasp, and ant associations, Moreau, R. E., *Ibis* (1936),

pp. 460–71; Maclaren, P. I. R., *Ibis* (1950), pp. 564–6; and Durango, S., *Ibis* (1949), p. 140.

4. For mixed colonies of birds in acacia trees, Dickey, D. R., and Van Rossem, A. J., *Fieldiana: Zoology*, Vol. XXIII (1938), p. 360.

5. Davis, D. E., *Auk*, Vol. LVII, 1940; pp. 179–218, and Davis, D. E., *Quarterly Review of Biology*, Vol. XVII (1942), pp. 115–35.

6a. Murphy, R. C., *Oceanic Birds of South America*, New York, 1936.

6. Sladen, W. S. L., *Nature*, Vol. CLXXI (London, 1953), pp. 952–5.

7. Allen, R. P., *National Audubon Society Research Report No. 5*, New York, 1956, p. 183.

8. For a review of social parasitism, Miller, A. H., *Scientific Monthly*, Vol. LXII (1946), pp. 238–46. For cuckoos as social parasites, Chance, E. P., *The Truth about the Cuckoo*, London, 1940.

9. For cow-birds as social parasites, Friedmann, H., *United States National Museum Bulletin 233* (1963). Also Friedmann, H., *The Cowbirds*, Springfield, Illinois, 1929.

10. For honey guides as social parasites, Friedmann, H., *United States National Museum Bulletin 208* (1955).

11. For weaver-birds as social parasites, Friedmann, H., *United States National Museum Bulletin 223* (1960).

12. For ducks as social parasites, Friedmann, H., *Proceedings of the United States National Museum*, Vol. LXXX (Washington, D.C., 1932), Art. 18, pp. 1–7.

13. For egg mimicry of cuckoo, Southern, H. N., 'Mimicry in Cuckoos' Eggs', in Evolution as a Process, edited by Huxley, J., and others, London, 1954, pp. 219–31.

Chapter 13. Wandering, Homing, and Orientation

The following is a selected bibliography:

1. Griffin, D. R., 'Bird Navigation', in *Recent Studies in Avian Biology*, edited by Wolfson, A., Urbana, Illinois, 1945, pp. 154–97.

2. Grinnell, J., 'The Role of the "Accidental"', *Auk*, Vol. XXXIX (1922), pp. 373–80.

3. Kramer, G., 'Long Distance Orientation', in *Biology and Comparative Physiology of Birds*, edited by Marshall, A. J., Vol. II, New York and London, 1961, pp. 341–71.

4. Matthews, G. V. T., *Bird Navigation*, London, 1955.

5. Sauer, E. G. F., 'Celestial Navigation by Birds', in *Scientific American*, Vol. CLXIX (August 1958), pp. 42–7.

1. For New Guinea swifts and altitude variation, Rand, A. L., *American Museum Novitates*, No. 890 (1936), pp. 1–14. Also Rand, A. L., *Bulletin of the American Museum of Natural History*, Vol. LXXIX (1942), p. 458.

2. For circumglobal wandering in far southern waters, Downes, M. C., and others, *Emu*, Vol. LIV (Sydney, Australia, 1954), pp. 257–62.

3. Alexander, W. B., and Fitter, R. S. R., *British Birds*, Vol. XLVIII (1955), pp. 1–14.

4. Witherby, H. F., *British Birds*, Vol. XXII (1928), pp. 6–13.

5. For dovekie invasions, American coast, Murphy, R. C., and Vogt, W., *Auk*, Vol. L (1933), pp. 325–49. Also for summary in North Atlantic, Fisher, J., and Lockley, R. M., *Sea-Birds*, Boston, 1954, pp. 127–31.

6. Kenyon, K. W., and Rice, D. W., *Condor*, Vol. LX (1958) pp. 3–6.

7. Mazzeo, R., *Auk*, Vol. LII (1953), pp. 200–201.

8. For summary of some records of homing of transported birds, reference 4, pp. 19–37.

9. For homing of pigeons, reference 1, pp. 177–81.

10. Matthews, G. V. T., *Ibis* (1961), pp. 211–30.

11. For a discussion of Ising on Coriolis force, reference 1, pp. 155–9; also Beecher, W. J., *Scientific Monthly*, Vol. LXXIX (1954), pp. 27–30.

12. For a discussion of Yeagley's theories on magnetism, reference 1, pp. 159–63.

13. Frisch, Karl von, *Bees, Their Vision*, Ithaca, New York, 1950.

14. For sun orientation, reference 3, pp. 347–8, 354–62, 365–7.

15. For nocturnal orientation, reference 3, pp. 362–7.

16. Matthews, G. V. T., *Journal of Experimental Biology*, Vol. XXX (1953), pp. 370–96.

Chapter 14. Migration and Hibernation

The following is a selected bibliography:

1. Dorst, J., *The Migrations of Birds*, London, 1961.

2. Farner, S. D., 'The Annual Stimulus for Migration: Experimental and Physiological Aspects', in *Recent Studies in Avian*

Biology, edited by Wolfson, A., Urbana, Illinois, 1955, pp. 198–237.

3. Lincoln, F. C., *Migration of Birds*, Garden City, New York, 1952.

4. Lowery, G. H., and Newman, R. J., 'Direct Studies of Nocturnal Bird Migration', (See note 2 above), pp. 238–63.

1. For migration in North America, reference 3; in Eurasia, reference 1, pp. 37–96; in Africa, reference 1, pp. 143–4, 156–65; in Australia, reference 1, pp. 144–8; in South America, reference 1, pp. 141–2, 167–70.

2. For sea birds, reference 1, pp. 171–206.

3. For maps showing speed of migrating cliff swallow, reference 3, p. 17; of Canada goose, p. 22; of grey-cheeked thrush, p. 23.

4. Cooch, G., *Wilson Bulletin*, Vol. LXVII (1955), pp. 171–4.

5. For a summary of bird-ringing programmes of world, reference 1, pp. 18–36.

6. Reference 3, p. 21.

7. Nisbet, I. C. T., *Bird Banding*, Vol. XXXIV (1963), pp. 57–67.

8. On evolution of migration, reference 1, pp. 371–86.

9. On choice of direction, reference 1, pp. 320–70.

10. On timing of migration, reference 1, pp. 282–319. Also Marshall, A. J., 'Breeding Seasons and Migration', in *Biology and Comparative Physiology of Birds*, edited by Marshall, A. J., Vol. II, New York and London, 1961, pp. 307–39.

11. For migration of storks, reference 1, pp. 50–58, 253. Also Schüz, E., 'On the Northwest Migration Divide of the White Stork', *Proceedings XIII International Ornithological Congress* (Ithaca, New York, 1963), p. 477.

12. For orientation of migration, reference 1, pp. 320–70.

13. For timing of migration, reference 1, pp. 282–319. Also reference 2, p. 221.

14. Jaeger, E. C., *Condor*, Vol. LI (1949), p. 105.

15. For torpidity in birds, historical, McAtee, W. L., 'Torpidity in Birds', *American Midland Naturalist*, Vol. XXXVIII (1947), pp. 191 ff. For a summary of torpidity and hibernation, Pearson, O. P., *Bulletin of the Museum of Comparative Zoology at Harvard College*, Vol. CXXIV (1960), pp. 93–102.

Chapter 15. Predation and Parasites

The following is a selected bibliography:

1. Elton, C. S., *The Ecology of Invasions by Animals and Plants*, London, 1958.
2. Errington, P. L., 'Predation and Vertebrate Populations', in *Quarterly Review of Biology*, Vol. XXI (1946), pp. 144–77.
3. Herman, Carlton M., 'Diseases of Birds', in *Recent Studies in Avian Biology*, edited by Wolfson, A., Urbana, Illinois, 1955, pp. 450–68.
4. Lack, D., *The Natural Regulation of Animal Numbers*, London, 1954.
5. Meinertzhagen, R., *Pirates and Predators*, Edinburgh, 1959.
6. Olsen, O. W., *Animal Parasites: Their Biology and Life Cycles*, Minneapolis, Minnesota, 1962.
7. Rothschild, M., and Clay T., *Fleas, Flukes and Cuckoos, A Study of Bird Parasites*, New York, 1952.

1. For Eleanora's falcon nesting time and the autumn migration, Vaughn, R. V., *British Birds*, Vol. LIV (1961), pp. 235–8.
2. For sparrow-hawk predation on birds, reference 4, p. 155.
3. Reference 2, pp. 161–3.
4. Murie, A., 'The Wolves of Mt McKinley', in *Fauna of the National Parks of U.S.*, Fauna Series No. 5, Washington, D.C., 1944, pp. 126–8.
5. Allen, A. A., *Auk*, Vol. XLI (1927), pp. 1–16.
6. Stoddard, H. L., *The Bobwhite Quail*, New York, 1931, pp. 203–20.
7. For sea leopard and penguins, Murphy, R. C., *Oceanic Birds of South America*, New York, 1936, p. 414.
8. Reference 4, p. 157.
9. For ravages of a coyote that reached a duck-nesting island, Bent, A. C., *United States National Museum Bulletin 126* (1923), p. 79.
10. Shaw, C. E., *Zoonooz*, Vol. XXXIV, No. I (San Diego, California, 1961), pp. 1–7.
11. Rand, A. L., 'Pity Poor Pigeon: Host to a Community', *Chicago Natural History Museum Bulletin*, Vol. XXX, No. 8 (Chicago, 1959), pp. 6–7.
12. For pigeon parasites, Levi, W., *The Pigeon*, Sumter, South Carolina, 1957, pp. 381–448.
13. For life histories of many parasites, reference 6.
14. For roundworm life history, reference 7, pp. 179–87.

15. For fluke life history, reference 7, pp. 191–208.
16. Taylor, R. M., and others, *American Journal of Tropical Medicine and Hygiene*, Vol. V (1956), pp. 579–620.
17. Reference 1, pp. 21–4.
18. Wetmore, A., *National Geographic Magazine*, Vol. XLVIII (1925), pp. 77–108.
19. Reference 1, pp. 83–5.
20. For malaria and mosquitoes in Brazil, reference 1, pp. 19–20.
21. Reference 1, pp. 56–8.

Chapter 16. Vital Statistics

The following is a selected bibliography on population problems and vital statistics:

1. Farner, D. S., 'Birdbanding in the Study of Population Dynamics', in *Recent Studies in Avian Biology*, edited by Wolfson, A., Urbana, Illinois, 1955, pp. 397–449.
2. Gibb, J. A., 'Bird Populations', in *Biology and Comparative Physiology of Birds*, edited by Marshall, A. J., Vol. II, New York and London, 1961, pp. 413–46.
3. Hickey, J. J., 'Some American Population Research on Gallinaceous Birds', in *Recent Studies in Avian Biology*, edited by Wolfson, A., Urbana, Illinois, 1955, pp. 326–96.
4. Lack, D., *The Natural Regulation of Animal Numbers*, London, 1954.
5. Udvardy, M. D. F., 'An Evaluation of Quantitative Studies in Birds', *Cold Spring Harbor Symposia on Quantitative Biology*, Vol. XXII (Cold Spring Harbor, New York, 1957), pp. 301–11.
6. Wynne-Edwards, V. C., *Animal Dispersal in Relation to Social Behavior*, New York, 1962.

1. Rand, A. L., *Fieldiana: Zoology*, Vol. XXXIX (1957), pp. 41–5.
2. For status of black-capped chickadee and willow tit, Snow, D. W., 'The Specific Status of the Willow Tit', *Bulletin of the British Ornithologists' Club*, Vol. LXXVI (1956), pp. 29–31.
3. Mayr, E., *Auk*, Vol. LXIII (1946), pp. 64–9.
4. For whooping-crane data, Allen, R. P., *National Audubon Society Research Report No. 3*, New York, 1952, pp. 69–86.
5. Greenway, J. C., 'Extinct and Vanishing Birds of the World', International Committee for Wild Life Protection, Special Publication No. 13, New York, 1958.

6. Fisher, J., and Vevers, H. G., *Proceedings X International Ornithological Congress* (Uppsala, 1951), pp. 463–9.

7. For emperor-penguin numbers, Budd, G. M., *Proceedings of the Zoological Society of London* (1962), p. 382.

8. For *Melanocharis arfakiana* records, Mayr, E., and Rand, A. L., *Ornithologische Monatsberichte*, Vol. XLIV (1936), p. 44.

9. Murphy, R. C., *Oceanic Birds of South America*, New York, 1936, p. 621.

10. Neff, J. A., and Meanley, B., *Bird-Banding*, Vol. XXIX (1958), p. 59.

11. Gueniat, E., *Ornithologische Beobachter*, Vol. XLV (1948), pp. 89–97.

12. Fitzgerald, D. V., *Ibis* (1958), pp. 167–74. For a synopsis of quelea problems in Africa, Naude, T. J., *Proceedings First Pan-African Ornithological Congress* (1959), pp. 264–70; and Williams, J. G., 'The Quelea's Threat to African Grain Crops', *East African Agricultural Journal*, Vol. XIX (1954), pp. 133–6.

13. Meinertzhagen, R., *Pirates and Predators*, Edinburgh and London, 1959, p. 9.

14. For a table of selected population densities in different habitats, Welty, J. C., *The Life of Birds*, Philadelphia, 1962, p. 348.

15. Wing, L. W., *Natural History of Birds*, New York, 1956, p. 265.

16. Reference 4, p. 9.

17. Bump, G., and others, *The Ruffed Grouse, Life History, Propagation, Management*, Albany, New York, 1947, pp. 555–79.

18. For age at sexual maturity, reference 4, pp. 62–3.

19. For precocial breeding, Johnston, R. F., *Auk*, Vol. LXXIX (1962), pp. 269–70.

20. Mayr, E., *American Naturalist*, Vol. LXXIII (1939), pp. 156–79.

21. For sex ratio in game birds, reference 3, pp. 347–50.

22. Selander, R. K., *Condor*, Vol. LXII (1960), pp. 34–44.

23. For sex ratio and mortality, reference 4, pp. 107–13.

24. For nesting success of altricial birds, Nice, M. M., *Auk*, Vol. LXXIV (1957), pp. 305–21.

25. For young game-bird mortality, reference 3, pp. 338–9.

26. Emlen, J. T., *Journal of Wildlife Management*, Vol. IV (1940), pp. 92–9.

27. Reference 1, p. 440.

28. Reference 1, p. 440.

29. For oldest-known banded wild bird, Bergstrom, E. A., *Bird-Banding*, Vol. XXXIV, p. 101, 1963. For table of age records of

banded birds, Welty, J. C., *The Life of Birds*, Philadelphia, 1962, p. 345.

30. Newton, A., *A Dictionary of Birds*, London, 1893, p. 691 (footnote).

31. Flower, S. S., *Proceedings of the Zoological Society of London* (1938), pp. 195–235.

32. Budd, G. M., *Proceedings of the Zoological Society of London*, Vol. CXXXIX (1962), p. 382.

33. Brodkorb, P., *Bulletin of the Florida State Museum, Biological Sciences*, Vol. V, No. 3 (Gainesville, Florida, 1960), pp. 41–53.

34. Greenway, J. C., 'Extinct and Vanishing Birds of the World', American Commission on International Wild Life Protection, Special Publication No. 13, New York, 1958. Included is a discussion of extinction and related factors, pp. 29–137.

Chapter 17. Colour and Coloration

The following is a selected bibliography:

1. Cott, H. B., *Adaptive Coloration in Animals*, London, 1940.

2. Fox, H. M. and Vevers, G., *The Nature of Animal Colours*, London, 1960.

3. Portman, A., *Animal Camouflage*, Ann Arbor, Michigan, 1960. A short, readable account.

4. Rawles, M. E., 'The Integumentary System', in *Biology and Comparative Physiology of Birds*, edited by Marshall, A. J., Vol. I, New York and London, 1960, pp. 189–240; pp. 212–36 deal with pigments, structural colours, patterns, and their origins in birds.

1. Reference 1, p. 35.

2. Reference 1, pp. 5, 117.

3. Reference 1, p. 48.

4. Reference 1, p. 191.

5. Cott, H. B., *Proceedings of the Zoological Society of London*, Vol. CXVI (1946), pp. 371–524.

6. For pigment in plumage, reference 4, pp. 212–21.

7. For structural colour in plumage, reference 4, pp. 221–5. Also reference 2, pp. 5–21. For iridescence, Greenewalt, C. H., *Hummingbirds*, New York, 1960, pp. 169–200.

8. Conway, W. G., *Animal Kingdom*, Vol. LXI (New York, 1958), pp. 169–73.

9. For bioluminescence, Harvey, E. N., *Bioluminescence*, New York, 1952.

10. For luminescence in birds, McAtee, W. L., *American Midland Naturalist*, Vol. XXXVIII (1947), pp. 207–12.

11. Christmas, J. Y., *Auk*, Vol. LXXV (1958), p. 224.

12. For colour change in green hunting jay (*Kitta chinensis*), Deignan, H. G., *Ibis* (1938), pp. 769–72.

Chapter 18. Skin, Feathers, and Moult

1. For discussion of skin and feathers, Rawles, M. E., 'The Integumentary System', in *Biology and Comparative Physiology of Birds*, edited by Marshall, A. J., Vol. I, New York and London, 1960, pp. 189–240.

2. For plumage as insulation, Irving, L., *United States National Museum Bulletin 217* (1960), pp. 344–6.

3. Van Someren, V. G. L., *Fieldiana: Zoology*, Vol. XXXVIII (1956), p. 162.

4. For use of powder down by heron, Wetmore, A., *Condor*, Vol. XXII (1920), pp. 168–70.

5. For preen, or uropygial, glands, Rawles, M. E., 'The Integumentary System', in *Biology and Comparative Physiology of Birds*, edited by Marshall, A. J., Vol. I, New York and London, 1960, pp. 211–12.

6. For number of feathers, various species, Wetmore, A., *Auk*, Vol. LIII (1936), pp. 159–69; and Brodkorb, P., *Quarterly Journal of the Florida Academy of Sciences*, Vol. XII (1949), pp. 241–5.

7. For number of feathers on swan, Ammann, G. A., *Auk*, Vol. LIV (1937), pp. 201–2.

8. For number of feathers on penguin, Lowe, P., *Proceedings of the Zoological Society of London* (1933), pp. 487, 489.

9. For number of feathers and size of bird, Hutt, F. B., and Ball, L., *Auk*, Vol. LV (1938), pp. 651–7.

10. For seasonal variation in number of feathers, Wetmore, A., *Auk*, Vol. LIII (1936), p. 163.

11. For details of feather tracts (i.e., pterylography), Miller, A., *University of California Publications in Zoology*, Vol. XXXVIII (1931), pp. 124–30. For many species, Nitzsch, C. L., *Pterylography*, translated by Dallas, W. S., edited by Sclater, P. L., London, 1867.

12. For brief survey of moults and plumages, Stresemann, E., *Auk*, Vol. LXXX (1963), pp. 1–8. This is a thoughtful critique of a

more comprehensive paper published by Parkes, K., and Humphrey, P., *Auk*, Vol. LXXVI (1959), pp. 1–31. This last, however, uses an experimental nomenclature that is not recommended.

13. Crandall, L. S., *Zoologica*, Vol. XXVI (New York, 1941), pp. 7, 8.

14. For moult of emperor penguin, Murphy, R. C., *Oceanic Birds of South America*, New York, 1936, p. 363.

15. Jollie, M., *Auk*, Vol. LXIV (1947), pp. 549–76.

16. Wetmore, A., *Proceedings of the United States National Museum Bulletin 47* (1914), pp. 497–500.

Chapter 19. Flight, Walking, and Swimming

The following is a selected bibliography:

1. Brown, R. H. J., 'Flight', in *Biology and Comparative Physiology of Birds*, edited by Marshall, A. J., Vol. II, New York and London, 1961, pp. 289–305.

2. Dewar, J. M., *The Bird as a Diver*, London, 1924.

3. Greenewalt, C. H., 'Dimensional Relationships for Flying Animals', *Smithsonian Miscellaneous Collections*, Vol. CXLIV, No. 2, Washington, D.C., 1962, pp. 1–46.

4. Greenewalt, C. H., *Hummingbirds*, New York, 1960. Chapter III deals with hovering flight.

5. Meinertzhagen, R., 'The Speed and Altitude of Bird Flight', *Ibis*, Vol. XCVII (1955), pp. 81–117.

6. Savile, D. B. O., 'Adaptive Evolution in the Avian Wing', *Evolution*, Vol. XI (1957), pp. 212–24.

7. Storer, J. H., *The Flight of Birds*, Bloomfield Hills, Michigan, 1948.

8. Sutton, O. G., *The Science of Flight*, London, 1955.

1. For weight of muscles, Hartman, F. A., *Smithsonian Miscellaneous Collections*, Vol. CXLIII, No. 1 (1961), pp. 19, 89.

2. For aerodynamics of flight, reference 1 and reference 6.

3. Heinroth, O., and Heinroth, K., *The Birds*, Ann Arbor, Michigan, 1958, p. 150.

4. For wing area and bird weight, reference 3, pp. 1–46.

5. For rate of wing beat, reference 3, and reference 5, p. 111.

6. For speed of flight, reference 5, pp. 87–106 (tables).

7. Reference 5, p. 82.

8. For speed varying within species, reference 5, pp. 87–106 (tables).

9. Meinertzhagen, R., *Pirates and Predators*, Edinburgh, 1959, p. 139.
10. Behle, W., *Condor*, Vol. XXXVII (1935), p. 28.
11. Lockley, R. M., *Shearwaters*, London, 1942, p. 128.
12. Wetmore, A., *Proceedings of the United States National Museum*, Vol. LXXXVII (1939), p. 179.
13. For deep-diving records, reference 2, p. 15.
14. Murphy, R. C., *Oceanic Birds of South America*, New York, 1936, p. 384.
15. ibid.

Chapter 20. Voice and Display

The following is a selected bibliography:

1. Armstrong, E. A., *Bird Display*, New York, 1942. An introduction to the study of bird psychology.
2. Hartshorne, C., 'The Relation of Bird Song to Music', *Ibis*, Vol. C (1958), pp. 421–45.
3. Saunders, A. A., *A Guide to Bird Songs*, New York, 1951. Deals with North American birds.
4. Thorpe, W. H., *Bird-Song*, London, 1961.

1. For an example of multiple use of wing fluttering, Rand, A. L., *Auk*, Vol. LVIII (1941), p. 58.
2. Friedmann, H., *The Parasitic Cuckoos of Africa*, Washington Academy of Science, Monograph No. 1, Washington, D.C., 1948, pp. 128–9, 147–50, 181–5.
3. For duetting, reference 4, p. 49.
4. For mutual displays, reference 1, Chapter 10.
5. Jackson, F., *Birds of Kenya and Uganda*, London, 1938, p. 354.
6. For song-sparrow song classification, reference 3, p. 275. Also Saunders, A. A., *Wilson Bulletin*, Vol. LXIII (1951), pp. 99–109.
7. Benson, C. W., *Ibis*, Vol. XC (1948), pp. 48–71.
8. For general discussion of variation in song, reference 4, pp. 93–103.
9. Reference 4, p. 17.
10. For bird dances, reference 1 (Ch. 14).
11. Reference 4, p. 56.
12. Reference 2.
13. For innate song, reference 4, pp. 73, 77.
14. For learning of song, reference 4, pp. 66, 71.
15. Reference 4, p. 64.
16. For mimicry in birds, reference 2, p. 438, and reference 4, p. 113.

Chapter 21. Behaviour, Instinctive and Learnt

The following is a selected bibliography:

1. Emlen, J. T., 'The Study of Behavior in Birds', in *Recent Studies in Avian Biology*, edited by Wolfson, A., Urbana, Illinois, 1955, pp. 105–53.

2. Hinde, R. A., 'Behaviour', in *Biology and Comparative Physiology of Birds*, edited by Moshall, A. J., Vol. II, New York and London, 1961, pp. 373–411.

3. Huxley, J., 'Lorenzian Ethology', *Zeitschrift für Tierpsychologie*, Vol. XX (Berlin and Hamburg, 1963), pp. 402–9.

4. Thorpe, W. H., *Learning and Instinct in Animals*, London, 1963.

1. For an example see hatching of quail, Stoddard, H. L., *The Bobwhite Quail*, New York, 1931, p. 36.

2. For life history of Baltimore oriole, Bent, A. C., *United States National Museum Bulletin 211* (1958), pp. 247–66.

3. Rand, A. L., *Bulletin of the American Museum of Natural History*, Vol. LXXIX (1942), pp. 512 ff.

4. Anthony, A. W., *Auk*, Vol. XV (1898), p. 314.

5. Grohmann, J., *Zeitschrift für Tierpsychologie*, Vol. II (1938), pp. 132–44. Also reference 4, pp. 51–2.

6. Thorpe, W. H., *Bird-Song*, London, 1961, Chapter V. Also reference 4, pp. 370 ff.

7. For importance of learning in everyday life, reference 4, p. 316.

8. Oliver, W. R. B., *New Zealand Birds*, Wellington, New Zealand, 1955, p. 544.

9. Reference 4, pp. 314, 315.

10. Reference 4, pp. 332–8.

11. Eibl-Ebesfeldt, I., *Animal Kingdom*, Vol. LXVII (1964), pp. 11–13, four photographs.

12. For detour problems, reference 4, p. 339.

13. Reference 4, pp. 340–46.

14. Rand, A. L., *Bulletin of the American Museum of Natural History*, Vol. LXXVIII (1941), pp. 213–42.

15. For new traditions in waterfowl, Hochbaum; A., *Travel and Traditions of Waterfowl*, Newton, Massachusetts, 1955, pp. 217–36.

16. Bent, A. C., *U.S. National Museum Bulletin 191* (1946), p. 266.

17. For a survey of different approaches to bird behaviour, reference 4, Chapters 1 and 2; reference 2; and reference 3.

Chapter 22. Bird Geography

The following is a selected bibliography:

1. Darlington, P. J., *Zoogeography. The Geographical Distribution of Animals*. New York, 1957.
2. Sclater, P. L., 'On the General Geographical Distribution of the Members of the Class Aves', *Proceedings of The Linnaean Society of London, Zoology*, Vol. II (1859), pp. 130–45.
3. Wallace, A. R., *The Geographical Distribution of Animals*, London, 1876.
4. Wallace, A. R., *Island Life*, London, 1880.

1. For bird dispersal, continental patterns, and island patterns, reference 1, Chapters 5, 7, and 8.
2. For survey of the fossil record, Wetmore, A., 'Paleontology', *Recent Studies in Avian Biology*, edited by Wolfson, A., Urbana, Illinois, 1955, pp. 44–56.
3. Wetmore, A., *Smithsonian Miscellaneous Collections*, Vol. CXXXVIII, No. 4 (1959), p. 12.
4. ibid., pp. 10, 11.
5. Miller, A. H., *Condor*, Vol. LXV, pp. 289–99, Berkeley, California, 1963.
6. Sprunt, A., 'The Spread of the Cattle Egret', *Smithsonian Report for 1954*, Washington, D.C., 1955, pp. 259–76.
7. References 2, 3, and 4.
8. For Ethiopian Region, Chapin, J. P., 'Birds of the Belgian Congo', *Bulletin of the American Museum of Natural History*, Vol. LXV (1932), pp. 1–391. Also reference 1, pp. 428–.
9. For Oriental Region, reference 1, pp. 433–7.
10. For Australian Region, reference 1, pp. 449–52.
11. For Palearctic Region, reference 1, pp. 438–42.
12. For Nearctic Region, reference 1, pp. 442–6.
13. For Neo-tropical Region, reference 1, pp. 446–9.
14. For distribution of sea birds, Serventy, D. L., 'Geographical Distribution of Living Birds', in *Biology and Comparative Physiology of Birds*, edited by Marshall, A. J., Vol. I, New York and London, 1960, pp. 118–24.
15. For ecology and distribution, Hesse, R., Allee, W. C., and Schmidt, K. P., *Ecological Animal Geography*, New York and London, 1937.

Chapter 23. The Nature of Species

The following is a selected bibliography:

1. Huxley, J., *Evolution: The Modern Synthesis*, London, 1942.
2. Mayr, E., *Animal Species and Evolution*, Cambridge, Massachusetts, 1963.
3. Romer, A. S., *The Vertebrate Story*, Chicago, 1959.
4. Simpson, G. G., *The Meaning of Evolution*, New York, 1951.

1. For chronology of fossils, reference 3, p. 10.
2. For rate of evolution and environmental changes, reference 4, Chapter 5.
3. Brodkorb, P., *Bulletin of the Florida State Museum, Biological Sciences*, Vol. V, No. 3 (1960), pp. 47–9.
4. Darwin, C., *On the Origin of Species by Means of Natural Selection, or the Preservation of Favoured Races in the Struggle for Life*, London, 1859.
5. For the course of twentieth-century evolutionary thinking, reference 1 and reference 4.
6. For evaluation of bird-fossil record, Wetmore, A., 'Paleontology', *Recent Studies in Avian Biology*, edited by Wolfson, A., Urbana, Illinois, 1955, pp. 44–55.
7. Levi, W. M., *The Pigeon*, Sumter, South Carolina, 1957, Chapter III.
8. For Galápagos finches, Lack, D., *Darwin's Finches*, London, 1947.
9. For factors regulating population numbers, Lack, D., *The Natural Regulation of Animal Numbers*, London, 1954, pp. 1–343.
10. For sub-species of song sparrow, Miller, A. H., *Evolution*, Vol. X (1956), pp. 262–77.
11. For map of breeding colonies of Caspian tern, Voous, K. H., *Atlas of European Birds*, Amsterdam, 1960, p. 150.
12. For Philippine avifauna, Delacour, J., and Mayr, E., *Birds of the Philippines*, New York, 1946.
13. Rand, A. L., *Natural History Miscellanea*, No. CVII (Chicago, 1952), pp. 3–5.
14. Pough, R. H., *Audubon Bird Guide. Eastern Land Birds*, New York, 1946, pp. 63–5.
15. For effect of glaciation on species formation, Rand, A. L., *Evolution*, Vol. II, No. 4 (1948), pp. 314–21.

Chapter 24. Birds and Man

The following is a selected bibliography:

1. Armstrong, E. A., *The Folklore of Birds*, London, 1958. An inquiry into the origin and distribution of some magico-religious traditions.
2. Fisher, J., *A History of Birds*, Boston, 1954.
3. Sibley, C. G., 'Ornithology', in *A Century of Progress in the Natural Sciences 1853–1953*. California Academy of Science, San Francisco, 1955, pp. 629–59.
4. Walker, R. H., *Birds and Men. American Birds in Science, Art, Literature and Conservation, 1800–1900*, Cambridge, Massachusetts, 1955.

1. Cott, H. B., *Ibis*, Vol. XCV (1953), p. 426.
2. Rowan, M. K., *Ibis*, Vol. XCIV (1952), pp. 116–20.
3. Salomonsen, F., *The Birds of Greenland*, Copenhagen, 1950, p. 408.
4. Delacour, J., *The Pheasants of the World*, London, 1951, pp. 107–8.
5. Newton, A., *A Dictionary of Birds*, London, 1893, pp. 994–6.
6. For ancestors of domestic ducks and geese, Delacour, J., *Waterfowl of the World*, Vol. I, pp. 97–9 (geese), Vol. II, p. 43 (mallard), Vol. III, pp. 126–30 (Muscovy duck), London, 1954–9.
7. For guano in South America, Murphy, R. C., *Oceanic Birds of South America*. New York, 1936, pp. 286–95.
8. For guano, world-wide occurrence, Hutchinson, G. E., *Bulletin of the American Museum of Natural History*, Vol. XCVI (1950), pp. 1–554.
9. For some statistics on extent of plume trade, Henderson, J., *The Practical Value of Birds*, New York, 1934, pp. 103–7.
10. Phillips, J. C., *A Natural History of the Ducks*, Vol. IV, Boston, Massachusetts, 1936, pp. 98–103.
11. Rand, A. L., *Stray Feathers from a Bird Man's Desk*, Garden City, New York, 1955, pp. 38–41, 214.
12. Serventy, D. L., and Whittell, H. M., *A Handbook of the Birds of Western Australia*, Perth, W.A., 1948, p. 96.
13. Fisher, J., and Lockley, R. M., *Sea-Birds*, Cambridge, Massachusetts, 1954, pp. 93–9.
14. For various methods of catching birds, MacPherson, H. A., *A History of Fowling*, Edinburgh, 1897.
15. For the practice of falconry, Mitchell, E. B., *The Art and*

Practice of Hawking, Boston, Massachusetts, 1962 (first published in 1900). Also Woodford, M., *A Manual of Falconry*, Newton, Massachusetts, 1960.

16. For Dyaks and their belief in bird magic, Freeman, J. D., 'Iban Augury', in *Birds of Borneo*, by B. E. Smythies, Edinburgh and London, 1960, pp. 73–98.

17. Rand, A. L., *Stray Feathers from a Bird Man's Desk*, Garden City, New York, 1955, pp. 171–2.

18. Harrisson, T., 'Sarawak: A Calendar of Migratory Birds', in *Birds of Borneo*, by Smythies, B. E., Edinburgh and London, 1960, pp. 39–42.

19. Chapman, F. M., 'The Ornithology of Columbus' First Voyage', *Papers Presented to the World's Congress on Ornithology*, edited by Rood, E. I., and Coues, E., Chicago, 1896, pp. 181–5.

20. Greenway, J. C., *Extinct and Vanishing Birds of the World*, New York, 1958, p. 275.

21. Seton, E. T. [E. E. Thompson], 'The Birds of Manitoba', *Proceedings of the United States National Museum*, Vol. XII (1890), pp. 457–653.

22. Evans, A. H., *Turner on Birds*, Cambridge, 1903, pp. 1–223.

23. For birds of the Bible, Parmalee, A., *All the Birds of the Bible*, New York, 1959.

24. For a translation of a twelfth-century bestiary and comments on its history, significance, and influence, White, T. H., *The Book of Beasts*, London, 1954.

25. For a translation of Turner (from Latin), Evans, A. H., *Turner on Birds*, Cambridge, 1903.

26. For a brief survey of the history of world ornithology, Fisher, J., *A History of Birds*, Boston, 1954, pp. 1–205.

27. For comments on birds in English and American literature, Harrison, T. P., *They Tell of Birds. Chaucer, Spenser, Milton, Drayton*, Austin, Texas, 1950. Also Stuart, D. M., *A Book of Birds and Beasts, Legendary, Literary and Historical*, London, 1957. Also Welker, R. H., *Birds and Men. American Birds in Science, Art, Literature and Conversation, 1800–1900*, Cambridge, Massachusetts, 1955.

28. Rand, A. L., *Chicago Natural History Museum Bulletin*, Vol. XXIX, No. 8 (1958), pp. 6–7.

Appendix I. Classification

The following is a selected bibliography:

1. Austin, O. L., *Birds of the World*, New York, 1961. All families illustrated with beautiful art work.

2. Gilliard, E. T., *Living Birds of the World*, Garden City, New York, 1958. Illustrated with colour photographs.

3. Mayr, E., and Amadon, D., 'A Classification of Recent Birds', *American Museum Novitates*, No. 1496 (1951), pp. 1–42. Another point of view in regard to many details.

4. Storer, R. W., 'The Classification of Birds', in *Biology and Comparative Physiology of Birds*, edited by Marshall, A. J., Vol. I, New York, 1960, pp. 57–92. A discussion of orders and families.

5. Van Tyne, J., and Berger, A. J., *Fundamentals of Ornithology*, New York, 1959. Chapter XII is devoted to a discussion of 'Taxonomy and Nomenclature', Chapter XIII to 'The Classification of World Birds by Families', with a black-and-white of a species for each family.

6. Wetmore, A., 'A Classification for the Birds of the World', *Smithsonian Miscellaneous Collections*, Vol. CXXXIX, No. 11 (1960). This is the standard reference.

Scientific Names of Birds Mentioned

albatross. Family Diomedeidae.

albatross, Laysan. *Diomedea immutabilis*.

albatross, royal. *Diomedea epimorpha*.

albatross, wandering. *Diomedea exulans*.

anhinga. *Anhinga anhinga*.

ani. A cuckoo, genus *Crotophagus*.

auk. Family Alcidae.

auk, great. *Pinguinus impennis*.

auk, little. *Plautus alle*

barbet. Family Capitonidae.

bateleur. An eagle, *Terathopius ecaudatus*.

bee eater. Family Meropidae.

bee eater, least. *Melittophagus pusillus*.

bird of paradise. Family Paradisaeidae.

bird of paradise, blue. *Paradisaea rudolphi*.

bird of paradise, king. *Cicinnurus regius*.

bird of paradise, magnificent. *Diphyllodes magnificus*.

bird of paradise, twelve-wired. *Seleucides ignotus*.

bittern. Family Ardeidae (part).

bittern, sun. Family Eurypygidae.

blackbird, American. Family Icteridae (part).

blackbird, crow. *See* grackle, New World.

blackbird, European. *Turdus merula*.

blackbird, icterid. *See* blackbird, American.

blackbird, red-winged. *Agelaius phoeniceus*.

blackcock. *See* grouse, black.

blue-bird, American. Genus *Sialia*.

blue-bird, fairy. Genus *Irena*.

bobolink. *Dolichonyx oryzivorus*.

bobwhite. *See* quail, bobwhite.

booby. Genus *Sula*.

bower-bird. Family Ptilonorhynchidae.

bower-bird, gardener. *Amblyornis inornatus*.

brambling. *Fringilla montifringilla*.

broadbill. Family Eurylaimidae.

budgerigar. *Melopsittacus undulatus*.

bulbul. Family Pycnonotidae.

bullfinch, European. *Pyrrhula pyrrhula*.

bunting. Family Fringillidae (part).

bunting, cirl. *Emberiza cirlus*.

bunting, corn. *Emberiza calandra*.

bunting, snow. *Plectrophenax nivalis*.

bustard. Family Otididae.

buzzard. Family Accipitridae (part).

cahow. *See* petrel, Bermuda.

canary. A finch, *Serinus canarius*.

canvas-back. *Aythya valisineria*.

cardinal. *Richmondena cardinalis*.

cariama. Family Cariamidae.

cassowary. Genus *Casuarius*.

cat-bird, American. *Dumetella carolinensis*.

chachalaca. Family Cracidae (part).

chaffinch. *Fringilla coelebs*.

chat. Genus *Saxicola*.

chat, palm. *Dulus dominicus*.

chat, robin. Genus *Cossypha*.

chickadee. *See* tit, great.

chickadee, black-capped. *Parus atricapillus*.

chicken, prairie. *Tympanuchus cupido*.

cockatoo, sulphur-crested. *Cacatua galerita*.

cock-of-the-rock. *Rupicola rupicola*.

coly. Genus *Colius*.

condor, Andean. *Vultur gryphus*.

condor, California. *Gymnogyps californianus*.

coot. Genus *Fulica*.

cormorant. Family Phalacrocoracidae.

cormorant, flightless. *Phalacrocorax harrisi*.

cormorant, great. *Phalacrocorax carbo*.

cotinga. Family Contingidae.

coucal. A cuckoo, genus *Centropus*.

cow-bird. Parasitic icterid blackbirds of the genera *Molothrus*, *Tangavius*, and *Psomocolax*.

cow-bird, bay-winged. *Molothrus badius*.

cow-bird, brown-headed. *Molothrus ater*.

cow-bird, screaming. *Molothrus rufo-axillaris*.

crake, Argentine. *Laterallus leucopyrrhus*.

crane. Family Gruidae.

crane, whooping. *Grus americana*.

creeper, tree. Family Certhiidae.

crossbill. Genus *Loxia*.

crossbill, red. *Loxia curvirostra*.

crow. Genus *Corvus*.

crow, American. *Corvus brachyrhynchos*.

crow, Indian. *Corvus macrorhynchos*.

cuckoo. Family Cuculidae.

cuckoo, black-billed. *Coccyzus erythropthalmus*.

cuckoo, common European. *Cuculus canorus*.

cuckoo, glossy, of Africa. Genus *Chrysococcyx*.

cuckoo, guira. Genus *Guria*.

cuckoo, yellow-billed. *Coccyzus americanus*.

curassow. Family Cracidae (part).

curlew, Eskimo. *Numenius borealis*.

dickcissel. *Spiza americana*.

dipper. Genus *Cinclus*.

diver, great northern. *See* loon, common.

dodo. *Raphus cucullatus*.

dove. Family Columbidae (part).

dove. *See* pigeon.

dove, Florida ground. *Columbigallina passerina*.

dove, mourning. *Zenaidura macroura*.

dove, rock. Ancestor of domestic pigeon. *Columba livia*.

dovekie. *Plautus alle*.

drongo. Family Dicruridae.

duck. Family Anatidae (part).

duck, black-headed. *Heteronetta atricapilla*.

duck, domestic. *See* mallard *and* duck, Muscovy.

duck, Labrador. *Camptorhynchus labradorium*.

duck, Muscovy. *Cairina moschata*.

duck, speckled. *Anas flavirostris*.

duck, steamer. *See* steamer duck.

duck, tree. Genus *Dendrocygna*.

duck, wood. *Aix sponsa*.

eagle. Family Accipitridae (part).

eagle, bald. *Haliaeetus leucocephalus*.

eagle, golden. *Aquila chrysaetos*.

eagle, Verreaux's. *Aquila verreauxi*.

egret. Genus *Egretta*. Also, other plumed, white herons.

egret, cattle. *Bubulcus ibis*.

eider. Family Anatidae (part).

eider, common. *Somateria mollissima*.

emu. *Dromiceius novae-hollandiae*.

falcon. Family Falconidae (part).

falcon, Eleanora's. *Falco eleanorae*.

falcon peregrine. *Falco peregrinus*.

falcon, pigmy. *Poliohierax semitorquatus*.

finch. Family Fringillidae (part).

finch, Galápagos. Sub-family Geospizinae.

finch, purple. *Carpodacus purpureus*.

finch, rosy. *Leucostica tephrocotis*.

finch, snow. *Montifringilla taczanowski*.

finch, weaver. Family Ploceidae (part).

finch, woodpecker. *Camarhynchus pallidus*.

fin-foot. *See* sun-grebe.

flamingo. Family Phoenicopteridae.

flicker. Genus *Colaptes*.

flicker, red-shafted. *Colaptes cafer*.

flicker, yellow-shafted. *Colaptes auratus*.

flower-pecker. Family Dicaeidae.

flower-pecker, obscure. *Melanocharis arfakiana*.

fly-catcher, Acadian. *Empidonax virescens*.

fly-catcher, least. *Empidonax minimus*.

fly-catcher, New World. *See* flycatcher, tyrant.

fly-catcher, Old World. Family Muscicapidae.

fly-catcher, scissor-tailed. *Muscivora forficata*.

fly-catcher, tyrant. Family Tyrannidae.

fowl, domestic. *See* fowl, jungle.

fowl, Guinea. Family Numididae.

fowl, jungle. Ancestor of domestic fowl, *Gallus gallus*.

francolin. Genus *Francolinus*.

frigate bird. Family Fregatidae.

frogmouth. Family Podargidae.

fulmar. *Fulmarus glacialis*.

gallinule. Family Rallidae (part).

gallinule, Florida. *Gallinula chloropus*.

gannet. *Moris bassanus*.

gnat-catcher. Genus *Polioptila*.

goldcrest. *See* kinglet.

goldfinch, American. *Spinus tristis*.

goldfinch, European. *Carduelis carduelis*.

goose. Family Anatidae (part).

goose, blue. *Chen caerulescens*.

goose, brent. *Branta berniclas*.

goose, Canada. *Branta canadensis*.

goose, Chinese. *Cygnopsis cygnopsis*.

goose, domestic. *See* goose, Chinese *and* goose, greylag.

goose, greylag. *Anser anser.*
goose, Ross. *Chen rossii.*
goose, snow. *Chen hyperborea.*
goose, swan. *See* goose, Chinese.
goose, white-fronted. *Anser albifrons.*
goshawk, African. Genus *Melierax.*
goshawk, northern. *Accipiter gentilis.*
grackle, boat-tailed. *Cassidix mexicanus.*
grackle, New World. Family Icteridae (part).
grass-wren. *Amytornis goyderi.*
grebe. Family Podicipedidae.
grebe, Lake Atitlán. *Podilymbus gigas.*
grebe, Lake Titicaca. *Centropelma micropterum*
grebe, pied-billed. *Podilymbus podiceps.*
grosbeak, evening. *Hesperiphona vespertina.*
grouse. Family Tetraonidae.
grouse, black. *Lyrurus tetrix*
grouse, ruffed. *Bonasa umbellus.*
grouse, sharp-tailed. *Pedioecetes phasianellus.*
guan. Family Cracidae (part).
gull. Family Laridae (part).
gull, herring. *Larus argentatus.*
gull, ivory. *Pagophila eburnea.*
gull, western. *Larus occidentalis.*

hawfinch. Genus *Coccothraustes.*
hawk. Family Accipitridae.
hawk, American sparrow. *Falco sparverius.*
hawk, Cooper's. *Accipiter cooperii.*
hawk, duck. *See* falcon, peregrine.
hawk, European sparrow. *Accipiter nisus.*
hawk, fish. *See* osprey.
hawk, harrier. *Gymnogenys typicus (Polyboroides typicus).*
hawk, marsh. *Circus cyaneus.*

hawk, red-shouldered. *Buteo lineatus.*
hen, heath. Eastern race of prairie chicken.
hen, prairie. *See* chicken, prairie.
heron. Family Ardeidae (part).
heron, black-crowned night. *Nycticorax nycticorax.*
heron, great blue. *Ardea herodias.*
heron, night. Family Ardeidae (part).
hoatzin. Family Opisthocomidae.
honey creeper, Hawaiian. Family Drepanididae.
honey eater. Family Meliphagidae.
honey guide. Family Indicatoridae.
honey guide, common. *Indicator indicator.*
hoopoe. *Upupa epops.*
hornbill. Family Bucerotidae.
hornbill, ground. *Bucorvus abyssinicus.*
hornbill, Oriental. *Rhinoplax vigil.*
humming-bird. Family Trochilidae.
humming-bird, Anna's. *Calypte anna.*
humming-bird, bee. *Mellisuga helenae.*
humming-bird, ruby-throated. *Archilochus colubris.*

ibis. Family Threskiornithidae.
ibis, scarlet. *Eudocimus ruber.*
ibis, wood. *Mycteria americana.*

jacamar. Family Galbulidae.
jacana. Family Jacanidae.
jay. Family Corvidae (part).
jay, blue. *Cyanocitta cristata.*
jay, Canada. *Perisoreus canadensis.*
jay, grey. *See* jay, Canada.
jay, green hunting. *Kitta chinensis.*
jay, Mexican brown. *Psilorhinus morio.*
junco. Genus *Junco.*
junco, slate-coloured. *Hyemalis.*

kagu. Family Rhynochetidae.

kestrel. *Falco tinnunculus.*

kill-deer. *Charadrius vociferus.*

king-bird. *Tyrannus tyrannus.*

kingfisher. Family Alcedinidae.

kinglet. Genus *Regulus.*

kite. Family Accipitridae (part).

kite, swallow-tailed. *Elanoides forficatus.*

kiwi. Genus *Apteryx.*

lammergeier. *Gypaetus barbatus.*

lapwing. *Vanellus vanellus.*

lark. Family Alaudidae.

lark, horned. *Eremophila alpestris.*

leaf-bird. Family Chloropseidae.

lily-trotter. *See* jacana.

longclaw. Genus *Macronyx.*

loon. Genus *Gavia,* family Gaviidae.

loon, common. *Gavia immer.*

lorikeet, bat. Genus *Loriculus.*

lory. Family Psittacidae (part).

love-bird, African. Genus *Agapornis.*

lyre-bird. *Menura novae-hollandiae.*

macaw. Genus *Ara.*

magpie. *Pica pica.*

magpie, bell. Family Cracticidae.

magpie, lark. Family Grallinidae.

mallard. *Anas platyrhynchos.*

manakin. Family Pipridae.

martin. Family Hirundinidae (part).

martin, house. *Delichon urbica*

martin, purple. *Progne subis.*

martin, sand. *See* swallow, bank.

meadowlark. Genus *Sturnella.*

megapode. Family Megapodiidae.

merganser. Genus *Mergus.*

merganser, American. *Mergus merganser.*

mesites. Family Mesitornithidae.

moa. Family Dinornithidae.

mocking-bird. *Mimus polyglottos.*

moorhen. *See* gallinule, Florida.

motmot. Family Momotidae.

mouse-bird. *See* coly.

mutton-bird. *See* shearwater, slender-billed.

mynah. Family Sturnidae (part).

mynah, talking. *Gracula religiosa.*

nightingale. Genus *Luscinia.*

nightjar. Family Caprimulgidae.

nutcracker, thick-billed. *Nucifraga caryocatactes.*

nuthatch. Genus *Sitta,* family, Sittidae.

oil-bird. *Steatornis caripensis.*

old-squaw. *Clangula hyemalis.*

oriole, Baltimore. *Icterus galbula.*

oropendola. Family Icteridae (part)

osprey. *Pandion haliaetus.*

ostrich. *Struthio camelus.*

oven-bird. In Central and South America, an oven-bird, Family Furnariidae (part).

oven-bird. In North America, a wood warbler, *Seiurus aurocapillus,* Family Parulidae.

owl, barn. Family Tytonidae.

owl, barred. *Strix varia.*

owl, eagle. *Bubo bubo.*

owl, great horned. *Bubo virginianus*

owl, little, of Pallas Athene. *Athene noctua.*

owl, screech. *Otus asio.*

owl, short-eared. *Asio flammeus.*

owl, snowy. *Nyctea scandiaca.*

owl, typical. Family Strigidae.

owlet frogmouth. Family Aegothelidae.

oyster-catcher. Genus *Haematopus.*

oyster-catcher, European. *Haematopus ostralegus.*

paradise, bird of. *See* bird of paradise.

parakeet, Carolina. *Conuropsis carolinensis.*

parakeet, hanging. *See* lorikeet, bat

parrot. Family Psittacidae.

parrot, African grey. *Psittacus erithacus.*

parrot, Amazon. Genus *Amazona.*

parrot, kea. *Nestor notabilis.*

parrot, monk. *Myiopsitta monachus.*

partridge, grey. *Perdix perdix*

peacock. *See* peafowl.

peafowl. *Pavo muticus.*

pelican. Family Pelecanidae.

pelican, American white. *Pelecanus erythrorhynchos.*

pelican, brown. *Pelecanus occidentalis.*

pelican, European white. *Pelecanus onocrotalus.*

penguin. Family Spheniscidae.

penguin, Adélie. *Pygoscelis adeliae.*

penguin, emperor. *Aptenodytes forsteri.*

petrel, Bermuda. *Pterodroma cahow.*

petrel, Leach's. *Oceanodroma leucorhoa.*

petrel, storm. Family Hydrobatidae.

petrel, South Trinidad. *Pterodroma arminjoniana.*

phainopepla. *Phainopepla nitens.*

phalarope. Family Phalaropodidae.

pheasant. Family Phasianidae (part).

pheasant, argus. *Argusianus argus.*

philepittas. Family Philepittidae.

piculet, rufous. *Sasia abnormis.*

pigeon. Family Columbidae.

pigeon, domestic. *See* dove, rock.

pigeon, passenger. *Ectopistes migratorius.*

pipit. Family Motacillidae (part).

pipit, meadow. *Anthus pratensis.*

pipit, tree. *Anthus trivialis.*

pitta. Genus *Pitta.*

plantain eater. *See* turaco.

plover. Family Charadriidae.

plover, American golden. *Pluvialis dominica.*

plover, black-bellied. *Squatarola squatarola.*

plover, grey. *See* plover, black-bellied.

plover, New Zealand shore. *Thinornis novae-seelandiae.*

plover, ringed. *Charadrius hiaticola.*

plover, spur-winged. *Hoplopterus spinosus.*

plover, upland. *Bartramia longicauda.*

poorwill. *Phalaenoptilus nuttalii.*

potoo. Family Nyctibiidae.

prion. A petrel, genus *Pachyptila.*

ptarmigan. Genus *Lagopus.*

quail. Family Phasianidae (part).

quail, bobwhite. *Colinus virginianus.*

quail, bustard. Family Turnicidae.

quail, button. *See* quail, bustard.

quail, California. *Lophortyx californicus.*

quail, Gambel's. *Lophortyx gambelii.*

quail, mountain. *Oreortyx picta.*

quelea. *Quelea quelea.*

rail. Family Rallidae.

raven. *Corvus corax.*

rhea. Family Rheidae.

rifle-bird. *Craspedophora magnifica* (a bird of paradise).

roadrunner. *Geococcyx californianus.*

robin, American. *Turdus migratorius.*

robin, European. *Erithacus rubecula.*

roller. Family Coraciidae.

roller, cuckoo. Family Leptosomatidae.

roller, ground. Family Brachypteraciidae.

rook. *Corvus frugilegus.*

ruff. *Philomachus pugnax.*

sanderling. *Crocethia alba.*

sandgrouse. Family Pteroclidae.

sandpiper. Family Scolopacidae (part).

sandpiper, Baird's. *Erolia bairdii.*

woodcock, American. *Philohela minor*.

woodcock, European. *Scolopax rusticola*.

woodcreeper. *See* wood-hewer.

wood-hewer. Family Dendrocolaptidae.

wood hoopoe. Family Phoeniculidae.

woodpecker. Family Picidae.

woodpecker, acorn. *Melanerpes formicivorus*.

woodpecker, California. *See* woodpecker, acorn.

woodpecker, downy. *Dendrocopos pubescens*.

woodpecker, great spotted. *Dendrocopos major*.

woodpecker, green. *Picus viridis*.

woodpecker, red-headed. *Melanerpes erythrocephalus*.

wood pewee. *Contopus virens*.

wren. Family Troglodytidae.

wren, cactus. *Campylorhynchus brunneicapillum*.

wren, house. *Troglodytes aedon*.

wren, New Zealand. Family Acanthisittidae.

wren-tit. Family Chamaeidae.

yellow-legs, lesser. *Totanus flavipes*.

INDEX

References to illustrations are in *italics*.

MORE ABOUT PENGUINS
AND PELICANS

Penguinews, which appears every month, contains details of all the new books issued by Penguins as they are published. From time to time it is supplemented by *Penguins in Print*, which is a complete list of all available books published by Penguins. (There are well over four thousand of these.)

A specimen copy of *Penguinews* will be sent to you free on request, and you can become a subscriber for the price of the postage. For a year's issues (including the complete lists) please send 30p if you live in the United Kingdom, or 60p if you live elsewhere. Just write to Dept EP, Penguin Books Ltd, Harmondsworth, Middlesex, enclosing a cheque or postal order, and your name will be added to the mailing list.

Note: *Penguinews* and *Penguins in Print* are not available in the U.S.A. or Canada

KES

Barry Hines

Billy Casper is a boy with nowhere to go and nothing to say;
part of the limbo generation of school leavers too old for
lessons and too young to know anything about the outside
world. He hates and he is hated. His family and friends are
mean and tough and they're sure he's going to end up in big
trouble. But Billy knows two things about his own world.
He'll never work down the mines and he does know about
animals. His only companion is his kestrel hawk, trained
from the nest, and, like himself, trained but not tamed, with
the will to destroy or be destroyed.

This is not just another book about growing up in the
North. It's as real as a slap in the face to those who think
that orange juice and comprehensive schools have taken the
meanness out of life in the raw working towns.

Not for sale in the U.S.A.

ADVENTURE LIT THEIR STAR

The Story of an Immigrant Bird

Kenneth Allsop

Shortly after the Second World War ornithologists noticed that the little ringed plover – a rare bird new to England – was attempting to establish itself as a permanent breeder. Curiously enough, these pioneer birds chose to colonize a particularly messy stretch of land on the outskirts of London, thus making things difficult both for themselves and for those attempting to protect them from the depredations of man and animal.

Kenneth Allsop, an actual observer at the time, has recounted this story in a fictionalized form. Chief among those involved in the little plover's battle for survival is Richard Locke, a convalescent R.A.F. pilot determined to outwit an egg thief. Scrupulously accurate in detail, compassionate without being sentimental, this novel captures the intensity of wildlife drama.

Not for sale in the U.S.A.